LEBANON

Through Writers' Eyes

LEBANON

Through Writers' Eyes

Edited by

T. J. GORTON AND
A. FÉGHALI GORTON

ELAND

First published in 2009 by Eland Publishing Ltd,
61 Exmouth Market, London ECIR 4QL

Editorial Content © T. J. Gorton and A. Féghali Gorton 2009

All extracts © of the authors, as attributed in
the text and acknowledgements

ISBN   978 1 906011 27 7

Map © Reginald Piggott
Typeset in Great Britain by Antony Gray
Printed in Spain by GraphyCems, Navarra

Contents

TWO
Orient of the Mind: Travellers from the West

THREE
Identities

Lebanon

SYRIA

Mediterranean

Sea

N

El Qoubaiyet
Halba

El Mina
El Minie
Tripoli
Zgharta

NORTH
Sir ed Danniye
LEBANON
Hermel
R. Orontes

Batroun
Amioun
Bcharre

Ibail
R. Ibrahim
Afqa
BEKAA
Baalbek

Jounie
MOUNT
Dog R. Bikfaiya
Zahle

Beirut
(Beyrouth)
Broummana
LEBANON
Rayak

Aley
Hammana
Anjar

Damour
Beit ed Dine

Sidon
(Saida)
Joun
Niha
Rachaiya
Damascus
Jezzine

Nabatiye
Mount Hermon

Tyre
(Sour)
SYRIA

Nahariya

ISRAEL

Mount Lebanon

Anti Lebanon Mts.

R. Litani

SOUTH LEBANON

NABATIYE

Mount Hermon

— · — International boundary		═══ Expressway
——— Other main roads		+++ Railways

0   5   10   15   20   25 miles
0   10   20   30   40 km

Photo credits

Pages 25, 31, 41, 178: Directorate-General of Antiquities, Ministry of Culture, Beirut

Pages 68, 286: Manoug Alemian

Pages 75, 105, 133, 190, 197, 214, 281: from Michel Fani, Liban 1880–1914: Atelier photographique de Ghazir

Pages 12, 18, 63, 99, 155, 164, 180, 205, 259: T. J. Gorton

Acknowledgements

We would like to thank all the authors for making this collection possible by allowing us to use their material, and gratefully acknowledge permission to reprint copyright material as follows:

Dar An-Nahar Publishing House in Beirut for permission to quote from *Friday, Sunday* by Khaled Ziyade and from *Lebanon: Poems of Love and War* by Nadia Tueni; Colin Thubron, the Aitken Alexander Agency and the Random House Group Ltd. for the extracts from *Hills of Adonis* by Colin Thubron; University of California Press for the extract from *Memory for Forgetfulness: August, Beirut, 1982* by Mahmoud Darwish; Interlink Publishing for permission to reprint an extract from *The Stone of Laughter* by Hoda Barakat; Columbia University Press for permission to quote from *An Arab-Syrian Gentleman and Warrior in the period of the Crusades* by Usama ibn Munqidh, translated by Philip K. Hitti; Caravan Books for permission to use an extract from *The Druze Faith* by Sami N. Makarem; the Random House Group Ltd. for permission to include an extract from *An Evil Cradling* by Brian Keenan; HarperCollins Publishers Ltd for permission to use an extract from *From the Holy Mountain* by William Dalrymple and from *Dreams of Water: my family, my life, my Lebanon* by Nada Awar Jarrar and Quartet Books for permission to use the extract from *The Rock of Tanios* by Amin Maalouf.

In addition we thank Rose Baring and Barnaby Rogerson of Eland Books, whose patience and suspension of disbelief made this book conceivable. Thanks also to the staff of the British Library (Asian and African Room and Rare Books) for their unfailing competence and helpfulness. Among the friends who read all or part of the draft for us and saved us from all kinds of errors: Robert Irwin, and L. P. Harvey; also Drew Oliver, who found our American traveller. Peter Gubser and Joseph Raidy also contributed.

View of Byblos from the door of the Crusader Castle

Introduction

Lebanon remains familiar to most Westerners through horrific images of the civil war that convulsed the tiny country from 1975 to 1990, with heart-rending stories of hostages and lurid news coverage of massacres, destruction and human suffering. Two decades have now passed, but Lebanon cannot manage to stay out of the headlines for long, like a soccer or film star with a temper. One still reads of the 'Lebanonisation' of Bosnia or Iraq; but one increasingly reads of collaboration between formerly hostile population groups, of feuds and disagreements settled and power increasingly allocated at the ballot box. The headlines, bad or good, are (not unusually) far from being the whole story.

A comprehensive solution to the country's dire political problems is still not on the horizon, but there is a noticeable if timid revival of tourism. It is once again possible to visit most parts of the country. After all the years of turmoil, the 'Events' as they are called, many people have difficulty imagining what they would find there. The far-reaching changes of the last thirty years, seen against a background of abiding constants, mean that surprises await almost anyone, whether coming new to the country or coming back after a long absence or exile. What should you look for? What will you find?

Some of the places are obvious, such as Beit ed-Din (palace of the Druze Emirs who ruled Lebanon in the nineteenth century), up in the parasol-pine-forested Shouf Mountains. If you should (and you should, if you can afford to) stay at the Palace of the Emir Amin, a sort of mini-Beit ed-Din, now transformed into a luxury hotel, you might be forgiven for thinking that the 'Events' had never happened, or were long ago. Go on to spend a beach day at one of the resorts just south of Byblos. Margarita in hand, watch the sun set into the Mediterranean, the Crusader castle catching the last rays in its amber sandstone, mellowed by nearly a millennium of nestling like a parvenu among Phoenician, Greek, Roman, Persian and Arab ruins. Stroll through Beirut's 'Centre-Ville', the slightly antiseptic redeveloped downtown area, with sidewalk cafés and 'archaeological parks'. Tour the lush American University of Beirut campus with its graceful Moorish architecture and cosmopolitan student body (and, incidentally, a gem of a small archaeological museum). Visit Baalbek, antique Heliopolis; Tripoli with its Crusader Castle of Saint-Gilles and bustling port; the legendary Cedars, still worth a visit though the dominant impression is of how few remain; the Canaanite Temple of Aphaca at Afka; broad-shouldered Mount Sannine, hovering oblique to the sunset in tawny regal solitude above the trees; the Anti-Lebanon, arid and austere to the east, dropping down into the broad and Biblical Bekaa Valley with its dreamy bride, Baalbek, and delicate Umayyad colonnade at Anjar beckoning out towards the desert.

Beirut is a world of its own, seeming to thrive on contradiction – and conflict. A Mediterranean port-cum-microcosm of the Middle East: rich and poor, diverse and turbulent, touching and repellent. Donkeys and Ferraris, hurried bankers, palsied beggars and strutting thugs; veiled ladies in black elbowing past golden girls in miniskirts. Any elegance it may have had when it was the sleepy port painted by David Roberts has been superseded by its modern avatar as a sprawling, chaotic, dusty, noisy sacrifice to unbridled commerce, ruthless geopolitics and automotive gridlock. Not without interest or even charm, in parts, but a heady potion all the same. Beirut must be experienced; but, fortunately, Beirut is not all there is to Lebanon.

This Mountain of Lebanon

Like the hedgehog, Lebanon knows one Big Thing, and that big thing is of course the mountain, Mount Lebanon or just Lebanon as Antiquity knew it. The west-facing littoral known in the West as the Levant or the Orient – both meaning 'rising sun' – passes, on its way down to Egypt, through modern-day Turkey, Syria, Lebanon, and Israel/Palestine. The narrow, fertile coastal plain rises more or less abruptly into hills or mountains a few kilometres inland. The highest by far of those seaward-facing mountain ranges is in the middle:

Lebanon, rising to over 3,000 metres. On the highest peaks, there are pockets of eternal snow, but the copious snows that do melt feed springs and streams and rivers that water the coastal plain and give it an extraordinary fertility, a legendary beauty. On the other side, facing east, the slopes are more abrupt and arid, leading down to the fertile upland valley of the Bekaa, itself hemmed in on the east by another mountain chain called the Anti-Lebanon or Hermel. Beyond, far below, lies Syria, and the ancient tracks of the frankincense or silk roads leading across the desert to Petra, Palmyra, Damascus, Aleppo, and beyond, towards Iraq, Arabia and Persia.

In Central Europe or the Andean countries, such a mountain would be, if not commonplace, at least less of a marvel. But in the Middle East, snowy mountains and trackless forests were – are – more than a novelty. They struck the ancients as marvellous in every sense. For many centuries, most human activity was confined to the arable coastal plain, with its string of natural ports. The forest and wildlife of the mountain was exploited as a boundless natural reserve. From the earliest recorded times, however, we find hermits and anchorites and solitary madmen, rebels and fugitives and fanatics of all kinds, taking refuge in the lofty wilderness, living in the caves overlooking the holy rivers: Kadisha ('holy' in every Semitic language); and the Adonis River, the name redolent of beauty, thwarted love, meddlesome gods, tragic death and mystical rebirth. It is as though the former nomads of the desert and steppe, lifting up their eyes unto the hills, found it natural that gods or God would live up there, and the mystical among them would climb up to be closer to the divine.

The texts in this book span three millennia and then some. If Lebanon cannot manage stability, it has perennity. Empires rise, dynasties fall, ideas and faiths come in from the sea or desert, then clash and wither in a high-speed newsreel that defies synopsis. So, other than in passing – as we present the texts in each section of this book – we will let the writers speak for themselves and for their historical moment. And those writers are themselves an unruly lot. Natives tend to the mystical, while expatriates describe the place they visited to see if the rumours were true (like Herodotus), or the country they had to go through to get to the Holy Land (like many of the 18th-

and 19th-century travellers). The more literary of our travelling writers dwell on natural beauty, while journalists and politicians record the perversity of men who persist in destroying the thing they profess to love.

                         *   *   *

This book is organised thematically: first, texts from Antiquity and the Middle Ages to the end of the Crusades. Next, the country seen through the prism of several centuries of Western travellers, who saw in Lebanon varying proportions of the real country, an imagined 'Orient', and themselves. The third part we have called 'Identities'. In it one steps aside from the world of Oriental Travel to something closer to the grittier world of real people and events. One of the main aims of this book is to try to understand what it means to be Lebanese, or at least, what Lebanon variously means to its people. Chosen to reflect the country's religious, political, and literary identities, these texts are mostly written by locals – of various times, religions and political leanings. The literary selections are grouped under the title 'People of the Book': writing (of diverse kinds, from mystic prose to orally-composed popular poetry) by post-nineteenth-century natives of Lebanon, including some expatriates or exiles.

We end with 'Wars'. Of these, there have been all too many, their causes mostly now forgotten or meaningless to us; so we have started with the inter-communal strife of the 1860s. These events are described by observers, willing or unwilling participants, bystanders and invaders. Some are highly partisan, some less so. If we had expurgated or avoided all evidence of bias this would have been a very short section indeed. It, and the book, end with selections from recent fiction by Lebanese women writers; perhaps, as we suggest, not coincidentally. Many of these are set during the recent war – but Lebanon has been at or close to or recovering from war for much of the time since 1975. The best of these writers transcend their setting in time and place, and reflect Lebanon, its people, and perhaps the rest of us, under a brilliant, unforgiving spotlight.

Note on translation. As is now traditional in this series, in the case of texts in languages other than English, a published English version as close as possible to the time of the original has been preferred. Some of these are therefore written in the language of the time of Shakespeare or Milton, and we hope that the charm of these early texts will outweigh any difficulties. We have not regularised spelling but have respected the text as published wherever possible.

Many of the travellers whose stories we present had to rely on interpreters to make themselves understood, and to understand. There were, and are, many excellent translators at the service of the Levantine traveller; but the temptation to produce a culturally adapted version is sometimes too strong, and one suspects that some of the accounts, however entertaining, may have owed quite some debt to the interpreter. In his masterful *Eothen*, Charles Kinglake shows us how it works:

> *Pasha.* – The Englishman is welcome; most blessed among hours is this, the hour of his coming.
>
> *Dragoman* (to the Traveller). – The Pasha pays you his compliments.
>
> *Traveller.* – Give him my best compliments in return, and say I'm delighted to have the honour of seeing him.
>
> *Dragoman* (to the Pasha). – His Lordship, this Englishman, Lord of London, Scorner of Ireland, Suppressor of France, has quitted his governments, and left his enemies to breathe for a moment, and has crossed the broad waters in strict disguise, with a small but eternally faithful retinue of followers, in order that he might look upon the bright countenance of the Pasha among Pashas – the Pasha of the everlasting Pashalik of Karagholookoldour.
>
> *Traveller* (to the Dragoman). – What on earth have you been saying about London?

Baalbek

ONE

Phoenix and Cedar:
Ancient and Medieval Views

From the face of the mountain
The cedars raise aloft their luxuriance.
Good is their shade, full of delight

GILGAMESH

LEBANON FROM ANTIQUITY TO THE MIDDLE AGES

Lebanon's first appearance under anything like that name is in about 3000 BC, when the Great Pyramids of Egypt rise at Gizeh. Historical records begin to divide the land of Canaan into 'lowlands' and 'highlands', with the latter referring to what we know as Mount Lebanon, '*RMNN*' in Ancient Egyptian, '*labna-a-ni*' in Assyrian texts. There is little description of Mount Lebanon as such, dense forests inhabited only by hunters and woodsmen; but one feels its presence even in late Bronze Age Egyptian texts. The mountain's cedar and other timber provided the city-states of the Phoenician coast with a seemingly inexhaustible reserve of tradable (and especially exportable) goods, in addition to the famous purple or red textiles manufactured on the coast. These were dyed with the rotting bodies of crustaceans called murex, a process that gave off a smell so pungent one could smell it while approaching Tyre from the sea, even before the gleaming island-city came into sight. Mounds of bleached murex shells still punctuate the beaches around Tyre.

During the most peaceful and prosperous centuries in Phoenicia (1200-800 BC), 'Lebanon' still meant the mountain as opposed to the coast. 'Phoenicia' – at least partly cognate with the Greek *phoinix*, but in the meaning 'red' or 'purple', rather than anything to do with the bird of legend – evoked a string of coastal city-states loosely linked by language and trade: Aradus (Arwad in modern Syria), Gubal (Byblos), Berytus (Beirut), Sidon and Tyre. These shared a common pantheon with three principal deities, presided over by a Chief God that was different (better, of course) from their neighbours' counterpart; 'Lebanon' was still an image of sublime, inaccessible beauty. Phoenicia became the greatest seafaring and trading nation of antiquity, globalising the economy of the known world without feeling the need to conquer or govern an empire of foreign subjects. The Phoenicians established trading-posts and colonies all around the Mediterranean, teaching the Greeks to use the alphabet, visiting the Scilly Isles and Cornwall for tin, exploring beyond Gibraltar as far as West Africa. In the late ninth century BC, Tyre established a settlement at Carthage in centrally-located North Africa. The colony later became a power in its own right, more militarised than the mercantile mother-city of Tyre ever was, provoking the fatal umbrage of Rome.

As the ages came and went, so did successive invaders. Each carved a stela at the Dog River, lingered awhile, and went their way. First the Egyptians, who asserted a loose hegemony for a millennium or so; then Babylonians and Assyrians and Persians, continental empires that found it expedient to use Phoenician merchant and military navies for their own purposes, often leaving the coastal city-states to govern themselves.

In spite of the Phoenicians' long-standing affinity for Greek culture, the advent of the Persians in about 539 BC was accepted with typical pragmatism – geography not being negotiable. The long black galleys of Tyre and Sidon helped Persia against Greece during the Persian Wars, a close-run thing right up to Salamis in 480 BC. By the time of Herodotus' visit to Tyre a generation later, they had identified their traditional deities with members of the Greek pantheon: Herakles with Melkart, Aphrodite with Astarte.

In 332 BC, Alexander nonetheless had to force his way in. The siege of Tyre, when he built under fire the causeway that still links the former island city to the mainland, was the longest and most difficult of his career (the Sidonians, cousins and competitors of the Tyrians, helped him). After Alexander, the philhellene cultural leanings of this Semitic population were given free rein. Greek became the language of the aristocracy and of the famous school of philosophy and law at Beirut, though the people continued to speak Phoenician until late Roman times. Several Greek philosophers had Phoenician roots, including the first Stoic, Zeno. Buried with honours where he taught, in Athens, his epitaph reads:

> And if thy native country was Phoenicia,
> What need to slight thee? Came not Cadmus thence,
> Who gave to Greece her books and arts of writing?

But the loveliest ancient illustration of the enduring cosmopolitanism of the Levant might be another epitaph, that of yet another Hellenistic philosopher and epigrammatist, Meleager (of Tyre, buried on Cos):

> If I am a Syrian,[1] what of it? We all dwell in one country: the world
> …
> Stranger, pass quietly by, the old man slumbers
> Amongst the pious dead, lulled in the common sleep.
> This is Meleager, son of Eucrates …
> If you are a Syrian, *Salam!* If a Phoenician, *Naidios!*
> If you are a Greek, *Chaire!* the meaning is the same.[2]

Phoenicia prospered under the Pax Romana, and suffered under the increasingly turbulent times from the third century AD. During Imperial times, substantial human settlement began to creep up the slopes of Mount Lebanon, terracing the hillsides for farming and pasturing goats and sheep. Even Roman bigwigs had the good taste to enjoy its beauty; one had the misfortune to die there. This is

---

1　'Syria' was used from Antiquity until the early twentieth century to mean the geographical (never the political) region of the Levant and its hinterland, comprising Lebanon, Palestine and Syria 'proper'.
2　*The Greek Anthology*, Book VII, no. 417.

attested by a funerary monument erected at Niha, with its (perhaps literally) heart-stopping views. Berytus continued its intellectual career, switching from Greek to Latin but remaining the most important centre of jurisprudence of any Roman province. It and Heliopolis (Baalbek, or Ba'al Beq'a, 'Lord of the Bekaa') were renowned for Latin eloquence, 'islands of Latinity in a sea of Oriental Hellenism'.

The pagan religion of Antiquity was replaced by Christianity in Lebanon, as in the rest of the Roman Empire; once again, local elements merged with the new creed (Tammuz/Adonis died in winter to be reborn in the spring …). Life in Lebanon was relatively un-affected by the transition from Roman rule to that of Byzantium; the most dramatic events of the centuries between Rome and Islam were a series of devastating earthquakes in the sixth century. These destroyed Heliopolis/Baalbek and Beirut, including its famous law school, which never recovered.

When the Byzantine world was convulsed by theological disputes in the sixth and seventh centuries AD, more people began to settle up on the mountain. Among these were the Maronites: fleeing Byzantine persecution, they preferred to leave their ancestral homes in the plain for a wilderness, rather than give up their belief in the single nature of the *will* of Christ. Once tolerated, the 'monothelite' compromise was now regarded as heresy. Lebanon became part of the Islamic world around 640 AD, mostly without resistance, each town or city negotiating its status with the nascent Muslim polity. Arabic is close to the Aramaic then spoken by the people in Phoenicia; the local Christians hoped, with initial justification, that their new Semitic rulers would be less keen than the Byzantines on persecuting them for their theology, so long as they paid their taxes and kept the peace.

Several centuries of obscurity followed, as the Arabs, concentrating on extending and consolidating their empire, showed little interest in high mountains – no place or climate for their kind of warfare – or forests inhabited by fierce sectarians and wild animals. Later, the Maronites were joined by political refugees like the Jarajimah (a Christian military sect which became a thorn in the side of first Byzantium, then Islam, until it was destroyed by an Arab expeditionary force). Then came others, such as the Druze, Shi'i and other groups refusing to conform to the majority religion of the region – by now, Sunni Islam. Non-conformists would flee persecution in Syria or Palestine and take residence on the mountain, sealing Lebanon's vocation as refuge for religious and political exiles, mystics, outcasts and general trouble-makers.

Sinuhe (*c.*1875BC)

About 1960 BC, during the Egyptian Middle Kingdom, a minor official named Sinuhe was attending the funeral of the pharaoh Amen-em-het. Suddenly, he overheard a member of the Royal Family saying something alarmingly derogatory about him, and immediately decided to pre-empt disgrace or worse. He fled the country, visiting the gateway to Phoenicia, Byblos, and spent many years in Asia, at a place which has been identified with the fertile Bekaa Plain separating the twin ranges of Lebanon and Anti-Lebanon. As an old man, he was finally invited to return to Egypt, which he did gladly, and recorded his story for posterity. Several papyri survive; it is not known how much fiction, and how much truth they contain; but if fiction, it was plausible enough to become part of the literary heritage of the time (judging by the numerous copies made in Antiquity).

I was a henchman who followed his lord, a servant of the Royal harim attending on the hereditary princess, the highly-praised Royal Consort of Sesostris in the pyramid-town of Khnem-esut, the Royal Daughter of Amenemmes in the Pyramid-town of Ka-nofru, even Nofru, the revered.

In year 30, third month of Inundation, day 7, the god attained his horizon [*Pharoah died*], the King of Upper and Lower Egypt Sehete-pebre. He flew to heaven and was united with the sun's disk; the flesh of the god was merged in him, who made him. Then was the Residence hushed; hearts were filled with mourning; the Great Portals were closed; the courtiers crouched head on lap; the people grieved …

Message had been sent to the Royal Children who were with him in this army, and one of them had been summoned. And lo, I stood and heard his voice as he was speaking, being a little distance aloof; and my heart became distraught, my arms spread apart, trembling having fallen on all my limbs. Leaping I betook myself thence to seek me a hiding-place, and placed me between two brambles so as to sunder the road from its traveller. I set out southward . . .

Land gave me to land. I set forth to Byblos, I pushed on to Kedme. I spent half a year there; then Enshi son of Amu, prince of Upper Retenu, took me and said to me: Thou farest well with me, for thou hearest the tongue of Egypt. This he said, for that he had become aware of my qualities, he had heard of my wisdom; Egyptian folk, who were there with him, had testified concerning me. And he said to me: 'Wherefore art thou come hither? Hath aught befallen at the Residence?' And I said to him: 'Sehetepebre is departed to the horizon, and none knoweth what has happened in this matter' ... 'But thou, behold, thou art here; thou shalt dwell with me, and I will entreat thee kindly.'

And he placed me even before his children, and mated me with his eldest daughter. He caused me to choose for myself of his country, of the best that belonged to him on his border to another country. It was a goodly land called Yaa. Figs were in it and grapes, and its wine was more abundant than its water. Plentiful was its honey, many were its olives; all manner of fruits were upon its trees. Wheat was in it and spelt, and limitless cattle of all kinds. Great also was that which fell to my portion by reason of the love bestowed on me. He made me ruler of a tribe of the best of his country. Food was provided me for my daily fare, and wine for my daily portion, cooked meat and roast fowl, over and above the animals of the desert; for men hunted and laid before me in addition to the quarry of my dogs. And there were made for me many dainties, and milk prepared in every way ...

There came a mighty man of Retenu [*Highlands of Canaan, Lebanon*] and flaunted me in my tent. He was a champion without a peer, and had subdued the whole of Retenu. He vowed that he would fight with me, he planned to rob me, he plotted to spoil my cattle, by the counsel of his tribesfolk ...

[*Sinuhe defeats the challenger and takes his possessions*]

I became great thereby, I grew large in my riches, I became abundant in my flocks. Thus God hath done, so as to shew mercy to him whom he had condemned, whom he had made wander to another land. For today is his heart satisfied. A fugitive fled in his season; now the report of me is in the Residence. A laggard lagged because of hunger; now give I bread to my neighbour. A man left his country because of nakedness; but I am clad in white raiment and linen. A man sped for lack of one whom he should send; but I am a plenteous owner of slaves. Beautiful is my house, wide my dwelling-place; the remembrance of me is in the Palace.

[*Sinuhe is invited to return to Egypt, which he does, and is received with great honour*]

ॐ

The Journey of Wenamon to Phoenicia (*c.*1100 BC)

Wenamon, an official of the Temple of Amon at Karnak, lived sometime not too long before the Twenty-First Dynasty of the New Kingdom (eleventh century BC). He tells in this narrative how he was sent to Byblos on the Phoenician coast to procure cedar-wood for the ceremonial barge of the god. Egypt was divided into petty principalities at the time, and he was sent off without adequate money, credentials or armed force. His efforts to talk himself out of a pinch when he found himself in the clutches of a grasping Prince of Byblos are both amusing and reminiscent of the very similar quandary in which Cornelius de Bruyn would find himself nearly three millennia later, at the hands of the Agha of Tyre ...

Year 5, fourth month of the third [Summer] season, day 16. The day on which Wenamon, the eldest of the hall of the house of Amon, lord of the Thrones of the Two Lands, set forth to fetch the timber for the great noble barge of Amen-Re, King of the Gods, which is upon the river ... On the day of my arrival at Tanis at the palace of Nesubenebded and Tentamon, I gave them the writing of Amen-Re, King of the Gods.

They caused them to be read in their presence and they said: 'We

will surely do as Amen-Re, King of the Gods, our lord has said.' …
I went down upon the great Syrian sea in the fourth month of the
third season. And I arrived at Dor, a city of the Thekel,[3] and Beder,
its prince, caused to be brought to me much bread, a jar of wine, and
a joint of beef. Then a man of my ship fled having stolen one vessel
of gold worth 5 deben,[4] four jars of silver worth 20 deben, and a bag
of silver, 11 deben; total of what he stole, gold 5 deben, silver 31
deben.

I arose in the morning and went to the abode of the prince, and said
to him: 'I have been robbed in thy harbor. Since thou art the king of
this land, thou art therefore its investigator. Search for my money, for
indeed the money belongs to Amen-Re, King of the Gods, the lord of
the lands … '

He said to me: 'To thy honour and thy excellence! But behold, I
know nothing of this complaint which thou hast lodged with me. If
the thief belonged to my land, he who went on board thy ship, that he
might steal thy treasure, I would repay it to thee from my treasury till
they find thy thief by name; but the thief who robbed thee belongs to
thy ship. Tarry a few days here with me, and I will seek him.'

[*Wenamon departs against the Prince of Dor's advice; stopping in at Tyre,
he arrives at Byblos; on the way he finds a Thekel ship containing 30 debens
of silver, which he confiscates pending return of his own*] … I hid Amon-of-
the-Road[5] and placed his possessions within it. And the prince of
Byblos sent to me saying: 'Remove thyself from my harbor.' And I
sent to him saying: 'Where shall I go? … If thou canst find a ship to
carry me, let me be taken back to Egypt.' And I spent nineteen days in
his harbor and he continually sent me daily, saying: 'Remove thyself
from my harbor … '

When morning came, he sent and had me brought up, while the
god was in the tent on the shore of the sea. And I found him sitting in

3 Dor = a town on the coast of Palestine; Thekel or Tjekker = one of the fierce
   Sea Peoples who had migrated there a century or two earlier, and who were
   obviously hostile to Egypt at the sunset of its imperial power.
4 1 deben = 91 grammes.
5 the 'portable' effigy of the god.

his upper chamber with his back against a window, while the waves of the great Syrian sea beat behind him. And I said to him: 'Kindness of Amon.'

He said to me: 'Behold [*if*] thou art true, where is the writing of Amon, which is in thy hand? Where is the letter of the High Priest of Amon, which is in thy hand?' I said to him: 'I gave them to Nesubenebded and Tentamon.' Then he was very wroth.

Then I was silent in this great hour. He answered and said to me: 'On what business hast thou come hither?' I said to him: 'I have come after the timber of the great and august barge of Amon-Re, king of gods. Thy father did it, thy grandfather did it, and thou wilt also do it.' So spake I to him.

He said to me: 'They did it, truly. If thou give me something for doing it, I will do it. Indeed my agents transacted the business; the Pharaoh … sent six ships, laden with the products of Egypt, and they were unloaded in their storehouses. And thou also shalt bring something for me.'

He had the journal of his fathers brought in, and he had them read before me. They found 1,000 deben of every kind of silver, which was in his book.

He said to me: 'If the ruler of Egypt were the owner of my property, and I were also his servant, he would not send silver and gold, saying: "Do the command to Amon." It was not the payment of tribute which they exacted of my father. As for me, I am myself neither thy servant nor am I the servant of him that sent thee. If I cry out to the Lebanon, the heavens open, and the logs lie her on the shore of the sea … '

[*A long speech of Wenamon follows, in which he claims Egypt as the home of civilisation, and claims Lebanon for Amon*] … But I said to him: 'Let my scribe be brought to me, that I may send him to Nesubenebded and Tentamon, the rulers whom Amon hath given to the north of his land, and they will send all that of which I shall write unto them, saying: "Let it be brought," until I return to the south and send thee all thy trifles again.' So spake I to him.

He gave me my letter into the hand of his messenger. He loaded in the keel, the head of the bow and the head of the stern, with four other hewn timbers, together seven; and he had them taken to Egypt. His messenger went to Egypt and returned to me, to Syria in the first month of the second season.

[*Nesubenebded and Tentamon send substantial quantities of gold, silver, linen, papyrus, ox-hides, rope, lentils, and fish*] The prince rejoiced, and detailed 300 men and 300 oxen, placing overseers over them, to have the trees felled. They spent the second season therewith ... In the third month of the second season (seventh month) they dragged them [*to*] the shore of the sea. The prince came forth and stood by them.

He sent to me, saying: 'Come.'

I presented myself before him, and he answered and said unto me: 'Behold the command which my fathers formerly executed, I have executed, although for thy part hast not done for me that which they fathers did for me. Behold there has arrived the last of the timber, and there it lies. Do according to my desire and come to load it, for they will indeed give it to thee.'

I went to the shore of the sea, to the place where the timbers lay; I spied eleven ships, coming from the sea, belonging to the Thekel, saying: 'Arrest him! Let not a ship of his pass to Egypt!' I sat down and began to weep. The letter scribe came out to me, and said to me: 'What is the matter with thee?' I said to him: 'Surely thou seest these birds which twice descend upon Egypt. Behold them. They come to the pool, and how long shall I be here, forsaken? For thou seest surely those who come to arrest me again.'

He went and told it to the prince. The prince began to weep at the evil words which they spoke to him. He sent out his letter-scribe to me and brought me two jars of wine and a ram.

He sent to me, Tento, an Egyptian singing-girl, who was with him, saying: 'Sing for him; let not his heart feel apprehension.'

He sent to me, saying: 'Eat, drink, and let not they heart feel apprehension. Thou shalt hear all that I have to say unto thee in the morning.'

Morning came, he ... stood in their midst and said to the Thekel: 'Why have ye come?' They said to him: 'We have come after the stove-up ships which thou sendest to Egypt with our ... comrades.' He said to them: 'I cannot arrest the messenger of Amon in my land. Let me send him away, and ye shall pursue him, to arrest him.'

He loaded me on board, he sent me away ... to the harbor of the sea. The wind drove me to the land of Alasa [*Cyprus*]; those of the city came forth to me to slay me ... [*Wenamon had a fraught journey home, where he again had to talk his way out of a tight situation; but he eventually made it home as the publication of his story demonstrates*]

∞

The Bible
For the Old Testament prophets and psalmists, Lebanon was a potent symbol: lofty, wild, inaccessible, a place of man-eating beasts and wilderness; but also of limpid streams, cool and fragrant beauty far above the dust and pollution of the world, not to mention the best wine, all sung in the most sensual tone in the Song of Solomon. The Phoenician coastal city-states with their mercantile and maritime vocation and relatively secular devotion to the accumulation of wealth, was another thing altogether. When Ezekiel fulminates against foreign nations in general, he is at his most vitriolic when it comes to Tyre, to be obliterated from the earth on account of the 'iniquity of thy traffick'.

I Kings 5:1–18
And Hiram king of Tyre sent his servants unto Solomon; for he had heard that they had anointed him king in the room of his father; for Hiram was ever a lover of David. And Solomon sent to Hiram, saying, Thou knowest how that David my father could not build an house unto the name of the LORD his God for the wars which were about him on every side, until the LORD put them under the soles of his feet.

But now the LORD my God hath given me rest on every side, so that there is neither adversary nor evil occurrent.

And behold, I purpose to build an house unto the name of the LORD my God, as the LORD spake unto David my father, saying, Thy son, whom I will set upon thy throne in thy room, he shall build an house unto my name. Now therefore command thou that they hew me cedar trees out of Lebanon; and my servants shall be with thy servants; and unto thee will I give hire for thy servants according to all that thou shalt appoint; for thou knowest that there is not among us any that can skill to hew timber like unto the Sidonians.

And it came to pass, when Hiram heard the words of Solomon, that he rejoiced greatly, and said, Blessed be the LORD this day, which hath given unto David a wise son over this great people. And Hiram sent to Solomon, saying, I have considered the things which thou sentest to me for: and I will do all thy desire concerning timber of cedar, and concerning timber of fir. My servants shall bring them down from Lebanon unto the sea: and I will convey them by sea in floats unto the place that thou shalt appoint me, and will cause them to be discharged there, and thou shalt receive them: and thou shalt accomplish my desire, in giving food for my household.

So Hiram gave Solomon cedar trees and firs according to all his desire. And Solomon gave Hiram twenty thousand measures of wheat for food to his household, and twenty measures of pure oil; thus gave Solomon to Hiram year by year.

And the LORD gave Solomon wisdom as he promised him: and there was peace between Hiram and Solomon; and they two made a league together. And king Solomon raised a levy out of all Israel; and the levy was thirty thousand men. And he sent them to Lebanon, ten thousand a month by courses; a month they were in Lebanon, and two months at home; and Adoniram was over the levy. And Solomon had threescore and ten thousand that bore burdens, and fourscore thousand hewers in the mountains; beside the chief of Solomon's officers which were over the work, three thousand and three hundred, which ruled over the people that wrought in the work.

And the king commanded, and they brought great stones, to lay the foundation of the house. And Solomon's builders and Hiram's builders did hew them, and the stonesquarers; so they prepared timber and stones to build the house.

Joshua 13:4–6

From the south, all the land of the Canaanites, and Mearah that is beside the Sidonians, unto Aphek, to the borders of the Amorites; And the land of the Giblites, and all Lebanon, toward the sunrising, from Baal-glad under mount Hermon into the entering into Hamath.

Gilded bronze statuettes of Phoenician gods, from Byblos, Temple of the
Obelisks – Middle Bronze Age

All the inhabitants of the hill country from Lebanon into Misrephoth-ma'im, and all the Sidonians, them will I drive out from before the children of Israel; only divide it thou by lot unto the Israelites for an inheritance, as I have commanded thee.

Song of Solomon 4:7–15

Thou art all fair, my love, there is no spot in thee. Come with me from Lebanon, my spouse, with me from Lebanon: look from the top of Amana, from the top of Shenir and Hermon, from the lions' dens, from the mountains of the leopards.

Thou hast ravished my heart, my sister, my spouse; thou hast ravished my heart with one of thine eyes, with one chain of thy neck. How fair is thy love, my sister, my spouse! How much better is thy love than wine! And the smell of thine ointments than all spices!

Thy lips, O my spouse, drop as the honeycomb: honey and milk are under thy tongue; and the smell of thy garments is like the smell of Lebanon. A garden enclosed is my sister, my spouse; a spring shut up, a fountain sealed. Thy plants are an orchard of pomegranates, with pleasant fruits; camphire, with spikenard. Spikenard and saffron; calamus and cinnamon, with all trees of frankincense; myrrh and aloes, with all the chief spices: a fountain of gardens, a well of living waters, and streams from Lebanon.

Awake, O north wind; and come, thou south; blow upon my garden, that the spices thereof may flow out. Let my beloved come into his garden, and eat his pleasant fruits.

Ezekiel 27:2–9; 26:3–13

Now, thou son of man, take up a lamentation for Tyrus; And say unto Tyrus, O thou that art situate at the entry of the sea, which art a merchant of the people for many isles, Thus saith the Lord God; O Tyrus, thou hast said, I am of perfect beauty. Thy borders are in the midst of the seas, thy builders have perfected they beauty. They have made all thy ship boards of fir trees of Senir: they have taken cedars from Lebanon to make masts for thee … The inhabitants of Zidon [*Sidon*] and Arvad were thy mariners: thy wise men, O Tyrus, that were in thee, were thy pilots. The ancients of Gebal [*Byblos*] and the wise men thereof were in thee thy calkers: all the ships of the sea with their mariners were in thee to occupy thy merchandise ...

Thine heart was lifted up because of thy beauty, thou hast corrupted thy wisdom by reason of thy brightness: I will cast thee to the ground, I will lay thee before kings, that they may behold thee. Thou has defiled thy sanctuaries by the multitude of thine iniquities, by the iniquity of thy traffick; therefore will I bring forth a fire from the midst of thee, it shall devour thee, and I will bring thee to ashes upon the earth in the sight of all them that behold thee.

Behold, I am against thee O Tyrus, and will cause many nations to come up against thee, as the sea causes his waves to come up. And they shall destroy the walls of Tyrus, and break down her towers ... And they shall make a spoil of thy riches, and make a prey of thy merchandise: and they shall break down thy walls, and destroy thy pleasant houses: and they shall lay thy stones and thy timber and thy dust in the midst of the water. And I will cause the noise of thy songs to cease; and the sound of thy harps shall be no more heard.

Homer: *The Odyssey* (Book xv)

Homer provides us with a vibrant picture of the economic and human geography of the Greek world, and quite a few details about those non-Greek nations that were allies with Troy. In the Odyssey, *the world beyond Magna Graecia and the Trojan confederation is portrayed, if at all, in a mixture of fantasy and reality, with one exception: the Phoenicians. They are consistently and realistically depicted as master mariners, makers and purveyors of useful and decorative crafts and sharp traders generally. In Book xiii, 277, he stresses the honesty of one crew of Phoenician sailors, possibly as an exception to the rule; more characteristically, in Book xiv, 291 we have a 'man of Phoenicia, well versed in guile, a greedy knave'. But the nicest Homeric story about Phoenicians, and a Sidonian lady of hard-tried virtue, possibly set on the Syro-Lebanese coast, comes in Book xv, when Odysseus meets up with Eumaeus on his way from Calypso to Ithaca and his date with the Suitors. The 'isle they call Syria, near Ortygia' ('quail-island') is more likely to refer to somewhere on the Syrian coast, than to Syracuse/Ortygia in Sicily. This passage is given in Chapman's sinewy translation, still the best in our opinion at conveying the archaising Homeric atmosphere of the Age of Heroes, pregnant with wild surmise.*

There is an Isle above Ortygia
(if thou hast heard) they call it Syria –
Where once a day the Sun moves backwards still.
Tis not so great as good, for it doth fill
The fields with Oxen, fils them still with Sheepe,
Fils roofes with wine, and makes all Corne there cheap:
No Dearth comes ever there, nor no Disease,
That doth with hate us wretched mortals sease.
But when men's varied Nations, dwelling there
In any City, enters th'aged years,
The Silver-bow-bearer [the Sun] and she
That beares as much renowne for Archery
Stoope with their painless shafts, and strike them dead,
As one would sleepe, and never keepe the bed.
In this Isle stands two Cities, betwixt whome
All things that of the soile's fertility come
In two parts are divided. And both these,
My Father ruld (Ctiesius Ormenides),
A man like the immortals. With these States
The crosse-biting Phoenicians traffick'd rates
Of infinit Merchandize in ships brought there,
In which they then were held exempt from pere.

'There dwelt within my Father's house a Dame
borne a Phoenician, skilful in the frame
of Noble Huswiferies, right tall, and faire.
Her the Phoenician great-wench-net-layer
With sweet words circumvented as she was
Washing her Linnen. To his amorous passe
He brought her first, shor'd from his Ship to her,
To whom he did his whole life's love prefer,
Which of these brest-exposing Dames the harts

Deceives, though fashion'd of right honest parts.
He askt her after, What she was, and whence?
She passing presently the excellence
Told of her Father's Turrets, and that she
Might boast her self sprung from the Progeny
Of the rich Sidons, and the daughter was
Of the much-year-revenew'd Arybas –
But that the Taphian Pirats made her prize
As she return'd from her field-huswiferies,
Transfer'd her hither, and at that man's house
Where now she liv'd for value precious
Sold her to th'Owner. He that stole her love
Bad her againe to her birth's seate remove,
To see the faire roofes of her friends againe,
Who still held state and did the port maintaine
Her self reported. She said: 'Be it so,
So you and al that in your ship shall roe
Sweare to returne me in all safety hence.'

'All swore; th'Oath past with every consequence,
She bad: "Be silent now, and not a word
Do you or any of your friends afford,
Meeting me afterward in any way,
Or at the washing Fount, lest some display
Be made and told the old man, and he then
Keepe me straight bound, to you and to your men
The utter ruine plotting of your lives.
Keepe in firme thought then every word that strives
For dangerous utterance. Haste your ship's ful freight
Of what you Trafficke for, and let me straight
Know by some sent friend: 'She hath all in hold' –
And (with my selfe) I'le bring thence all the gold
I can by meanes finger: and beside,
I'le do my best to see your freight supplide
With some wel-weighing burthen of mine own.
For I bring up in house a great man's sonne,

As crafty as my selfe, who will with me
Run every way along, and I will be
His leader till your Ship has made him sure.
He will an infinite price procure,
Transfer him to what languag'd men you may." '

'This said, she gat her home, and they made stay
A whole yeare with us, Goods of great availe
Their ship enriching. Which now fit for saile,
They sent a Messenger t'informe the Dame:
And to my father's house a fellow came,
Full of Phoenician craft, that to be sold
A Tablet brought, the body all of Gold,
The Verge all Amber. This had ocular view
Both by my honor'd Mother and the crew
Of her house-handmaids, handl'd, and the price
Beat, askt, and promist. And while this device
Lay thus upon the Forge, this Jeweller
Made privy signes (by winkes and wiles) to her
That was his object, which she tooke, and he
(his signe seeing noted) hied to Ship. When she
(my hand still taking, as she used to do
to walke abroad with her) convai'd me so
Abroad with her, and in the Portico
Found cups, with tasted Viands, which the guests
That used to flocke about my Father's feasts
Had left. They gone (some to the counsaile Court,
Some to heare newes amongst the talking sort)
Her theft three bowles into her lap convaid,
And forth she went. Nor was my wit so staid
To stay her, or my selfe. The Sun went downe,
And shadowes round about the world were flowne,
When we came to the haven, in which did ride
The swift Phoenician Ship – whose faire broad side
They boorded straight, took us up, and all went
Along the moyst waies. Winde Saturnius sent.

Six dayes we day and night sayl'd; but when Jove
Put up the seventh day, She that shafts doth love
Shot dead the woman, who into the pumpe
Like to a Dop-Chicke [moorhen] div'd, and gave a thumpe
In her sad settling. Forth they cast her then
To serve the Fish and Sea-calves, no more Men –
But I was left there with a heavy hart.
When winde and water drove them quite apart
Their owne course, and on Ithaca they fell,
And there poore me did to Laertes sell:
And thus these eyes the sight of this Isle prov'd.'

ﻉ

Herodotus: *The Histories* (*c.*450 BC)

Herodotus was an active antiquarian, not a library historian: he actually travelled to Lebanon to check up on the worship of Heracles/Melkart there, and gives us the first of several accounts of the blood-tinged river staining the sea on the anniversary of the death of the youthful Adonis. He had great respect for the seafaring prowess of the Phoenicians and Carthaginians, and recounts their story of circumnavigating Africa, which he doubted because they said they 'had the sun on their right hand'. In fact this is strong evidence in their favour, as they sailed west around the Cape.

The Phoenicians who came with Cadmus – amongst them came the Gephyraei – introduced into Greece, after their settlement in the country, a number of accomplishments, of which the most important was writing, an art till then, I think, unknown to the Greeks. At first they used the same characters as all the other Phoenicians, but as time went on, and they changed their language, they also changed the shape of their letters. *Book V, 58*

To satisfy my wish to get the best information I possibly could on this subject, I made a voyage to Tyre in Phoenicia, because I had heard there was a temple there of great sanctity, dedicated to Heracles. I visited the temple and found that the offerings which adorned it were numerous and valuable, not the least remarkable being two pillars, one of them of pure gold, the other of emerald which gleamed in the dark with a strange radiance. In the course of conversation with the priests I asked how long ago the temple had been built, and found by their answer that they, too, did not share the Greek view; for they said that the temple was as ancient as Tyre itself, and that Tyre already stood for two thousand three hundred years. I also saw another temple there, dedicated to the Thasian Heracles; and I also went to Thasos, where I found a temple of Heracles built by the Phoenicians who settled there after they had sailed in search of Europa. *Book II, 43–45*

⚜

Lucian: *de Dea Syria* (*c.*150 BC)

Lucian, writing in the second century BC, was a modern man of his time, a wry observer of the human condition. He wrote a long piece about the temples and cults in Syria (that is, of course, modern Syria, Lebanon, and parts of Anatolia, Mesopotamia and Palestine). This is largely given over to the stories behind the rites, and the similarities between Egyptian religion and that of what he called Syria: a sort of Frazer avant la lettre. *Lucian's language in this text is not his own clear Attic, but an archaising parody of Herodotus, who wrote about as long before Lucian as Chaucer did before our time. We were tempted to present him in a Chaucerian-English translation, such as Professor Harmon's in the Loeb Classics series, cited in the Bibliography. But even in modern English we can appreciate the irony when Lucian parodies Herodotus' breathless enthusiasm for old temples: 'I saw the temple, and it was old'.*

At Byblos, I saw the great temple of Aphrodite of Byblos. That is where they worship Adonis, and I found out about the manner of their rites. I was told that this is the region where Adonis was killed by the boar, and in memory of that tragic event, every year the people beat their breasts and mourn and perform rituals, and there is great sorrow throughout the land. Then when the breast-beating and weeping is over, they make sacrifices to Adonis, as though he were dead; the next morning, they recite to each other that he lives. They then take him in a procession out of doors, and shave their heads like the Egyptians do for the death of Apis. Any woman who does not wish to shave her head must instead do penance for one day, during which she must offer her body for sale (to strangers only); her hair is considered to be an offering to Aphrodite.

There are nonetheless some men of Byblos who maintain that the Egyptian god Osiris is buried nearby them, and that the mourning and rites are actually held to honour Osiris and not Adonis. They believe this for the following reason: every year, a head is taken by sea from Egypt to Byblos, covering that distance in seven days. The winds that drive it are sent by the Goddess, so that it never deviates from its course but sails straight to Byblos. This is a complete marvel, and indeed occurs every year, and so it happened while I was in that city, and saw the head, made of papyrus.

There is yet another marvel, a river – called Adonis – that flows from Mount Lebanon down to the sea. The waters of this river lose their normal friendly colour and run with blood every year, making the sea-water quite crimson; a symbol, as it were, of the mourning of the people of Byblos. Indeed, they say that is the season of Adonis' wounding, and that it is his blood spilling into the water that turns it red, hence the river's name. Or so, at least, the common people say; but personally, I tend to agree with one man of Byblos, who attributed it to another cause, saying: 'The Adonis River runs through Mount Lebanon, O stranger, and the soil up there is quite brown. The strong winds that blow this time of year carry the soil into the river, so that the reddish soil makes the water look bloody. So the changed colour is not due to blood, as they say, but to the earth.' That is what the man of Byblos told me; and that may sound reasonable, but it still seems awfully odd to me that the wind should start to blow just at the right season.

I also went from Byblos up onto Mount Lebanon on a day-trip, because I had heard that there was an old temple to Aphrodite that Cinyras had founded; I saw the temple, and it was old.

Translated by T. J. Gorton

⁂

Strabo: Geography (c.20BC)

Strabo died in about 23 AD, having lived through the incorporation into the Roman Empire of his hometown Amaseia (Amasya in modern Turkey) on the Black Sea. In his Geography he spent a lot of energy defending the geography of Homer against that of Herodotus, but allowing for that he gives a remarkably clear and accurate description of the Phoenician coast around the time of Christ, including the dye-works smell which made Tyre an 'unpleasant' place to live.

The whole country above Seleucis, extending towards Egypt and Arabia, is called Coele-Syria ['*hollow' Syria*], but peculiarly the tract bounded by Libanus and Antilibanus, of the remainder one part is the coast extending from Orthosia as far as Pelusium [Tineh], of the remainder one part ... is called Phoenicia, a narrow strip of land along the sea; the other, situated above Phoenicia in the interior between Gaza and Antilibanus, and extending to the Arabians, called Judaea ... Next to Berytus is Sidon, at the distance of 400 stadia. Between these places is the river Tamyras [*nahr Damur*] and the grove of Asclepius and Leontopolis.

Next to Sidon is Tyre, the largest and most ancient city of the Phoenicians. This city is the rival of Sidon in its magnitude, fame, and antiquity, as recorded in many fables. For although poets have celebrated Sidon more than Tyre (Homer, however, does not even mention Tyre), yet the colonies sent into Africa and Spain as far as, and beyond, the Pillars, extol much more the glory of Tyre. Both however were formerly, and are at present, distinguished and illustrious cities, but which of the two should be called the capital of Phoenicia is a subject of dispute among the inhabitants. Sidon is situated upon a fine naturally-formed harbour on the mainland.

Tyre is wholly an island, built in nearly the same manner as Aradus. It is joined to the continent by a mound, which Alexander raised, when he was besieging it. It has two harbours, one close, the other open, which is called the Egyptian harbour. The houses here, it is said, consist of many stories, of more even than at Rome; on the occurrence, therefore, of an earthquake, the city was nearly demolished. It sustained great injury when it was taken by siege by Alexander, but it rose above these misfortunes, and recovered itself both by the skill of the people in the art of navigation, in which the Phoenicians in general have always excelled all nations, and by (the export of) purple-dyed manufactures, the Tyrian purple being in the highest estimation. The shellfish from which it is procured is caught near the coast, and the Tyrians have in great abundance other requisites for dyeing. The great number of dyeworks renders the city unpleasant as a place of residence, but the superior skill of the people in the practice of this art is the source of its wealth. Their independence was secured to them at a small expense to themselves, not only by the kings of Syria, but

also by the Romans, who confirmed what the former had conceded. They pay extravagant honours to Hercules. The great number and magnitude of their colonies and cities are proofs of their maritime skill and power.

The Sidonians are said by historians to excel in various kinds of art, as the words of Homer also imply [*XXIII, 743*]. Besides, they cultivate science and study astronomy and arithmetic, to which they were led by the application of numbers (in accounts) and sight sailing, each of which (branches of knowledge) concerns the merchant and seaman.

ﺣﻚ

Josephus: *Antiquities of the Jews* (c.65AD)

Flavius Josephus was born in Jerusalem, in about 37 AD, and lived through times that were as momentous in his native Palestine as elsewhere in the Roman world. His The Antiquities of the Jews *gives a first-hand account of the state of things up to about 66 AD. He is not specifically concerned with Lebanon – this was the time of the Jewish War and the destruction of the Temple, Masada and other seminal upheavals in Jewish history. But he does provide a nice account of the attitude of the late first-century emperors to Phoenicia, at a time when Syro-Lebanese influences were increasingly evident. The influx of these swarthy parvenus with their Semitic take on pagan religion prompted Juvenal to complain: 'the Syrian Orontes has long since poured its waters into the Tiber, bringing with it its lingo and its manners'. In the passage chosen, Josephus describes the predilection of Kings Agrippa I and II (the last descendants of Herod the Great) for the city of Beirut, site of the most influential law school of any province; and the magnificent buildings the Agrippas built there to house lavish entertainments and spectacular gladiatorial contests.*

Now as Agrippa [*I*] was a great builder in many places, he paid a peculiar regard to the people of Berytus; for he erected a theater for them, superior to many others of that sort, both in Sumptuousness and elegance, as also an amphitheater, built at vast expenses; and besides these, he built them baths and porticoes, and spared for no costs in any of his edifices, to render them both handsome and large. He also spent a great deal upon their dedication, and exhibited shows upon them, and brought thither musicians of all sorts, and such as made the most delightful music of the greatest variety. He also showed his magnificence upon the theater, in his great number of gladiators; and there it was that he exhibited the several antagonists, in order to please the spectators; no fewer indeed than seven hundred men to fight with seven hundred other men and allotted all the malefactors he had for this exercise, that both the malefactors might receive their punishment, and that this operation of war might be a recreation in peace. And thus were these criminals all destroyed at once …

About this time it was that king Agrippa [*II*] built Cesarea Philippi[6] larger than it was before, and, in honor of Nero, named it Neronlas. And when he had built a theater at Berytus, with vast expenses, he bestowed on them shows, to be exhibited every year, and spent therein many ten thousand [*drachmae*]; he also gave the people a largess of corn, and distributed oil among them, and adorned the entire city with statues of his own donation, and with original images made by ancient hands; nay, he almost transferred all that was most ornamental in his own kingdom thither. This made him more than ordinarily hated by his subjects, because he took those things away that belonged to them to adorn a foreign city.

6 Banias, ancient Paneia – the birthplace of Pan – just over the modern border with Syria.

THE MIDDLE AGES: ARAB AND FRANKISH TRAVELLERS OF CRUSADER TIMES

It is a long jump from Josephus to the Crusades. But jump one must, as the Lebanese and their visitors are uncharacteristically silent during the end of Byzantine rule and the first few centuries of Islam. But then came the time when medieval Europe conjured up, and achieved, the fantastic dream of a People's Army that would march half-way around the known world to take back the Holy Places for Christ (and the all-too-secular ambitions of their leaders). In the crucible of those bloody centuries were forged many of the hostile and ignorant attitudes that characterise East–West relations today – on both sides.

The Crusades were supposedly about the Holy Land, but much of their drama unfolded in and around present-day Lebanon; Lebanon's subsequent personality – and personality problems – were more shaped by those two centuries of convulsion than those of any other modern state. This is partly because some of its substantial Christian population identified with the Franks, as they called the Crusaders irrespective of national origin, sharing with them useful local knowledge and thereby alienating their Muslim neighbours. This seed of disharmony, along with the abiding memory of the slaughter of Muslim and Jewish civilians at Jerusalem, is arguably the most lasting legacy of the Crusades.[7] The very nature of a Crusader state made its survival more tenable if its defence could be assured or at least assisted directly from the sea; thus the string of coastal cities from Tripoli to Tyre were among the last to be permanently re-conquered.

Lebanon now has, along with Syria, the best examples of Crusader architecture. These range from Beaufort (*ash-Shaqif*) in the far South, currently – perhaps one should say once again – a military area which you can't visit without an army, to the ones you can: the famous castles of St-Gilles in Tripoli, the *Château de la Mer* in Byblos, or the wonderfully preserved fortress lording over the seafront in Sidon,

---

7 As the historian Steven Runciman put it: 'When, later, wiser Latins in the East sought to find some basis on which Christian and Muslim might work together, the memory of the massacre stood always in their way.' (*The First Crusade*, p. 238)

rebuilt by Saint Louis (King Louis IX of France). Besides the stone witnesses, are the flesh-and-blood ones: extensive Christian families named Franjieh ('Frankish'), or Duaihi ('from Douai'), or the sonorous Bardawil ('Baldwin').

Nasir-I-Khusrau: *Diary of a Journey through Syria and Palestine* (1047 AD)

A Shi'i Muslim from Persia, Nasir-i-Khusrau, came through the Levant in the mid-eleventh century; his story is interesting from several points of view, not least as a last snapshot of the Near East just before the First Crusade opened that eventful chapter in Levantine history. He was mainly interested in the state of his fellow Shi'is in the region.

From Aleppo to Tripoli is forty leagues, and, by the way we marched, we reached the latter city on Saturday, the 5th of Sha'aban (February 6th). The whole neighbourhood of the town is occupied by fields, and gardens, and trees. The sugar-cane grows here luxuriously, as likewise orange and citron trees; also the banana, the lemon, and the date.

They were, at the time of our arrival, extracting the juice of the sugar-cane. The town of Tripoli is so situate that three sides thereof are on the sea, and when the waves beat, the sea-water is thrown up onto the very city walls. The fourth side, which is towards the land, is protected by a mighty ditch, lying eastward of the wall, in which opens an iron gate, solidly built. The walls are all of hewn stone, and the battlements and embrasures are after the like work. Along the battlements are placed balistae ('*arradah*), for their fear is of the Greeks, who are wont to attempt the place in their ships. The city measures a thousand cubits long, by the like across. Its hostelries are four and five stories high, and there are even some that are of six. The private houses and bazaars are well built, and so clean that one might take each to be a palace for its splendour.

Every kind of meat and fruit and eatable that ever I saw in all the land of Persia, is to be had here, and a hundred degrees better in quality. In the midst of the town is the great Friday Mosque, well kept, and finely adorned, and solidly constructed. In the Mosque court is a

large dome, built over a marble tank, in the middle of which is set a
brazen fountain. In the bazaar, too, they have made a watering-place,
where, at five spouts, is abundant water for the people to take from;
and the overflow, going along the ground, runs into the sea. They say
there are twenty thousand men in this city, and the place possesses
many adjacent territories and villages. They make here very good
paper, like that of Samarkand, only of better quality.

The city of Tripoli belongs to the (Fatimite) Sultan of Egypt. The
origin, as I was told, of this is that when, a certain time ago, an army
of the Infidels from Byzantium had come against the city, the Muslims
from Egypt came and did fight the Infidels, and put them to flight.
The Sultan of Egypt has remitted his right to the land-tax (*kharaj*) in
the city. There is always a body of the Sultan's troops in garrison here,
with a commander set over them, to keep the city safe from the
enemy. The city, too, is a place of customs, where all ships that come
from the coasts of the Greeks and the Franks, and from Andalusia, and
the Western lands (called Maghrib), have to pay a tithe to the Sultan;
which sums are employed for the rations of the garrison. The Sultan
also has ships of his own here, which sail to Byzantium and Sicily and
the West, to carry merchandise. The people of Tripoli are all of the
Shi'ah sect. The Shi'ahs in all countries have built for themselves fine
mosques. There are in this place houses like Ribats (which are
caravanserais, or watchstations), only that no one dwells therein on
guard, and they call them Mash-hads (or places of martyrdom). There
are no houses outside the city of Tripoli, except two or three of the
Mash-hads that are above described.

From Jubail we came on to Bairut. Here I saw an arch of stone so
great that the roadway went out through it; and the height of the arch
I estimated at fifty ells (*Gez*). The side walls of the arch are built of
white stone, and each block must be over a thousand Manns (or about
a ton and a half) in weight. The main building is of unburnt brick,
built up a score of ells high. Along the top of the same are set marble
columns, each eight ells tall, and so thick that with difficulty could two
men with their arms stretched embrace the circumference. Above
these columns they have built arcades, both to right and to left, all of
stones, exactly fitted, and constructed without mortar or cement. The

great centre arch rises up between, and towers above the arcades by a height of fifty cubits. The blocks of stone that are used in the construction of these arches, according to my estimate, were each eight cubits high and four cubits across, and by conjecture each must weigh some seven thousand Manns (or about ten tons). Every one of these stones is beautifully fashioned and sculptured after a manner that is rarely accomplished, even in (soft) wood.

Except this arch no other (ancient) building remains. I inquired in the neighbourhood what might have been the purpose thereof; to which the people answered that, as they had heard tell, this was the Gate of Pharaoh's garden; also that it was extremely ancient.

All the plain around this spot is covered with marble columns, with their capitals and shafts. These were all of marble, and chiselled, round, square, hexagonal, or octagonal; and all in such extremely hard stone that an iron tool can make no impression on it. Now, in all the country round there is apparently no mountain or quarry from which this stone can have been brought; and, again, there is another kind of stone that has an appearance of being artificial, and, like the first stone, this, too, is not workable with iron. In various parts of Syria there may be seen some five hundred thousand columns, or capitals and shafts of columns, of which no one now knows either the maker, or can say for what purpose they were hewn, or whence they were brought.

From Bairut we came on to the city of Sidon (Saida), likewise on the seashore. They cultivate here much sugar-cane. The city has a well-built wall of stone, and four gates. There is a fine Friday Mosque, very agreeably situated, the whole interior of which is spread with matting in coloured designs. The bazaars are so splendidly adorned that, as I first saw them, I imagined the city to be decorated for the arrival of the Sultan, or in honour of some good news. When I inquired, however, they said it was customary for their city to be always thus beautifully adorned. The gardens and orchards of the town are such that one might say each was a pleasance laid out at the fancy of some king. Kiosks are set therein, and the greater number of the trees are of those kinds that bear fruit.

Five leagues from Sidon we came to Tyre (Sur), a town that rises on the shore of the sea. They have built the city on a rock (that is in the sea), after such a manner that the town-wall, for one hundred yards only, is upon the dry land, and the remainder rises up from out the very water. The walls are built of hewn stone, their joints being set in bitumen in order to keep the water out. I estimated the area of the town to be a thousand (cubits) square, and its caravanserais are built of five and six stories, set one above the other. There are numerous fountains of water; bazaars are very clean; also great is the quantity of wealth exposed. This city of Tyre is, in fact, renowned for wealth and power among all the maritime cities of Syria. The population for the most part are of the Shi'ah sect, but the Kadi (or judge) of the place is a Sunni. He is known as the son of Abu 'Akil, and is a good man, also very wealthy. They have erected a Mash-had (a shrine, or place of martyrdom) at the city gate, where one may see great quantities of carpets and hangings, and lamps and lanterns of gold and silver.

٭

Ibn al-Qalanisi: *The Damascus Chronicle of the Crusades* (c.1150AD)

When the Frankish armies of the First Crusade marched down the Levantine coast on their way to Jerusalem, they found much to marvel at. Such was the disunity and turmoil among the petty principalities as the two-century-old Fatimid hegemony unravelled – and Turks and Turkomans of various stripes muscled in from the East – that many of the cities the Crusaders marched past chose to buy their peace. Instead of fighting the motley army, they provided it with food, money and guides, and sent it on its way to someone else's back yard. Jerusalem taken, the Crusaders came back twenty years later to besiege Tyre. We have chosen extracts from two versions of the siege and capture of Tyre, one from each side. The defenders' story is told first by Ibn al-Qalanisi, a contemporary Damascene man of letters.

In this year [1124] the Franks gained possession of the port of Tyre by capitulation … [*The Franks*] set about gathering their forces and making preparations to besiege and invest it. When the governor was informed of what was afoot, he, realizing that he could not resist the Franks nor hold out against their siege on account of the shortage of troops and provisions in the town, wrote to apprise al-Amir, lord of Egypt, of this.

Thereupon it was judged necessary to restore the government of Tyre to Zahir al-Din Atabek, in order that he should take measures for its defence and protection and for the warding off [*of the Franks*] from it, as he had been wont to do. The diploma of investiture was written in his name, and he deputed as its governors a body of men who had neither ability, capacity, nor bravery. In consequence of this its affairs fell into disorder, and the desire of the Franks was directed towards it. They set about forming a camp and making preparations for the blockade, and having encamped outside the city in First Rabi' of this year (18th April to 17th May), they blockaded it by fighting and siege until the supplies of food in the city ran short and its provisions were exhausted. Zahir al-Din marched with the 'askar [*army*] to Banyas for the defence of Tyre. Letters were despatched to Egypt with appeals for assistance to be sent to the city, but when day after day passed their hearts sank and the citizens came to the brink of destruction. Zahir al-Din, being made aware of the true state of affairs and the impossibility of remedying the critical situation in the town, and despairing of assistance being sent to it, opened negotiations with the Franks, and finessed, cajoled, threatened, and incited, until an agreement was reached to surrender the city to them, on the conditions that all who were in it should be given a guarantee of security, and that those of the troops and citizens who desired to depart should do so with as much of their property as they could remove, and those who desired to stay should stay.

The atabek then took up a position with his 'askar facing the Franks and the gate of the city was opened, and permission given to the people to depart. Each of them carried with him all light property that he was able to carry and left all heavy property behind. They filed out thus between two ranks, without a single Frank molesting any one of them, until the entire body of troops and citizens had left, and none remained behind but those who were too weak to leave. They were dispersed throughout the country and some of them came to Damascus. The date of the surrender of the city was 23rd First Jumada 518 (7th or 8th July, 1124).[8]

---

8 Not the same date given by William of Tyre. One would think the Archbishop would know; but the other sources agree with Ibn al-Qalanisi.

William of Tyre: *History of the Deeds Done Beyond the Sea* (*c.* 1170AD)

The invaders' version of the story is told (from eyewitness accounts) a generation later by the city's Archbishop, William, and his chronicle is a lively, if partisan, testimony.

When they [*the Crusaders, marching to Jerusalem*] had come within about six miles of Tripoli, they chose their campsite and pitched their tents. There came to them envoys from the Governor of Tripoli, who held that city and the surrounding countryside in fealty to the Caliph of Egypt. He had altogether put aside his previous haughty attitude, presuming to confront our leaders on equal terms. His messengers were under no such illusion, but entreated them to accept the Governor's offer of valuable consideration and remove themselves from his territory; he offered to give them fifteen thousand bezants [*gold coins*], to free from prison such of our soldiers as he had captured, and to make them other precious gifts: horses and mules, woven silk cloth and diverse vases. They in turn promised not to molest the Governor's three cities (Arka, Tripoli and Beirut [*Byblos in the Latin version*]). In addition to the above, he sent them oxen and cows and sheep and plenty of other food, so that they would not need to plunder the countryside as they marched.

At that time the army was joined by certain Syrians who live up on Mount Lebanon, an exceedingly high mountain that lies near the cities just mentioned. They are of our religion, and are extremely honest and loyal people; they had come to greet our leaders and rejoice with them concerning their recent victory. The leaders of the army called them to them, and entreated them to indicate which was the best way to Jerusalem from there. They conferred amongst themselves for a while, weighing the advantages of the various alternative routes, and finally said that the coast road was the best, inasmuch as their ships could follow their progress and provide security and comfort … The Syrians thus walked at the head of the army; the Governor of Tripoli also sent some of his own people, who knew the country very well. Thus they followed the sea, leaving Mount Lebanon on their left hand …

On the third day they came to the city of Beirut, and camped on the bank of a river which runs by it. The Governor of the city offered them a considerable sum of money, and provided plenty of provisions at a very reasonable price, in order that they should spare the crops and the trees. The next day they reached Sidon, and pitched their camp along the river. Those of Sidon were decidedly hostile to the army, and sent out a group of armed horsemen to taunt our ranks. Our knights finally lost patience, riding out against them and killing quite a few. After that they left us alone and we had a restful night. In the morning, so as not to tire the foot-soldiers, the army stayed where it was, sending out foraging-parties who brought back food for the men and fodder for the horses, as well as kine and various other valuables ... They then crossed the river and came to Tyre ...

[*Twenty years later, the army returns to Tyre, having conquered Jerusalem*]

Our army moved boldly up to the city and surrounded it as best we could, given that it lies in the sea, with but one entrance from the landward ... The citizens of Tyre were noble and rich, for since ancient times they have been acquiring wealth through trading and from pilgrims, and the city had become exceedingly wealthy. In addition, all the people who had been forced to flee their homes in Caesarea and other coastal cities which had fallen to the Christians, had sought refuge in Tyre, bringing with them their valuables. They thought themselves to be safe there, for no-one dreamt that such a well-fortified city would ever be taken by the Christians [*Latin version: 'and had bought homes for themselves there at a very high price'*] ...

When the Tyrians realised that they could not endure such privations much longer, they started to gather together to debate as to the best way to put an end to their sufferings. Some said that they would be allowed to go in safety if they surrendered the city, and that it would be better to go away with their wives and children to some other city which was in Muslim hands, rather than to die of hunger as they were doing. After this discussion had gone on for some time, the proposal was read aloud before the nobles and leaders of the city, so that all could hear. And so it was unanimously agreed that they should sue for peace ...

After much negotiation, a peace was finally agreed, the terms of which were that all those inhabitants of the city who so desired, could leave with their wives and children, and all their goods they could carry; and they would be given a safe-conduct to friendly territory. If, on the other hand, there were any who chose to remain and live under the Christians, they could stay and would retain all their homes and property. When the rank and file of the army heard that the peace agreement would allow the Turks to stay with their property, and they would have no plunder, there was great anger among them. They said openly that their barons had betrayed them and had taken large bribes in order to agree such a peace, while the poor men, who had suffered all the hardship, would not gain a single thing from this conquest. Feelings grew so violent that there was nearly a great scuffle between the poor and the rich members of the army. Things finally calmed down, and our forces entered the city on the basis I described. To commemorate the victory, the King's standard was hung on the highest tower near the city gate, while the banner of the count [*doge*] of Venice was placed on the tower known as the Green Tower; and on the other, called the tower of the Tannery, was raised the standard of the count of Tripoli …

The party of knights that was supposed to conduct the Turks to safety came into the city for that purpose, but the townspeople said they would not leave before they had a chance to see the Christian army. You should have seen them, thronging out of the city where they had been shut up for so long, and how they went around looking at the tents and the weapons of our soldiers, the siege-machines and the wooden siege-towers which had caused them so much injury. The barons of the army were also eager to see that which they had heard so much about, and all this was of great comfort to them after the terrible struggle they had endured. Our people went about the town, eagerly climbing the towers and walking along the walls; they saw the port, so nobly built within the walls, and observed the damage which their siege-engines had wrought there. In all the storehouses of the city, the only corn they found was fifteen [*Latin: five*] measures of wheat, which was hardly anything at all. For their part, our leaders had nothing but praise for these people who had steadfastly held out for so long. The city was shared out in three parts: two for the King, and one to the Venetians, in accordance with their prior agreement. As I said before, the city was taken on the next-to-last day of June, in the year of Our Lord 1124, the sixth year of the reign of Baldwin, the second king of Jerusalem.

Translated (from the Old French version) by T. J. Gorton

ﻣﺘ

Benjamin of Tudela: *Itinerary* (*c.*1170AD)

Two travellers from Spain came through the Levant during the heyday of the Latin Kingdom, visiting Lebanon when substantial parts of it were in Crusader hands. They were Ibn Jubair, a Muslim (as he never tires of reminding us), who called his homeland al-Andalus (see the following extract); and Benjamin, a Rabbi from Tudela, who called his country Sefarad. Like his Shi'i predecessor, Nasir-i-Khusrau, the Rabbi Benjamin was principally concerned with enumerating his co-religionaries in each town and describing their condition.

Thence [*from Latakia*] it is two days' journey to Gebal (Gebela), which is Baal-Gad, at the foot of Lebanon. In the neighbourhood dwells a people called Al-Haahishim [*Assassins*]. They do not believe in the religion of Islam, but follow one of their own folk, whom they regard as their prophet, and all that he tells them to do they carry out, whether for death or life. They call him the Sheik Al Hashishim, and he is known as their Elder. At his word these mountaineers go out and come in. Their principal seat is Kadmus, which is Kedemoth in the land of Sihon. They are faithful to each other, but a source of terror to their neighbours, killing even kings at the cost of their own lives. The extent of their land is eight days' journey. And they are at war with the sons of Edom who are called the Franks, and with the ruler of Tripolis, which is Tarabulus el Sham. At Tripolis in years gone by there was an earthquake, when many Gentiles and Jews perished, for houses and walls fell upon them. There was great destruction at that time throughout the Land of Israel, and more than 20,000 souls perished.

Thence it is a day's journey to the other Gebal (Gubail) [*Byblos*], which borders on the land of the children of Ammon, and here there are about 150 Jews. The place is under the rule of the Genoese, the name of the governor being Guillelmus Embriacus. Here was found a temple belonging to the children of Ammon in olden times, and an idol of theirs seated upon a throne or chair, and made of stone overlaid with gold. Two women are represented sitting, one on the right and one on the left of it, and there is an altar in front before which the Ammonites used to sacrifice and burn incense. There are about 200 Jews there, at their head being R. Meir, R. Jacob, and R. Simchah. The place is situated on the sea-border of the land of Israel. From there it is two days' journey to Beirut, or Beeroth, where there are about fifty Jews, at their head being R. Solomon, R. Obadiah, and R. Joseph.

Thence it is one day's journey to Saida, which is Sidon, a large city, with about twenty Jews. Ten miles therefrom a people dwell who are at war with the men of Sidon; they are called Druses, and are pagans of a lawless character. They inhabit the mountains and the clefts of the rocks; they have no king or ruler, but dwell independent in these high places, and their border extends to Mount Hermon, which is a three days' journey. They are steeped in vice, brothers marrying their sisters, and fathers their daughters. They have one feast-day in the year, when they all collect, both men and women, to eat and drink together, and they then interchange their wives. They say that at the time when the soul leaves the body it passes in the case of a good man into the body of a newborn child, and in the case of a bad man into the body of a dog or an ass. Such are their foolish beliefs. There are no resident Jews among them, but a certain number of Jewish handi-craftsmen and dyers come among them for the sake of trade, and then return, the people being favourable to the Jews. They roam over the mountains and hills, and no man can do battle with them.

From Sidon it is half a day's journey to Sarepta (Sarfend), which belongs to Sidon. Thence it is a half-day to New Tyre (Sur), which is a very fine city, with a harbour in its midst. At night-time those that levy dues throw iron chains from tower to tower, so that no man can go forth by boat or in any other way to rob the ships by night. There is no harbour like this in the whole world. Tyre is a beautiful city. It contains about 500 Jews, some of them scholars of the Talmud, at their head being R. Ephraim of Tyre, the Dayan, R. Meir from Carcassonne, and R. Abraham, head of the congregation. The Jews own sea-going vessels, and there are glass-makers amongst them who make that fine Tyrian glass-ware which is prized in all countries.

In the vicinity is found sugar of a high class, for men plant it here, and people come from all lands to buy it. A man can ascend the walls of New Tyre and see ancient Tyre, which the sea has now covered, lying at a stone's throw from the new city.

And should one care to go forth by boat, one can see the castles, market-places, streets, and palaces in the bed of the sea. New Tyre is a busy place of commerce, to which merchants flock from all quarters.

ﻤﺖ

Ibn Jubair: *Travels* (1184 AD)

When Ibn Jubair visited Tyre and gave us his Muslim's-eye view of Lebanon during the Crusades, including a marvellous vignette of a Frankish wedding, Tyre had already been in Christian hands for sixty years.

Beyond are the Mountains of Lebanon, of towering height and great length, extending along the sea coast. On their slopes are castles belonging to the heretical Isma'ilites, a sect which swerved from Islam and vested divinity in a man.

Their prophet was a devil in man's disguise called Sinan, who deceived them with falsehoods and chimeras embellished for them to act upon. He bewitched them with these black arts, so that they took him as a god and worshipped him. They abased themselves before him, reaching such a state of obedience and subjection that did he order one of them to fall from the mountain top he would do so, and with alacrity that he might be pleased. God in His power allows to stray those whom He wills, and guides whom He wishes. Glory to Him to whom we turn for protection from seducement in religion, asking His protection from the straying of the heretics. There is no

Lord but He, and only He should be worshipped. Mount Lebanon is the frontier between Muslim lands and those of the Franks, for beyond it lie Antioch, Latakia, and others of their cities – may God restore them to the Muslims. On the slopes of this mountain is a fortress called Hisn al-Akrad.[9] It belongs to the Franks, and from it they make raids on Hamah and Hims whence it can be seen ... We arrived at the city of Hamah in the high forenoon of Saturday and lodged in one of the khans in its suburb.

Any stranger in [*Mount Lebanon*] whom God has rendered fit for solitude may, if he wishes, attach himself to a farm and live there the pleasantest life with the most contented mind. Bread in plenty will be given to him by the people of the farm, and he may engage himself in the duties of an imam or in teaching, or what he will, and when he is wearied of the place, he may remove to another farm, or climb Mount Lebanon or Mount Judi and there find the saintly hermits who nothing seek but to please Great and Glorious God, and remain with them so long as he wishes, and then go where he wills. It is strange how the Christians round Mount Lebanon, when they see any Muslim hermits, bring them food and treat them kindly, saying that these men are dedicated to Great and Glorious God and that they should therefore share with them. This mountain is one of the most fertile in the world, having all kinds of fruits, running waters, and ample shade, and rarely is it without a hermit or an ascetic. And if the Christians treat the opponents of their religion in this fashion, what think you of the treatment that the Muslims give each other?

One of the astonishing things that is talked of is that though the fires of discord burn between the two parties, Muslim and Christian, two armies of them may meet and dispose themselves in battle array, and yet Muslim and Christian travellers will come and go between them without interference. In this connection we saw at this time, that is the month of Jumada 'l-Ula, the departure of Saladin with all the Muslims' troops to lay siege to the fortress of Kerak, one of the greatest of the Christian strongholds lying astride the Hejaz road

9 Literally, 'the Fortress of the Kurds', the Arab name for 'Krak des Chevaliers' in present-day Syria.

and hindering the overland passage of the Muslims. Between it and Jerusalem lies a day's journey or a little more. It occupies the choicest part of the land in Palestine, and has a very wide dominion with continuous settlements, it being said that the number of villages reaches four hundred. This Sultan invested it, and put it to sore straits, and long the siege lasted, but still the caravans passed successively from Egypt to Damascus, going through the lands of the Franks without impediment from them. In the same way the Muslims continuously journeyed from Damascus to Acre (through Frankish territory), and likewise not one of the Christian merchants was stopped or hindered (in Muslim territories).

The Christians impose a tax on the Muslims in their land which gives them full security; and likewise the Christian merchants pay a tax upon their goods in Muslim lands. Agreement exists between them, and there is equal treatment in all cases.

The soldiers engage themselves in their war, while the people are at peace and the world goes to him who conquers. Such is the usage in war of the people of these lands; and in the dispute existing between the Muslim Emirs and their kings it is the same, the subjects and the merchants interfering not ...

Two days we tarried at this place,[10] and then, on Thursday the 12th of Jumada, corresponding with the 20th of September, we set forth across country to Sur [*Tyre*]. On our way we passed by a great fortress called al-Zab [*al-Zib* or *Casal Imbert*] which dominates the continuous villages and farms, and by a walled town called Iskandarunah [*Iscandelion*]. We sought a ship which we had learnt was bound for Bijayah [*Bougie (Algeria)*] and on which we wished to embark. And so we alighted at this town on the evening of that same Thursday, for the distance between the two cities (of Acre and Tyre) is thirty miles. We lodged in a khan in the town prepared for the reception of pilgrims.

A note on the city of Sur [Tyre] – May God Most High destroy it

This city has come proverbial for its impregnability, and he who seeks to conquer it will meet with no surrender or humility. The Franks

10   Acre, described as 'full of refuse and excrement'.

prepared it as a refuge in case of unforeseen emergency, making it a strong point for their safety. Its roads and streets are cleaner than those of Acre. Its people are by disposition less stubborn in their unbelief, and by nature and habit they are kinder to the Muslim stranger. Their manners, in other words, are gentler. Their dwellings are larger and more spacious ...

An alluring worldly spectacle deserving of record was a nuptial procession which we witnessed one day near the port in Tyre. All the Christians, men and women, had assembled, and were formed in two lines at the bride's door. Trumpets, flutes, and all the musical instruments, were played until she proudly emerged between two men who held her right and left as though they were her kindred. She was most elegantly garbed in a beautiful dress – from which trailed, according to their traditional style, a long train of golden silk. On her head she wore a golden diadem covered by a net of woven gold, and on her breast was a like arrangement. Proud she was in her ornaments and dress, walking with little steps of half a span, like a dove, or in the manner of a wisp of cloud. God protect us from the seduction of the sight. Before her went Christian notables in their finest and most splendid clothing, their trains falling behind them. Behind her were her peers and equals of the Christian women, parading, in their richest apparel and proud of bearing in their superb ornaments. Leading them all were the musical instruments. The Muslims and other Christian onlookers formed two ranks along the route, and gazed on them without reproof. So they passed along until they brought her to the house of the groom; and all that day they feasted.

We thus were given the chance of seeing this alluring sight, from the seducement of which God preserve us.

We then returned by sea to Acre and landed there on the morning of Monday the 23rd of Jumada, being the first day in October. We hired passages on a large ship, about to sail to Messina on the island of Sicily. My God Most High, in His power and strength, assure the easing and lightening (of our way).

During our stay in Tyre we rested in one of the mosques that remained in Muslim hands. One of the Muslim elders of Tyre told us that it had been wrested from them in the year 518 [*27th of June,*

1124], and that Acre had been taken twelve [*actually twenty*] years earlier [*24th of March, 1104*], after a long siege and after hunger had overcome them. We were told that it had brought them to such a pass – we take refuge in God from it – that shame had driven them to propose a course from which God had preserved them. They had determined to gather their wives and children into the Great Mosque and there put them to the sword, rather than that the Christians should possess them. They themselves would then sally forth determinedly, and in a violent assault on the enemy, die together. But God made His irreversible decree, and their jurisprudents and some of their godly men prevented them.

They thereupon decided to abandon the town, and to make good their escape. So it happened, and they dispersed among the Muslim lands. But there were some whose love of native land impelled them to return and, under the conditions of a safeguard which was written for them, to live amongst the infidels, 'God is the master of His affair' [*Koran XII, 21*].

Glorious is God, and great is His power. His will overcomes all impediments. There can be no excuse in the eyes of God for a Muslim to stay in any infidel country, save when passing through it, while the way lies clear in Muslim lands. They will face pains and terrors such as the abasement and destitution of the capitation and more especially, amongst their base and lower orders, the hearing of what will distress the heart in the reviling of him [*Muhammad*] whose memory God has sanctified, and whose rank He has exalted; there is also the absence of cleanliness, the mixing with the pigs, and all the other prohibited matters too numerous to be related or enumerated. Beware, beware of entering their lands. May God Most High grant His beneficent indulgence for this sin into which (our) feet have slipped, but His forgiveness is not given save after accepting our penitence. Glory to God, the Master. There is no Lord but He.

Among the misfortunes that one who visits their land will see are the Muslim prisoners walking in shackles and put to painful labour like slaves. In like condition are the Muslim women prisoners, their legs in iron rings. Hearts are rent for them, but compassion avails them nothing ...

By an unhappy chance, from the evils of which we take refuge in God, we were accompanied on our road to Acre from Damascus by a Maghribi from Buna in the district of Bougie who had been a prisoner and had been released by the agency of Abu 'I-Durr and become one of his young men. In one of his patron's caravans he had come to Acre, where he had mixed with the Christians, and taken on much of their character. The devil increasingly seduced and incited him until he renounced the faith of Islam, turned unbeliever, and became a Christian in the time of our stay in Tyre. We left to Acre, but received news of him. He had been baptised and become unclean, and had put on the girdle of a monk, thereby hastening for himself the flames of hell, verifying the threats of torture, and exposing himself to a grievous account and a long distant return (from hell). We beg Great and Glorious God to confirm us in the true word in this world and the next, allowing us not to deviate from the pure faith and letting us in His grace and mercy, die Muslims.

This pig, the lord of Acre whom they call king, lives secluded and is not seen, for God has afflicted him with leprosy. God was not slow to vengeance, for the affliction seized him in his youth, depriving him of the joys of his world. He is wretched here, 'but the chastisement of the hereafter is severer and more lasting' [*Koran XX, 127*]. His chamberlain and regent is his maternal uncle, the Count, the controller of the Treasury to whom the revenues are paid, and who supervises all with firmness and authority. The most considerable amongst the accursed Franks is the accursed Count, the lord of Tripoli and Tiberias [*Raymond III*]. He has authority and position among them. He is qualified to be king, and indeed is a candidate for the Office.

He is described as being shrewd and crafty. He was a prisoner of Nur al-Din's for twelve years or more, and then ransomed himself by the payment of a great sum in the time of the first governorship of Saladin, to whom he admits his vassalage and emancipation ...

The cities of Acre and Tyre have no gardens around them, and stand in a wide plain that reaches to the shores of the sea. Fruits are brought to them from the orchards that are in the neighbourhood. They possess broad lands and the nearby mountains are furnished with farmsteads from which fruits are brought to them. They are very rich cities. At the eastern extremity of Acre is a torrent course, along the banks of which extending to the sea is a sandy plain, than which I have seen no more beautiful sight. As a course for horses there is none to compare with it. Every morning and evening the Lord of the town rides over it, and there the soldiers parade – destroy them, God. Beside Tyre's landward gate is a fresh spring down to which a stairway leads. The wells and cisterns of the town are many, and there is no house without one. May God Most High, in His grace and favour, restore to it and to its sister (cities) the word of Islam.

On Saturday the 28th of Jumada, being the 6th of October, with the favour of God towards the Muslims, we embarked on a large ship, taking water and provisions. The Muslims secured places apart from the Franks. Some Christians called 'bilghriyin' [*from the Italian pellegrini = pilgrims*] came aboard.

They had been on the pilgrimage to Jerusalem, and were too numerous to count, but were more than two thousand. May God in His grace and favour soon relieve us of their company and bring us to safety with His hoped-for assistance and beneficent works; none but He should be worshipped. So, under the will of Great and Glorious God, we awaited a favouring wind and the completion of the ship's stowing.[11]

---

11 On his way home Ibn Jubair's ship is wrecked off the coast of Sicily, where he is saved by the personal intervention of King William II ('the Bad'); his time on that island features in *Sicily: through writers' eyes*, written and edited by Horatio Clare, pp. 76 ff.

Usama ibn Munqidh: *Autobiography* (*c*.1180)

Once the Crusader fiefs were well-established, trade picked up and frater-
nization between Muslims and Franks was quite common, as the text from
Usama ibn Munqidh shows. The wry disdain shown by the urbane Syrian for
the uncouth Franks and their primitive medical skills, his sneering at their
loose attitude to feminine decency, are a fascinating commentary (though he
did express respect for some aspects of Frankish life).

The lord of al-Munaytirah [*in Mount Lebanon, above Byblos*] wrote to
my uncle asking him to dispatch a physician to treat certain sick
persons among his people. My uncle sent him a Christian physician
named Thabit. Thabit was absent but ten days when be returned. So
we said to him, 'How quickly has thou healed thy patients!' He said:
'They brought before me a knight in whose leg an abscess had grown;
and a woman afflicted with imbecility. To the knight I applied a small
poultice until the abscess opened and became well; and the woman I
put on diet and made her humor wet. Then a Frankish physician came
to them and said, "This man knows nothing about treating them." He
then said to the knight, "Which wouldst thou prefer, living with one
leg or dying with two?" The latter replied, "Living with one leg." The
physician said, "Bring me a strong knight and a sharp ax." A knight
came with the ax. And I was standing by. Then the physician laid the
leg of the patient on a block of wood and bade the knight strike his leg
with the ax and chop it off at one blow. Accordingly he struck it –
while I was looking on – one blow, but the leg was not severed. He
dealt another blow, upon which the marrow of the leg flowed out and
the patient died on the spot. He then examined the woman and said,
"This is a woman in whose head there is a devil which has possessed
her. Shave off her hair."

Accordingly they shaved it off and the woman began once more to
eat their ordinary diet – garlic and mustard. Her imbecility took a turn
for the worse. The physician then said, "The devil has penetrated
through her head." He therefore took a razor, made a deep cruciform
incision on it, peeled off the skin at the middle of the incision until the
bone of the skull was exposed and rubbed it with salt. The woman also

Ruins of crusader castle at Mseilha

expired instantly. Thereupon I asked them whether my services were needed any longer, and when they replied in the negative I returned home, having learned of their medicine what I knew not before ... '

The Franks are void of all zeal and jealousy ... Here is an illustration which I myself witnessed: I entered the public bath in Sur [*Tyre*] and took my place in a secluded part. One of my servants thereupon said to me, 'There is with us in the bath a woman.' When I went out, I sat on one of the stone benches and behold! the woman who was in the bath had come out all dressed and was standing with her father just opposite me. But I could not be sure that she was a woman. So I said to one of my companions, 'By Allah, see if this is a woman,' by which I meant that he should ask about her. But he went, as I was looking at him, lifted the end of her robe and looked carefully at her. Thereupon her father turned toward me and said, 'This is my daughter. Her mother is dead and she has nobody to wash her hair. So I took her in with me to the bath and washed her head.' I replied, 'Thou hast well done! This is something for which thou shalt be rewarded [*by Allah*]!'

Among the Franks are those who have become acclimatized and have associated long with the Muslims. These are much better than the recent comers from the Frankish lands. But they constitute the exception and cannot be treated as a rule.

*   *   *

High Life, High Spirits and High Jinks during the Crusades
Life was good, while it lasted, for the rulers and nobility of the Latin city-states, and nowhere better than in Tripoli. The counts of Toulouse knew how to live, and the ostentatious luxury displayed in the trousseau of Raymond's sister Mélisande for her planned wedding with the Byzantine Emperor shocked the clerical observer William of Tyre, who nonetheless recorded the brilliant occasion in his Chronicle. Slanders about the legitimacy of her birth caused the old Emperor to cancel the wedding, a slight from which the beauty never recovered. A century later, the Crusader States were on their last legs, having been reduced by Saladin to a string of squabbling statelets along the coast. King Louis IX of France, the future saint, spent a season in Lebanon, fortifying the castle at Sidon which is still known by his name, before dying

of dysentery on an equally doomed crusade to Tunisia. Even his liege-man and biographer Jean de Joinville found him dour and priestly, unresponsive to feelings of family affection; but that did not stop his feisty queen, Marguerite de Provence, from having a good laugh; nor Joinville and his peers from joyfully messing around with bears, among other things.

The Trousseau of Mélisande: from William of Tyre (c.1170 AD)

The King took the counsel of his closest friends as to which of the two damsels he should send to marry the Emperor. Their choice was unanimous. So he summoned his messengers and said that his desire and that of his counsellors was that their lord should wed Mélisande, the sister of [Raymond II] the count of Tripoli; she was a famously well-brought up virgin and a great beauty as well ... The Count of Tripoli was overjoyed, as was his wife, and so they prepared for her the richest possible trousseau for the damsel. The King himself and all his entourage outdid themselves in making it the most dazzling one ever. Dresses of the richest silk cloth of numerous kinds: scarlet, deep blue, green and brown, all in great abundance; golden tiaras, set with precious jewels, bejewelled belts and brooches and pins and rings, all exceedingly precious, as well as those other jewels which ladies hang from their ears, all most rich, of all these things they gave her many. There were also salvers, serving-spoons and all kitchen utensils in solid silver; harnesses and extremely costly saddles for men and ladies: description fails me as they were so rich and costly. The precious gifts offered her were greater than those ever assembled for any queen ...

The Woollen Relics: from Jean de Joinville (describing events c.1253 AD)

I entreated the King [Louis IX] to permit me to go on pilgrimage to Our Lady of Tortosa ... This he granted me, and after asking around, told me to buy a hundred lengths of wool-stuff [camelin] which he would give to the Cordeliers on our return to France. When we reached Tripoli, my knights asked me what I planned to do with the lengths of wool; 'Maybe,' I jested, 'I will steal them and make a handsome profit.' The Count of Tripoli (may God forgive him his sins!) received us with as much ceremony and honour as he could, and told my knights and me to take whatever rich presents we wished; but all we accepted were some holy relics, which I took to the King, along with the wool-stuff. But I did send four lengths of the wool to the Queen; the knight who brought them to her had wrapped them in white linen, and when she saw him coming into the room, she fell to her knees. The knight did likewise, but the Queen told him: 'Rise, Sir Knight; you should not kneel, since you are bearing holy relics.' The knight replied: 'But Majesty, these are not relics, only wool-stuffs which my lord sends to you!' When the Queen heard that, she and her ladies-in-waiting burst out laughing, and the Queen got up and told my knight: 'You tell your lord I hope he has a miserable day,[12] for having caused me to kneel before wool-stuffs!'

A Bear in the Barnyard: from Jean de Joinville

Let me tell you about the jokes that the Count of Eu played on us. I had arranged a house for my knights and me to eat in, in the open space near the gate [of Sidon]. Well, the gate itself was just near the lodging of the Count of Eu, who was exceedingly mischievous. He had a small crossbow made, with which he would shoot bolts into my house through the window. He would spy on us, and when we were at table eating our meal, would aim his crossbow to shoot down the length of our table, breaking our bowls and glasses.

Now, I had put in a good supply of hens and capons. I have no idea who gave it to him, but the Count had come into possession of a young she-bear, which he brought around and turned loose on my chickens. She had killed at least a dozen by the time we got there and found the serving-girl who watched after them, swatting the bear with her spindle …

Translated by T. J. Gorton

ﻋ

---

12 'maus jours li soit donnez'.

Ibn Battuta: *Travels* (*c.* 1325 AD)

During two voyages that took Ibn Battuta along the Lebanese coast, the
famous Tunisian traveller found almost nothing exotic enough to comment
on except the legend of a Sufi holy man whose tomb he visited near Beirut.
Sidon and Tiberias are described as 'ruins'. This is hardly surprising, coming
as it does in the aftermath of a century of warfare and destruction that led to
the final destruction of the Crusader states (one might also note that he was
on his way back from a long voyage to China and India).

I next visited Sidon and Tiberias ... ; the whole was, however, in ruins,
but the magnitude of it was sufficient to shew that it had been a large
place ... I next arrived at Beirut which is on the sea-shore, and then set
out to visit the tomb of Abu Yaakub Yusuf, who is supposed to have
been one of the kings of the west ... It is said that this Abu Yaakub
lived by weaving mats: it is also said, that he was hired to keep some
orchards in Damascus, for the sultan Nur Oddin the martyr, the
preceptor of Salah Oddin. After he had been some time in this
situation, Nur Oddin happened to come into the orchard, and to ask
the keeper for a pomegranate. He brought several, one after the other,
each of which, however, had the appearance of being sour. It was said
to him, have you been all this while in the orchard, and do not yet
know a sweet pomegranate from a sour one? He replied, I was hired
to keep the orchard, not to eat the pomegranates ... The sultan then
rose and embraced him, and made him sit by his side ...

   I next arrived at Tarabalas (Tripoli) in Syria, which is a large city,
and may be compared with Damascus.

Sidon in the 1950s

TWO

Orient of the Mind:
Travellers from the West
Fourteenth–Twentieth Centuries

When such a spacious mirror's set before him
He needs must see himself

Antony and Cleopatra

Before one can ask, What is the Orient?, one must first decide who one is, and where one is coming from; for the 'other shore', *l'autre rive* of the Mediterranean has always been a distorting mirror to the West, casting its mystic spell in the direction of the more down-to-earth, mercantile, secular shores of Europe. Those who succumbed to that hypnotic spell were sometimes harmless dreamers, or the scholarly or curious who, like Herodotus in his time, just had to go and see for themselves; and sometimes much less innocent voyagers, chasing empires, fortunes, or the keys to the gates of heaven. The ostensible and hidden reasons for going East evolved over time; but the stories brought back by those who returned, or told by those who were on the receiving end, speak volumes about all concerned as well as about the real countries behind the stage-set of dreams, legends and lies.

FOURTEENTH TO EIGHTEENTH CENTURIES

The century or two after the Crusades' final débâcle in about 1300 AD were understandably a difficult time for European cultural tourism in the Levant. Ironically, the fall of Constantinople to Mehmet the Conqueror in 1453 may have contributed both to the Renaissance, and to the European application of the new spirit of enquiry to practical spheres. The Ottomans were much slower to do so; this would eventually lead to the military and economic advances of the West and contribute to the relative decline of the sprawling Empire. The awakening of curiosity and enquiry in Europe initially coincided with a slightly less unwelcoming attitude in the vast Ottoman domain, now feeling secure at least in its Asian hinterland. First came pilgrims and envoys with an ecclesiastical mission. With the political fragmentation of Europe, the Church despaired of re-conquering Jerusalem through new Crusades, and instead sent missionaries with the covert aim of gnawing away at the edifice of Islam in the Levant through proselytism, cementing ties with local Christians. Then came intrepid merchants, and by the late sixteenth century, the odd European traveller without an official or a mercantile mission, travelling just to see, learn and report back to a public that was beginning to be interested.

In the background there is the series of bilateral Capitulations signed between the Sublime Porte (the Ottoman Government) and European powers, notably the Second French Capitulations in 1569 (the English would only get their first ones in 1580). The active and increasingly unrestricted presence of the European consuls and merchants is palpable as one reads the selections in chronological sequence. As portraits of Lebanon, they are of course partial. All the voyagers were Christians, and they naturally saw a lot more of the local Christians, especially Maronites, than of any other group: hence Regnault's absurd statement that the Maronites outnumbered the Muslims twenty or twenty-five to one. They gradually become better informed, even if still overly concerned with the Christian population, or with repeating preposterous stories about the secretive Druze. Only when we reach the mid-seventeenth century do we find a polyglot, relatively acculturated resident observer to give us a generally reliable inside story (d'Arvieux).

Our selections provide a chronological series of snapshots – ostensibly of Lebanon, incidentally of the state of European interest in and knowledge (or ignorance) of the Levant as it evolved over four centuries or so. They begin in the mid-fourteenth century, with the account of an almost certainly fictitious English knight, when Middle Eastern travel writing was a genre of fantasy literature. Three centuries later, in the late seventeenth and early eighteenth centuries, travel to the Levant was more feasible and frequent than a century earlier, but was still adventurous. Nor was there much the traveller could do to prepare for his visit other than to read the Classics and Scripture, and to de-brief any returned voyagers he might be fortunate enough to meet. From the middle of the seventeenth century, there were French, Italian and English consuls and 'factors' in all the principal ports and entrepôt cities. Their responsibilities included taking care of travellers, especially but not exclusively of their own nation: thus Henry Maundrell in 1697 is assisted by the English consul in Tripoli as well as the French one in Sidon (as was Cornelius de Bruyn in 1680).

By the seventeenth century (after the defeat of the Ottoman fleet at Lepanto in 1571, notably), the pace of Ottoman expansion, ebbing since Vienna, was perceived in the West as less threatening. Voyages of discovery became easier, if not yet commonplace; it even became feasible to travel to India overland, via Syria or Egypt. Travel conditions had improved to the extent that the Levant, from Damascus to the Holy Land, could be added to Grand Tour itineraries. Thoughtful travellers like Volney had an extensive literature of earlier voyagers and savants to draw on, though even in the nineteenth century, Scripture and Strabo are the constant references which would have been familiar to the reading public. The European urban classes became intensely curious about the 'Orient', assuring the success of the travellers whose stories follow. As with all travel writing, these tell as much about the writers, and their own societies and times, as about the places they visit:

'There is still one [*city*] of which you never speak.'

Marco Polo bowed his head.

'Venice,' the Khan said.

Marco smiled. 'What else do you believe I have been talking to you about?'[13]

'Sir John Mandeville': *Voyage* (*c.*1360)

Fraud or not, Mandeville's work was a bombshell when it was 'published' in Anglo-Norman French in about 1357 (the oldest extant manuscript dates from 1371). It was translated into several European languages including English (and Latin), printed as soon as printing began, and was still being reprinted in several of those languages well into the sixteenth century (in Italian, at Venice in 1537, for example). The text shows boundless ignorance about the Orient, with blanks often filled in with fantasy: that the compiler (possibly a Liège physician) could get away with some of his tall tales is an eloquent commentary. But there is a residue of reality: the compiler also cribbed from real travel stories such as that of Giovanni del Pian Carpini (the Pope's envoy to the Tatars in the late thirteenth century); the Historiae Orientis *of the Armenian Hetoum (1307); or, for the Levantine bits, from the pilgrim Wilhelm von Boldensele (1333). If its content is at least partly questionable – and it really should be seen as an encyclopedia of medieval belief and legend about the world – its influence was very real indeed: 'When the Santa Cruz sighted land on 12 October 1492, a copy of Mandeville's* Travels *lay beside Marco Polo's book in the admiral's day-cabin ... '*[14]

And men go by the mounts of Libanus, which lasts from Armenia the more towards the north unto Dan, the which is the end of the Land of Repromission toward the north, as I said before. Their hills are right fruitful, and there are many fair wells and cedars and cypresses, and many other trees of divers kinds. There are also many good towns toward the head of their hills, full of folk.

13   Borrowed from Italo Calvino, *Invisible Cities* (London: Vintage, 1997/New York: Harcourt Brace, 1974), p. 86.
14   *Mandeville's Travels*, M. C. Seymour (ed.), (Oxford: Clarendon Press, 1967), p. xx.

Between the city of Arkez and the city of Raphane is a river, that is called Sabatory; for on the Saturday it runs fast, and all the week else it stand still and runs not, or else but fairly. Between the foresaid hills also is another water that on nights freezes hard and on days is no frost seen thereon. And, as men come again from those hills, is a hill higher than any of the other, and they call it there the High Hill. There is a great city and a fair, the which is called Tripoli, in the which are many good Christian men, yemand [*using*] the same rites and customs that we use. From thence men come by a city that is called Beyrout, where Saint George slew the dragon; and it is a good town, and a fair castle therein, and it is three journeys from the foresaid city of Sardenak. At the one side of Beyrout sixteen mile, to come hitherward, is the city of Sydon. At Beyrout enters pilgrims into the sea that will come to Cyprus, and they arrive at the port of Surry or of Tyre, and so they come to Cyprus in a little space ...

From Tortouse pass men to Tripoli by sea, or else by land through the straits of mountains and fells. And there is a city that is called Gibilet. From Tripoli go men to Acres; and from thence are two ways to Jerusalem, the one on the left half and the other on the right half ...

From Cyprus, men go to the land of Jerusalem by the sea: and in a day and in a night, he that hath good wind may come to the haven of Tyre, that is now clept [*called*] Surrye. There was some-time a great city and a good of Christian men, but Saracens have destroyed it a great part; and they keep that haven right well, for dread of Christian men. Men might go more right to that haven, and come not in Cyprus, but they go gladly to Cyprus to rest them on the land, or else to buy things, that they have need to their living. On the sea-side men may find many rubies. And there is the well of the which holy writ speaketh of, and saith, *Fons ortorum, et puteus aquarum viventium*: that is to say, 'the well of gardens, and the ditch of living waters.'

In this city of Tyre, said the woman to our Lord, *Beatus venter qui te portavit, et ubera que succisti*: that is to say, 'Blessed be the body that thee bare, and the paps that thou suckedst.' And there our Lord forgave the woman of Canaan her sins. And before Tyre was wont to be the stone, on the which our Lord sat and preached, and on that stone was founded the Church of Saint Saviour.

And eight mile from Tyre, toward the east, upon the sea, is the city of Sarphen, in Sarepta of Sidonians. And there was wont for to dwell Elijah the prophet; and there raised he Jonas, the widow's son, from death to life. And five mile from Sarphen is the city of Sidon; of the which city, Dido was lady, that was Aeneas' wife, after the destruction of Troy, and that founded the city of Carthage in Africa, and now is clept Sidon sayete [*Saida*]. And in the city of Tyre, reigned Agenor, the father of Dido. And sixteen mile from Sidon is Beirout. And from Beirout to Sardenare is three journeys and from Sardenare is five mile to Damascus …

جٍ

Antoine Regnault: *Discours* (1548–9)

Our first passage written by someone who demonstrably made the journey he describes – and returned to give an intelligible account of it – is that of a Frenchman, Antoine Regnault. He made the pilgrimage to the Holy Land in 1548-9. Written in a terse, descriptive vein with many details of the religious practices he observed along the way, his diary is clearly the record of a man in an utterly exotic and rather threatening context, with only his faith to keep him going through all the discomfort and danger. His description of a strange cucumber-shaped fruit is like a riddle – until one realises it is a banana.

Tripoli of Syria is situated at the foot of the Lebanese mountains. This Tripoli is not the one in Barbary, as some think. On the sea port there is a square tower where the Turks inspect the goods coming in and out. The tribute of this port is farmed out for 60,000 Ducats a year, or so I heard, to Venetian, Genoan and Ragusan merchants who do their business at that place. The goods most commonly traded here are spices, ginger, pepper, and cinnamon, all coming from the markets in Aleppo, six days' journey away. These goods are brought to Aleppo by the Baldac caravan to India, passing through Armenia, Persia and Arabia. Other goods come to Tripoli by way of Damascus, including Turkish fustian.

Still other merchandise comes to Tripoli along the coast from

Qazhayya Monastery, in the wadi Qadisha, the 'Holy Valley';
photograph by Gérard de Martimprey, 1896

Tyre, Sidon, Caesarea, and Sarepta; the latter is presently the place
where the Jews have retired to await the coming of their Messiah. In
that country there is a great quantity of stuff, cotton and silk, all traded
as we heard by Christians, Greeks and Jews, who travel up and down
the coast on business and live along it. So at Tripoli large numbers of
people gather together in order to travel safely through the country,
in what are called caravans. Quite recently there has been constructed
a storehouse, or shed, where the merchandise coming from India is
kept safe, as well as other places where each nation of traders keeps its
goods, called *fondicque*s [*funduq*]. We retired to the Fondicque of the
French, which was held by Mathieu d'Aiguemorte, a merchant of
Marseilles; he acted as our Dragoman while we were there.

In the Lebanese and Armenian [*sic*] mountains roundabout Tripoli,
there are several nations of Christians, called Druges [*sic*], Maronites
and Armenians, so numerous that for every Turk or Saracen of this
country, one finds twenty or twenty-five Christians, often kept as
slaves. It was on these mountains that Noah's Ark came to land after
the Great Flood.

On Saturday twentieth July [*1549*], Piedefer, Pierre Blanc, Anthoine
Regnault, and Benjamin the Jew of Rhodes, along with Abraham,
Maronite Christian from Beirut, bargained with a Saracen to take us
overland as far as Beirut, at a distance of four long days' travel: about
forty French leagues, at a cost of eighteen *medin*s [*1/40 of a Ducat*]
each.

Before setting off we purchased provisions, given that there are no
inns such as we had found thus far on the journey, other than the
Carbachara [*kervansaray* or *caravansaray*], which are public houses
where all persons may lodge who happen to pass by there, whether
Christians, Turks or Jews; eminent persons or lowly ones alike, with
no need to pay. We had to wear our over-coats [*loudiers*], shearling-
coats [*esclauines*], or pelisses [*estramatz*] for sleeping in, as all one is
given in the Carbachara is a small empty room. Each traveller eats
what he brought, as there is nothing provided except soup, though a
few provide bread and some meat, for which you have to bring your
own dish. Everyone who travels through this country is expected to
wear a knife on his belt, and a spoon for the soup and other food. All

a Turk needs in the way of eating utensils is a rug on the ground, on which he sits. They do not make use of benches, chairs, tables or buffets, and usually have no bedsteads [*chalit*]. They have only a few cushions to lean on, and all they need is a pot to make soup in, a dish, and a leathern or wooden cup from which they drink.

We left Tripoli at about seven in the evening and journeyed all night, except for a rest of about two hours to eat our meal near the fountains.

The next day, twenty-first July, we continued our journey past a great mountain, passing several camels loaded with goods, at a small town at the foot of the mountain called Elpatron [*Batroun*]. Near the gate of some orchards, we had our picnic under some white mulberry trees; our Dragoman told us that a tax of four *medins* was paid each year for each mulberry tree, and of one *medin* for each olive-tree. After we finished eating, about fifty Moors came up and started mocking us Christians on account of our codpieces, which they find most bizarre and offensive. We then got on our mules and rode the rest of the day through great heat, following the seashore, over stones, rocks, and past very high mountains. About eight in the evening, we came to a tower where we could spend the night, each one of us in turn standing guard, for our Dragoman told us there were many thieves in this area.

We left that place at dawn, passing over a great bridge over a river [*Nahr el-Kalb*]. Near this we saw a carved stone, with some letters written in Turkish, telling of Solim the Turk [*Sultan Selim*], who paved the road and restored the bridge. There is also an old inscription in Roman letters made by the Emperor Antoninus Pius; as well as a rock carved into a column, where there was a stone dog which used to bark by magic [*par Nigromancie*] whenever it saw ships or galleys on the sea.

A little further there is a tower by which one must pass and pay a Cafare or toll, where each person has to pay one *medin*. Moors, however, are not required to pay so long as they know how to perform the rites according to Mohammedan Law. We continued on our way and came to Beirut, a sea port where our Dragoman made us get down and walk. The Saracens call us Chamupcaour, which means 'dirty Christian'; that is because they wash their feet, hands and face as often as possible. Christians do not perform any such ablutions. From there we proceeded to a small Monastery of Maronite Christians, in which there were two monks of the minor orders, and two converts living according to the Roman Church; they told us they were from the convent of Saint Francis on Mount Zion, in the province of Jerusalem.

In the environs of Beirut, the countryside is adorned with fruit trees, including sebesten [*cordia*], fig-trees, orange-trees, olive-trees, and pomegranates. There is also a small fruit grown there, like a cucumber, which is as sweet as sugar, and which they call Adam's apple; its leaves are six feet long ...

Thursday first August. We left ... Sidon at about midnight, and did not cease travelling until we came to the sea-port of Sour [*Tyre*], which appearances suggest was of some greatness in times past. One can see churches like ours, which are in ruins ... The countryside thereabouts is very beautiful, and fertile, full of meadows, woods, tilled fields, olives, pomegranates, pines, fountains, and this makes the air most pleasant ...

The following night we left Soure following the seacoast, and on Friday crossed mountains covered with rosemary, which are in the land of Aser. We entered Galilee near a town called Sarepta, and then the Mount Tabor near Nazareth. The inhabitants of the country usually wear a Houpelande, woven of pyed goat's wool, black and white, shapelessly hanging down to their calves. Their shirts hang out over their clothing; they wear sharp knives and keep their right arms always bare, to be ready to use their bows. We did not dare enter Sarepta for fear of the plague, which raged there; the inhabitants are Jews. We resumed our way past a tower, where there were several Turks, who made us pay a Cafare of one gold Ducat each ...

Translated by T. J. Gorton

❧

Girolamo Dandini: *Voyage to Mount Libanus* (1596)

An Italian priest, Girolamo Dandini, was appointed Papal Legate to Mount Lebanon by Pope Clement VIII in 1596. He had an easier journey than Regnault, and the future Cardinal found the time (and inclination) to give us detailed descriptions of feminine fashion among the Christian ladies of the mountain.

Of the Customs of the Maronites, and of their Manner of Living.

The Maronites will not suffer the Turks to live amongst them, altho' they be in all the rest of Syria, so that you cannot see one there; they are beholding for it to the great care of their Deacons, who spare neither their Purses nor their Lives to that purpose. There lives therefore upon their Mountains no other than the Christians, which they call Maronites, who have taken their name from a certain Abbot called Maron ... They do not inhabit great Cities, and magnificent Palaces, but little Villages, whereof there is a great number, and in divers places.

Their Houses are mean and little worth, not but that they have noble and rich Persons amongst them, but they are tyranniz'd so over by the Turks, that they are constrained to shun all manner of grandeur and ostentation; they make themselves poor that they may shun ill treatment, and they affect to go meanly clad. Their habit differs not from the other Levantines, which consists of a Turbant and a little Vest that descends down to the knees, or to the middle of the leg, and sometime they wear the *Spain* or *Aba* to cover it; they go ordinarily with their legs naked, although there be some who have Drawers on, according to the Turkish manner, with Shoes.

The Arms they use are the Bow, Harquebus [*blunderbuss*], Cimitar and Dagger; they are very tall men, of a natural sweetness, docible to Arms, and resemble the Italians more than other Nations. They use no Tables, nor Stools to sit on, but instead thereof sit down cross-legged upon Mats or Carpets spread upon the ground, and there eat and drink; instead of a Table-cloth they lay a round piece of leather, and cover it about with Bread, tho' there be but two or three to eat. They sit round, and put the Victuals in the middle; they eat just as the Turks do, making no use of Napkins, Knives, nor as much as Forks, but have only very pretty wooden Spoons; and when they drink the Glass goes round.

If any one eats in another's House, 'tis the Master of the House that waits, and serving every one with his Glass, so that he has no manner of repose at the Table. They drink often, however their Glasses are but small; the more they drink, the more honour they think they do their Host; and altho' the leather that serves for a Table-cloth, be taken up, yet they cease not to drink as long as there is any Wine in the Vessel. These leathern Table-cloths are neatly folded up with the drawing of a small cord that is round about them. If any one comes in after they are set at Table, when he has saluted the company he sits down, eats and drinks without any more ado, and 'twere a great incivility to do otherwise. They use no Sheets to their Beds they sleep in, but only cotton Coverlets; each fastens a string to the Coverlet, and so lies under it.

The Maronite women are civil and modest, their manner of Dress differs not much from the Italian; their Apparel descends to the ground, and covers their breasts and shoulders entirely; 'tis very plain, being but Cloth of white Cotton, or at best but a violet or blue colour, and sometimes a little wrought. They wear upon their Heads a kind of Linnen Veil, which covers all their hair both before and behind. If they meet by chance with a Man they know not, they shun him, or cover their faces with their Veil. There are many of them, who like the Turkish Women wear certain Bracelets upon their Arms and Legs, and others at the form of a Fillet at the Forehead, with small pieces of silver. They use not to curl their hair, nor to paint their faces, neither can you see any other like vanity amongst them; which is so much the more commendable in them, as the contrary is blame-worthy in our European Dames.

When they come to Church, they place not themselves amongst the Men, nor yet where they may see their faces, for all the Men sit at the upper part of the Church, and they stay near the door to get out first as soon as Service is done, to the end that they may not be seen of any. There is no Man stirs from his place till they be all gone forth. The country is altogether free from Debauched and Common Women, so that you can hear there no manner of discourse of Adulteries, or other the like Vices, which is a particular favour of God.

Their priests are as ignorant as the Common People, for they can but only read and write. Those amongst them are esteemed most Learned, who besides the Arabick language, which is the Mother-

EMIR FECHREDDIN, PRINCE DES DRVS

The Amir Fakhr ad-Din II Ma'an, from Eugène Roger, Voyage (1664)

Tongue, have some knowledge in the Caldee, which is regarded by them as the Latin is by us ... They have no convenience nor advantage of Printing, no more than all the rest of the Levant, which might have been of great use to publish and to multiply their Books; however, I think it is a great happiness to this Nation, and also to all Christianity, for that not having amongst them any knowing Persons; the rest of the Levant being filled with Jews, Turks, Armenians, Nestorians, Jacobites, Dioscarians, Eutychians, Cophts, Abissins, Greeks, Georgians, Melkites, and other Sects, their wicked Books would multiply too fast by the help of Printing ...

ﺟﻚ

George Sandys: *Journey* (1610)

This account by the scholarly Englishman George Sandys (1610), contains precious vignettes of daily life and of relations between civilians of various subject communities and the Turkish authorities. In his Lebanese pages, Sandys gives us a detailed eyewitness report on the personality and politics of the famous Emir of Mount Lebanon, the wily Druze Fakhr ad-Din II al-Ma'ni .

Beritus was so called of the idol Berith, but originally Geris of Girgasus fifth son unto Canaan. It was subverted by Tryphon, and reedified by the Romanes that there planted a Colony, and called it Julia Felix: who by the bounty of Augustus were endued with the priviledges of citizens of Rome. Agrippa there placed two legions, by whome, and his predecessor Herod, it was greatly adorned: as after with Christian Churches, and the sea of a Bishop; being under the Metropolitan of Tyrus. With the rest, it hath lost his beauty, but not his being; now stored with merchandize, and much frequented by foreinners.

But now returne we to Sidon, the most ancient citie of Phoenicia, built, as some write, by Sida ye daughter of Belus; according to others, by Sidon the first borne of Canaan. Some do attribute the building thereof to the Phoenicians, who called it Sidon, in regard of the plenty of fish which frequented those coasts: for Sidon signifieth fish in their language. In fame it contendeth with Tyrus, but exceedeth it in antiquitie & is more celebrated by the Ancient. The seate thereof is healthfull, pleasant and profitable: on the one side walled with the sea, on the other side with the fruitfull mountains that lie before Libanus: from whence fall many springs, wherewith they overflow their delicate orchards (which abound with all variety of excellent fruits) and when they list exclude them. The making of Cristall glasses was here first invented; made of the foresaid sand, brought hither before it would become fusable. Amongst others right famous, Sidon is honored with the birth of Boetius ... But this once ample Citie still suffering with the often changes of those countries, is at this day contracted into narrow limits: and only shewes the foundations of her greatnesse; lying Eastward of this that standeth, and overshadowed with olives. There is nothing left of antiquitie, but the supposed Sepulcher of the Patriarke Zebulon, included within a little Chappell amongst the ruines; and held (especially by the Jewes) in great veneration. The town now being, is not worth our description; the wals neither faire nor of force, the haven decayed, when at best but serving for gallies. At the end of the Peir stands a paltry block-house, furnished with sutable artillery. The Mosque, the Bannia, and Cane for Merchants, the only buildings of note.

The inhabitants are of sundry Nations and religions; governed by a succession of Princes, whome they call Emers ... As for this Emer, he was never known to pray, nor ever seene in a Mosque. His name is Faccardine; small of stature, but great in courage and atchievements: about the age of forty; subtill as a foxe, and not a little inclining to the Tyrant. He never commenceth battell, nor executeth any notable designe, without the consent of his mother ...

> Skilled in black Arts, she makes streames backward runne:
> The virtues knows of weeds; of laces spunne
> On wheeles; and poison of lust-stung mare.
> Faire dayes makes cloudie, and the cloudie faire;
> Starres to drop bloud; the Moune looke bloudily;
> And plum'd [alive] doth through nights shadowes fly.
> The dead calls from their graves to further harmes:
> And cleaves the solid earth with her long charmes.
>
> [*after Ovid*]

To his towne he hath added a kingly Signorie: what by his sword, and what by his stratagems. When Morat Bassa [*Murad Pasha*] (now principall Vizier) came first to his government of Damasco, he made him his, by his free entertainment and bounty; which hath converted to his no small advantage: of whome he made use in his contention with Frecke the Emer of Balbec, by his authority strangled. After that he pickt a quarrel with Joseph Emer of Tripoli, and dispossest him of Barut, with the territories belonging thereunto; together with Gazer, about twelve miles beyond it, a place by situation invincible ... The Grand Signior doth often threaten his subversion; which he puts off with a just, that he knows that he will not this years trouble him: whose displeasure is not so much provoked by his incroaching as by the revealed intelligence which he holds with the Florentine; whom he suffers to harbour within his haven of Tyrus (yet excusing it as a place lying wast, and not to be defended) to come ashore for the fresh-water, buyes of him underhand his prizes, and furnisheth him with necessaries. But designes of a higher nature have beene treated of betweene them, as is well known to certain merchants imployed in that businesse ...

It is said for a certainty, that the Turke will turne his whole forces upon him the next Summer: and therefore more willingly con-descends to a peace with the Persian. But the Emer is not much terrified with the rumour (although he seekes to divert the tempest by continuance of gifts, the favour of his friends & professed integrity): for he not a little presumeth of his invincible forts, well stored for a long warre; and advantage of the mountains: having besides forth thousand expert soldiers in continuall pay; part of them Moores, and part of them Christians: and if the worst should fall out, hath the sea to friend, and the Florentine. And in such an exigent intendeth, as is thought, to make for Christendome, and there to purchase some Signiory: for the opinion is, that he hath a masse of treasure, gathered by wiles and extortions, as well as from the Subject, as from the forreiner. He hath coined of late a number of counterfeit Dutch dollars, which he thrusteth away in payments, and offers in exchange to the merchant: so that no new Dutch dollars, though never so good, will now go currant in Sidon. He hath the fifth part of the increase of all things, the Christians & Jewes do pay for their heads two dollars apiece yeerely: and head money hee hath for all the cattell within his dominions. A severe Justicer: re-edified ruinous and replants depopulated places; too strong for his neighbors, and able to maintaine a defensive warre against the Turke: but that it is to be suspected that his people would fall from him in regard of his tyranny. Now as for the merchants, (who are for the most part English) they are entertained with all courtesie and freedome: they may travel without danger with their purses in their hands, paying for custome but 3. in the hundred. Yet these are but traines to allure them, and disguise his voracity; for if the owner of a Factor dye, as if the owner and he his heire, he will seize on the goods belonging to his Principals, and seeme to doe them a favour in admitting of a redemption under the value: so that they doe but labour for his harvest, and reape for his garners: For such, and such-like eatings they generally intend to forsake his Country ...

After five miles riding, we came to a small solitary Mosque not far from the sea; erected, as they say, over the widowes house that entertained Elias. Close by it are the foundations of Sarepta commended for her wines:

> Gazetick, Chian nor Falernan wine
> Have I: drink then of the Sareptan vine ...
>
> [*Sidonius*]

We crossed a little valley devided by the river Eleutherus (now called Casmeir) which derives his originall from Libanus, and glideth along with a speedy course through a strangely intricate channel guilty of the death of the Emperour Fredericke Barbarossa, who falling from his horse as he pursued the Infidels, and oppressed with the weight of his armour, was drowned therein and buried at Tyrus ...

Tyrus was said to be built by Tyrus the seventh son of Japhet; re-edified by Phoenix, made a colony of the Sidonians, and after the Metropolis of Phoenicia. The Citie was consecrated to Hercules, whose Priest was Sicheus. The citizens famous for sundry excellencies, and forreine plantations ...

A people fierce in warre [*Virgil*]

Nor were their women inexpert in their weapons.

> The Tyrian virgins quivers use to beare:
> And purple buskins, ty'd with ribands, weare   [*Virgil*]

Yet branded with two-fold imputation:

> Inconstant Tyrians –
> – Tyrians double-tongued,   [*Virgil*]

And no marvell, since their principall profession was merchandize …

჻

De Monconys: *Journal* (1647)

The Levant was still an obscure and mysterious place, where travellers as late as the Lyonnais diplomat Baron Balthasar de Monconys (1647) could hope to find secret potions and magic formulae to bring home. De Monconys is better known for having given one of only two known first-hand (but in his case, most uninformative) descriptions of a painting by Vermeer during the painter's lifetime.

Sidon, 18 November [1647]. The cotton market is held in the morning, in front of the French Warehouse [*khan*]. This is the finest I saw in the Frankish Levant, all of cut stone, square in shape and having seven spacious arcades with the stores below and above, a large gallery five paces wide, with each merchant's space behind them one next to the other, as in a cloister … On the 19th I went to the spun cotton market, which is held at a small square near the port; there is usually a huge crowd of women to be seen there, making it one of the principal amusements of the French. The 21st I left … for Beirut, sleeping along the road. At night I heard a mountain-dog howl; they say it has a fox's tail, and I was assured that some of them mount certain birds, which give birth to greyhounds from this coupling.

22 November. We sailed at moonrise, and got a little more sleep; then arrived at Beirut at 11 in the morning. It is a small town built on the sea, behind which rise the mountains of Kesrouan … The whole region is covered with trees, including fine mulberries, and handsome

pines, of which there is a forest planted in straight rows by the Emir
Fakhr ad-Din, who had his pleasure palace here, even though there is
no port worthy of the name.

23 November. We walked a league and a half from Beirut, heading
along the coast towards Tripoli; there is a small Chapel built where St.
George killed the Dragon. There formerly was a lake where that
creature lived, and now a small river runs under an arched bridge.
Halfway there one sees an old ruined house which, one is told, was the
King's Palace at that time; others say it was the place where the
maidens were kept while waiting to be devoured …

24 November. I stayed here on purpose to see a Jewess who was said
to know something of divination, and to be the only one around with
such knowledge; she merely threw a few drops of oil in a brass basin
of water, mumbled a few words, had me stick a finger in, then told me
to think to myself what it was that I desired. This I did, but she could
not divine what it was, telling me the sort of thing you would say to
any traveller, such as good omens for the voyage, safe return etc. In
the evening we went to see a local Jewish farmer, who was very cordial
to us, as I had been in contact with his Rabbi …

25 November. The Jewish farmer invited us to lunch, and in order
to retain us closed off the finest house in the City, built with vaulted
terraces along its whole length (as the rooms inside are also arranged).
The city is dark and dirty, rivulets running where horses pass down
the middle of its narrow streets …

27 November. A beautiful, clear and calm morning; I went to see M.
Faure and learned the following secrets: To stop a wound from
bleeding, put grated leather on it, from the hair-side. To make an
excellent eau de toilette ['*eau de fart*'], put balsam in brandy and leave
it several days, then pour off the water; when you're ready to use it, put
three drops in a glass of clear water, which becomes white as milk;
then wash yourself with it. To cure an epileptic, whisper into his ear,
or if you're not close enough for that, look him right in the eye and say
three times: '*memento Creatoris tui in nomine Patris*' …

Translated by T. J. Gorton

Eugène Roger: *Terre Sainte* (1664)

Eugène Roger, another (French) friar, found employment during his sojourn in the Holy Land, as a physician. He served as personal medic to Fakhr ad-Din, and (though he had left the region by the time), was the first to allege that a Lorraine cross was found on the Emir's person after his execution. This was much repeated by later travellers (such as d'Arvieux, who wrote later than Roger). Whatever his personal convictions, it seems unlikely that the wily Druze would commit such a risky faux pas. He did spend five years among the Medici and other power-brokers of the day – including the Pope – in an unsuccessful campaign to drum up support for European intervention in support of Lebanese independence from Turkey.

In all the Mount Lebanon, which is entirely inhabited by Maronites, there are forty monasteries, of which most are abandoned. In those which are not, there are only two or three monks left, tilling the land and the vineyards and raising silk worms; the old ones weave mats, and thus they live from their labour. Their monasteries are in wild places, among frightening rocks, where it seems that nature took pleasure in making such lonely and penitent places, but so lovely, that on looking at them one is inspired to devotion and to despise the world. Some of them appear to hang in the air, especially the one called Mar Salita, where Saint Alexis lived for seven years. Extremely difficult of access, to enter it you have to climb a ladder twenty-five feet tall … But of all of the inhabited ones, there is one called Mar Sarkis, so forbidding that words cannot describe it. Other than being situated in the highest and gloomiest mountains of Lebanon, in a place so wild you see more wild beasts than human beings. Furthermore, it is set within a sheer cliff-face, so that in order to enter you have to climb a ladder, and pass over a scaffold made of branches, which leads you into a hole in the rock. This acts both as door and window allowing a little air and light into a cavern, at the back of which there are a few steps carved in the rock. These take you up into another cavern which is used as a church, and where there is no light at all other than that of a small lamp burning in front of an altar. When I visited there with a Friar of our Order, it was inhabited by a Maronite monk named Ibrahim Sahiuni, that is, Abraham of Zion. Eighty years old, he had lived in this place for fifty of them, living the life of a veritable Anchorite, easier to admire than to imitate ...

It once happened that a rich Maronite was surprised urinating in a Turkish cemetery near Tripoli; for this crime, the Cadi sentenced him to be burned alive, or to renounce his faith, and become a Turk. Renounce he did, in order to save his life, and hoping that he would be able to leave that country and live in some unknown place, where he could continue to live in observation of the Christian faith; and so he did. But the Turks also insisted on making his wife and children renounce their faith and become Turks, which they were compelled to do.

When the Patriarch heard about this matter, he went to find the Emir Fechrreddin, and asked him to take this family under his protection. This he did, which allowed the children to come back to the Church ... For this they deserved to die, according to Muslim Law, but the Turks did not dare mistreat them, because of their fear of the Emir Fechrreddin ...

[*Execution of the Emir Fakhr ad-Din*]

The Emir [*having been sentenced to die on the spot*] asked for a quarter of an hour to make his peace with God. This the Sultan granted him, thinking he would pray in the Turkish manner. But when he saw the Emir kneeling, facing East and crossing himself, he shouted, telling his Mutes: 'Quickly, strangle this Christian pig!' This was carried out at once; his head was then cut off. As he was stripped of his robes, next to his breast they found a gold Cross shaped like those of Lorraine ...

Translated by T.J. Gorton

༶

Laurent d'Arvieux: *Memoirs* (1658–65)

The Chevalier Laurent d'Arvieux lived a good portion of his adult life in the Levant, finally as French Consul in Aleppo. Returning to Marseille to marry and then die – in 1702 – he spent his last years writing a six-volume autobiography. This is one of the best sources of informed description of life

*in the Levant during the heyday of the Ottoman Empire – though the
accuracy of some of his facts and descriptions has been challenged by a near-
contemporary Turkish commentator. Facts aside, his descriptions of the
musical and inter-ethnically convivial Beirutis singing drinking-songs
(zajals?) in their gardens of a summer evening, or the French merchants
running cabarets on the side, or the author's own narrow escape drinking his
way out of a Druze ambush-party, are unique. His description of Lebanon
dates from observations made around 1660; regrettably, only the portion of
his travels dealing with Tunis has been published more recently than 1800.*

Life in Sidon is exceedingly commodious, and very cheap. Beef and
mutton costs no more than two French *sous* a pound, hens are ten *sous*
apiece; chickens eight *sous* the brace; red partridges, fifteen *sous* the
brace. Of the latter there are plenty, as well as tiny *beccaficos* and
migratory and water birds. Game of all sorts is plentiful and very cheap
as well. Hunting is most conveniently undertaken, and every resident
Frenchman without exception takes pleasure in going hunting, failing
which he pays a local hunter who supplies his master's table easily and
abundantly.

The local fruits are grapes, figs, apricots, peaches, pears, cherries,
blackberries, bananas or 'Adam's figs', scammony figs, plums, and
others most abundant ...

[*The ceremonial arrival of a new French Consul to Sidon*]

The Turkish officers sent by the Governor led the procession, after
welcoming the new Consul on his behalf; they were followed by the
Dragomans, then the janissaries, then servants, one of whom led by
hand the horse which the Pasha of Gaza had presented to the new
Consul.

Then came the Merchants two by two, in order of seniority;
followed by the Consul in superb attire, riding an exceedingly fine bay
horse with a French-style harness which I had bought for him from
M. de Bricard. In this order we entered the city; the streets were
thronged with people, all making a most joyful clamour.

Thus we arrived to the Khan. The Consul received compliments
on behalf of the Pasha, the Mayor, and the Qadi, and was then led to
his apartments. All the monks and priests who had come from the

Chapel to the city gate welcomed him, and presented him with holy water. He kneeled on his *prie-dieu*, covered with red velvet, and a Te Deum was sung, attended by the whole French colony.

He then entered the great hall, sat on an armchair at the head of the table, and had all the Merchants sit around him ... The Minutes of the occasion were prepared and signed by all present, then the papers were cleared away and a magnificent meal was served buffet-style on the table, of which all present were invited to partake. We thus spent the remainder of the day as well as the night in a joyous and pleasant state; this entire ceremony took place on the 15th of March, 1659.

The Merchants have their quarters around the arcades; they are spacious and comfortable, each with its office; some of these, as well as some of the store-rooms on the ground floor, have been turned into kitchens complete with ovens. In these a number of Frenchmen took it upon themselves to open cabarets, which are always full of sailors.

To make this little Republic complete, two Physicians have set up there. They represent the three Orders of Medicine, that is, Physicians, Surgeons, and Apothecaries ... I shall say nothing about their ability, fearing to say either too little or too much. If those they killed could speak, they would give us more reliable news; but, here as elsewhere, their errors are hidden under the ground ... Lucky are they who had no need of their care, unless they were dear enough friends to them to deserve a quick and inexpensive death. If one judges the skill of a Physician by his filling of cemeteries, then it would be fair to say that these were skilful indeed ...

There are several fine mosques in [*Beirut*], including one brand new one just next to the Saray ... The Imams and other officials of this mosque are careful to choose the finest voices of the city to sing out the regular prayer-call from the minaret, every Thursday evening, and during the entire lunar month of Ramadan. This music strikes one at first as unpleasant, but once the ear becomes accustomed to it, and to their manner of singing, it becomes most pleasing to hear.

All the people of Beirut have good voices and are exceeding fond of singing songs. It is most agreeable to hear them of an evening, singing in their gardens where they are accustomed to eat and drink. They sing at the top of their voice, in the same key, sometimes in several parts, and pitched an octave from each other; they do this with a cup of wine in hand, singing away for up to a quarter of an hour before they raise it to their mouth. This is considered very gallant in the Orient ...

Except for the Jews,[15] all the Citizens of Beirut, no matter what their religion, live harmoniously together. They treat each other with courtesy, pay each other visits, and take their entertainment together. The Beirutis are not mean like the inhabitants of Sidon and the other coastal towns; those who live at Tripoli of Syria are more affable still, and their town seems the most like a great city ...

The Princes of the Druses have forever been of the House of Ma'n. The Emir Fakhr ad-Din (meaning 'Glory of Religion') was of this illustrious family, being the last descendant thereof along with his uncle Yunis, which means Jonas. He was only six or seven when his father died, making him ruler off the entire country with all its Cities and Forts from Carmel [*Haifa*] as far as Tripoli of Syria ...

Fakhr ad-Din was of modest stature, ruddy-faced, with large fiery eyes, an aquiline nose, small mouth, white teeth, a handsome face withal; his beard was a chestnut-blond colour, and he carried himself with greatness and majesty. He was exceedingly intelligent and witty, loving painting, poetry and music; he treated generously those scholars and artists he brought across from Europe.

The number of his wives makes it clear that the Emir was not – yet – a Christian, as they say he was later to become; or if he was, he was not living a very Christian life. Or, one could surmise that he had no Religion other than that of his Tribe, which had none, as I have already mentioned.

On returning to Beirut, I found myself in such a dangerous situation that I thought my adventures had come to an end. I might have taken ship and travelled more comfortably, but I had two horses I would have had to entrust to a servant, from whom they might have been stolen (or who might have stolen them himself), so I decided to travel overland.

---

15 D'Arvieux, like many of the seventeenth-century (Inquisition-era) travellers, includes a rather formalistic, but very insulting description of the Jewish communities he ran across.

Just after crossing the river at Damour, which is about half-way between Beirut and Sidon, I heard from some peasants that there were five hundred Druses waiting to ambush any traveller, and who had been cutting the throats of all the Turks who fell into their hands; nor did they treat others much better. They were hiding in a defile, the road closed on one side by a horrid precipice against the foot of which the sea beat fiercely, and on the other side by rocks with a thick wood interspersed. The path has been so worn by mules passing over it that horses must step into the holes left by the others' hooves, forcing one to proceed with painful slowness. Some peasants who had had a skirmish with those Druses a few hours earlier had told me the name of their Chief.

As soon as I was close enough to talk to him, I greeted him by name and in his language, as though I knew him well already. I dismounted, took him by the hand and all that, feigning astonishment that he did not recognise me: 'What?!' I said, 'Shaikh Mender, you do not recognise a Frank whom you saw so often at Saida in the days of the Emirs, you who shared my victuals along with Shaikh so-and-so,' and more in this vein. So impressed by my assurance was he, that he pretended to recognise me, and asked me smilingly whence I came and where I was going. I answered his questions, and then asked him in turn whether he would fancy helping me drain a bottle of wine and having something to eat with me. My valet was stuck to his horse, immobile as a statue, just waiting to have his throat cut and body thrown down the precipice, following all those others whose blood was still fresh around us.

I told the Shaikh to send one of his people to take my provisions from the saddle-bags on my valet's horse; he said my valet would do it better than his. I was pleased to hear this, as I had put a bag of silver I had received in Beirut under the provisions, the sight of which might have reawakened the greed of these people, whom I could see grumbling in their beards, and complaining of the forbearance of their Chief. My valet looked a little reassured. I told him to bring us food; fortunately, I had loaded his horse with four capacious leathern flasks of excellent wine which I had received as a gift, and another bottle of brandy. With these he brought a roast capon and some

bread. Some of the Shaikh's principal followers joined us, and the first
two bottles were soon empty. The other two were brought, and soon
all those present were in exceedingly good spirits; we kissed each other
most tenderly. They told me of their present good fortune, and
showed me the clothes of those whose throats they had so recently
finished cutting, and the booty they had acquired. Seeing that the
advancing hour made me think of continuing my journey in order to
arrive at Sidon before the closing of the gates, he told me I was free to
go whenever I pleased: but above all things, not to tell a soul of their
ambush. This I promised him, and I would have promised much
besides, had he asked me, in order to procure my removal from such
a dangerous place.

Translated by T. J. Gorton

ؤ

Cornelius De Bruyn: *Travels* (*c.*1680)

*Cornelius De Bruyn was a Dutch polymath, artist and traveller, whose two
books of travels in the East were enormously popular in the late seventeenth
and early eighteenth centuries; he was especially acclaimed for his drawings
of Persepolis in Iran.*

Whilst I was at Tripoli I was minded to go and see Mount Lebanon,
tho' every body thought such a journey in that Season of the Year to
be impracticable. However I was willing to try, and to this purpose I
set out January 12, attended with one of my Fellow-Travellers, who
had the same Curiosity with my self. We got a Horseback by break of
day, and at first we crossed a great Plain planted with Olive Trees, of
which there are great Quantities round about Tripoli. In the middle
of these Trees I saw the Ruins of an old Oyl-Mill, call'd Cabo, which
tho' at present ruinated, yet still serves for the same use: formerly
there was a Village in that place. Then we pass'd by the Borough of
Kistin and Cafare Cabel, which is a neat and ancient piece of ruins
behind which is to be seen the Mountain Covered with Snow. [...]
    After this we went by S. Marie's Grotto, and a little after Noon,

arrived at Canobin or Stinoba, which signifies a Convention of Monks [*coenobium*]. This Convent is seated very pleasantly on the Hill, with Trees round about it. Behind it is to be seen at a distance the Mountain of Lebanon, with the Snows that always cover it … 'Tis said the Emperor Theodosius founded this Monastery. Here is the residence of the Patriarch of Antioch, whose jurisdiction reaches over all the Maronite Christians of that Country and Region. The Person who held that Dignity when I was there was one of Worth and very Civil; his Name was Stephanus Petrus, he spoke very good Italian, having studied at Rome fourteen Years. He encourag'd us to continue our Journey, and told us, that if no Snow fell that Night, we should certainly arrive the next day at the Cedars …

I had the Curiosity of measuring the bigness of two of the most remarkable, and found that one was fifty seven Spans about, and the other was forty seven: Under one of those Trees I saw a heap of Stones, which the Monks who come thither from time to time make use of instead of an Altar, whereat to perform their Devotions. The Branches of these Trees spread themselves so far about, that a great number of People may shelter themselves under the shadow thereof. 'Tis of this that the Prophet Hosea makes mention, Ch. 14, 5 &c. When he says; *I will be as the dew unto Israel, he shall grow as the Lilly, and cast forth his Roots as Lebanon. His Branches shall spread, and his beauty shall be as the Olive-Tree, and his smell as Lebanon. They that dwell under his shadow shall return* …

After a great deal of trouble we arrived to the place where we had left our Horses, and made all the speed we could to get to the next Village, being glad we had got off so well, and when we were come thither, we made our selves amends for the fatigues we had endured upon the Mountain. After this we set forward on our Journey, and by Four in the Afternoon return'd to Canobin.

This is a very pleasant place, and tho' it was Winter when I was there, yet I must needs own, that I never saw any thing more Charming in my Life. I could have wish'd to have spent some Months there, if the time would have permitted me, but this could not be, for I had more than one reason to the contrary. Here are Partridges as tame as our Yard Fowls. They fly about ten Paces, and then alight on the ground again, and seem to have no manner of fear of a Man. But besides this, Canobin would be preferable to all other places on account of its Wines, which are the richest and finest in the World. They are of a very sweet red Colour, and so Oleaginous, that they stick to the Glass. The Prophet Hosea makes a comparison from them, when he says, Chap. 14, 7, *the scent thereof shall be as the Wine of Lebanon.*

They have these Wines sent thither from all parts, but the Grape of which they are made is very scarce. The other Wines are not near so good, tho' there is a greater plenty of them. Whereas the Patriarch seem'd to have a great respect for us, he order'd the best to be serv'd always up to us; I found it so good that I think I never tasted a more delicious Liquor in all my Life. Turn your Eyes on which side you will, you may see great Quantities of Waters falling down from the Top of the Mountains, after a most admirable manner. Solomon in his Song of Songs seems to refer to this, when he says, Chap. 4, 15. *A Fountain of Gardens, a Well of Living Waters, and Streams from Lebanon.* Some there are who believe it was here where Noah lived; and the Patriarch in his Discourse with us gave us to understand that he was of that Opinion. For proof thereof he alledged, that there are two Mountains adjacent to Anti-Lebanon, which at this very day are call'd, the one Cain, the other Abel …

I found myself so well at Tripoli, that I resolv'd to pass the Winter there … During my residence in Tripoli I was told a thing somewhat strange, which I will impart to the Reader. About a Year before my coming thither, there dyed a certain Turk, who liv'd a little out of the Town on the Seaside, near this Rivulet which we have said came from Mount Lebanon. A Sopha of plain Boards like a square Table serv'd him for a House, in which he had liv'd Seventeen Years, without ever going out of it. The People of the Country look upon him as a great Saint. And every Body strove to bring him Provision, and happy were those whose Victuals he was pleas'd to eat. But notwithstanding his Sanctity he had the Capriciousness to cast into the River what did not please him. That which is most remarkable was that he never spake; When Nature obliged him to ease his Body, it was without stirring from this Place, and he would have wallowed in his Ordure, if the Turks, who have otherwise such great horrour for all manner of filthiness, or uncleanness, had not thought it an honour to carry away that of the holy Man. Such Power has a vain presumption on the Minds of those Superstitious and Credulous Musulmen. But it were to be wished that this was only to be found among them, and that there were none amongst Christians, who suffer themselves to be deceiv'd by an affected semblance of Holiness ...

[*After visiting Acre*] Having made an Agreement with the Master of the Vessel that was bound to Tripoli, ... that he should put me ashore at Tyre and Sidon, called at present Saide, and that he should tarry some hours for me there, I went on Board towards Evening. About Midnight we set sail with a Land Wind. The next day being the 29th of April we passed by Cape Bianco, with a pretty favourable Wind, and at Noon we arrived before Sour or Tyre, where we came to an anchor. I have already said heretofore, speaking of this place, that they use a sort of Violence on Travellers, by extorting a certain sum of Money from them against all right and reason: having then been instructed by Merchants of that Coast, that one was not obliged to pay any thing, and that I might freely go ashore without any charge, I caused the Bark to put to Land, where I presently went ashore, where I found the Aga that Commanded there, sitting with some of his Men on the Sea-side. He came immediately to me, and demanded the Cafare, or Tribute. I told him the Franks owed no Tribute there, adding, that I had been there divers times without ever having paid any thing, neither did I think to pay any thing now.

The Aga not being contented herewith, commanded his Janissaries to carry me to the Castle; and as they were going to take me by the Arm, to execute his Order, I told them that they need not give themselves that trouble, for I was willing to go where the Aga would have me carried, but that I assured him that I would complain to the Bassa, of the Consul of Saide, of the injustice done to me here, for this place depends on the Bassa of Saide. And to the end I might make the Aga more thoughtful, and obtain my liberty more easily, I endeavour'd to make him believe, that I was a Merchant of Tripoli, and had lived there some Years, so that I knew very well what it was to pay Tribute in that place; but for all my reasons and cunning, he would not let me go without paying: But carried me to the Castle, where they put me into a Nasty hole full of Vermin, where I found a Greek Priest who was put there for the same cause.

In the mean time the Master of the Vessel called to me several times in Italian, that I must pay, and that the Consul of Saide would speedily cause my Money to be return'd, complaining at the same time that he could not depart without me, to which he added, that if I should send an express to the Consul of Saide, as I had a mind to do, the Aga would stop him there, and in the mean while feed me with Bread and Water. These considerations brought me at last, after having staid there two or three hours, to pay him the sum he demanded of me. After which I was brought a second time before the Aga, and then I said to him, that since he would proceed so unreasonably with me, he might as well take all I had from me, to which he answered, without any hesitation or passion, that he did not demand a penny more than his right. So I drew my Purse, and paid him about four Crowns, which is as much as he takes from every Person. That which vext me most in this affair was, that I knew very well there was nothing due to him, and that the Merchants of the Coast had entreated me earnestly not to pay, because that when the Turks have once begun to settle a thing, it is very difficult to take them off it again. So that I fear for the future the Franks will be obliged to pay this duty, although they should oppose it as well as I did, and by my Example cause themselves to be put in Prison …

ﵟ

Henry Maundrell: *Journey* (1697)

Henry Maundrell gives us detailed (if not always accurate) observations of his leisurely travels through Lebanon in 1697, and famously wishes that Fakhr ad-Din's renowned pleasure-garden at Beirut had had the benefit of an English gardener …

We had a very tempestuous night both of wind and rain, almost without cessation, and with so great violence, that our servants were hardly able to keep up our tents over us. But however, this accident

Wall decoration, Beit ad-Din

which gave us so much trouble in the night, made us amends with a curiosity which it yielded us an opportunity of beholding the next morning.

Wednesday, March 17. For by this means we had the fortune to see what may be supposed to be the occasion of that opinion which Lucian relates, concerning this river, viz. that this stream, at certain seasons of the year, especially about the feast of Adonis, is of a bloody colour; which the heathens looked upon as proceeding from a kind of sympathy in the river for the death of Adonis, who was killed by a wild boar in the mountains, out of which this stream rises. Something like this we saw actually come to pass: for the water was stain'd to a surprising redness, and, as we observ'd in travelling, had discolour'd the sea a great way into a reddish hue; occasion'd doubtless by a sort of minium, or red earth, lashed into the river by the violence of the rain, and not by any stain from Adonis's blood.

In an hour and a quarter from this river, we passed over the foot of the mountain Climax; where, having gone thro' a very rugged and uneven pass, we came into a large bay, called Junia. At the first entrance into the bay, is an old stone bridge, which appoints the limits

between the two bassalicks [*pashalik, Ottoman sub-province*] of Tripoli
and Sidon. At the bottom of the bay are exceeding high and steep
mountains, between which and the sea the road lies. These are the
mountains of Castravan [*Kesrouan*], chiefly inhabited by Maronites,
famous for a growth of excellent wine. The Maronite bishop of Aleppo
has here his residence in a convent, of which he is the guardian. We
saw many other small convents on the top of these mountains; one of
which, call'd Oozier, was, as we were here told, in the hands of ten or
twelve Latin fryars.

Towards the further side of the bay, we came to a square tower or
castle, of which kind there are many all along upon the coast, for
several days' journey from this place: they are said to have been built
by the empress Helena, for the protection of the country from pirates.
At this tower is to be paid a fourth caphar [*toll*]. It is receiv'd by
Maronites, a pack of rogues, more exacting and insolent in their office
than the very Turks themselves. A little beyond this place, we came to
a road cut thro' the rocks, which brought us out of the bay, having
been one hour and a quarter in compassing it. In an hour more, spent
upon a very rugged way close by the sea, we came to the river Lucus,
call'd also sometime Canis, and by the Turks at this day, Nahor Kelp.
It derives its name from an idol in the form of a dog or wolf, which was
worshiped, and is said to have pronounc'd oracles, at this place. The
image is pretended to be shewn to strangers at this day, lying in the
sea, with its heels upward: I mean the body of it – for its oracular head
is reported to have been broken off, and carried to Venice, where (if
fame be true) it may be seen at this day.

This river issues into the sea from between two mountains, excessive
steep and high; and so rocky, that they seem to consist each of one
entire stone. For crossing the river, you go up between these mountains
about a bow shot from the sea, where you have a good bridge of four
arches; near the foot of which is a piece of white marble, inlaid in the
side of a rock, with an Arab inscription on it, intimating its founder to
have been the emir Faccardine (of whom I shall have occasion to speak
more when I come to Beroot). Being passed the river, you immediately
begin to ascend the mountain (or rather great rock), hanging over it
on that side. To accommodate the passage, you have a path of above

two yards breadth cut along its side, at a great height above the water; being the work of the emperour Antoninus. For the promontory allowing no passage between it and the sea at bottom, that emperour undertook, with incredible labour, to open this way above; the memory of which good work is perpetuated by an inscription, engraven on a table plain'd in the side of the natural rock, not far from the entrance into the way …

In passing this way, we observ'd, in the sides of the rock above us, several tables of figures carv'd; which seem'd to promise something of antiquity: to be satisfied of which, some of us clamber'd up to the place, and found there some signs as if the old way had gone in that region, before Antoninus cut the other more convenient passage a little lower. In several places hereabouts, we saw strange antique figures of men, carv'd in the natural rock, in mezzo relievo and in bigness equal to the life …

It was our unhappiness to have at this place a very violent storm of thunder and rain, which made our company too much in haste to make any long stay here; by which misfortune I was prevented, to my great regret, from copying the inscription, and making such an exact scrutiny into this antiquity as it seem'd very well to deserve. I hope some curious traveller or other will have better success, in passing this way hereafter. The figures seem'd to resemble mummys, and were perhaps the representation of some persons buried hereabout; whose sepulchers might probably also be discover'd by the diligent observer.

The emir Faccardine had his chief residence in this place [*Beirut*]. He was in the reign of the sultan Morat, the fourth emir, or prince of the Druses; a people suppos'd to have descended from some dispers'd remainders of those christian armies, that engaged in the crusades, for the recovery of the Holy Land: who afterwards, being totally routed, and despairing of a return to their native country again, betook themselves to the mountains hereabout; in which their descendants have continued ever since.[16]

16 Henry is repeating a baseless legend that would derive 'Druze' from the Crusader contingent 'de Dreux' …

Faccardine being (as I said) prince of these people, was not contented to be penn'd up in the mountains; but by his power and artifice, enlarged his dominions down into the plain all along the sea coast as far as from this place to Acra. At last the grand seignior, grown jealous of such a growing power, drove the wild beast back again to the mountains, from whence he had broke loose; and there his posterity retain their principality to this day.

We went to view the palace of this prince, which stands on the north east part of the city. At the entrance of it is a marble fountain, of greater beauty than is usually seen in Turkey. The palace within consists of several courts, all now run much to ruin; or rather perhaps never finish'd. The stables, yards for horses, dens for lions and other salvage creatures, gardens, &c. are such as would not be unworthy of the quality of a prince in Christendom, were they wrought up to that perfection of which they are capable, and to which they seem to have been design'd by their first contriver.

But the best sight that this palace affords, and the worthiest to be remember'd, is the orange garden. It contains a large quadrangular plat of ground, divided into sixteen lesser squares, four in a row, with walks between them. The walks are shaded with orange trees, of a large spreading size, and all of so fine a growth both for stem and head, that one cannot imagine any thing more perfect in this kind ... Were this place under the cultivation of an English gardner, it is impossible any thing could be made more delightful ...

In another garden we saw several pedestals for statues; from whence it may be inferr'd, that this emir was no very zealous mahometan. At one corner of the same garden stood a tower of about sixty foot high; design'd to have been carried to a much greater elevation for a watchtower, and for that end built with an extraordinary strength, its walls being twelve foot thick. From this tower we had a view of the whole city: amongst other prospects it yielded us the sight of a large christian church, said to have been at first consecrated to St. John the Evangelist. But, it being now usurp'd by the Turks for their chief mosque, we could not be permitted to see it, otherwise than at this distance. Another church there is in the town, which seems to be ancient; but being a very mean fabrick is suffer'd to remain still in the hands of the Greeks … We found it adorn'd with abundance of old pictures.

We saw many granite pillars and remnants of mosaick floors; and in an heap of rubbish, several pieces of polish'd marble, fragments of statues, and other poor relicks of this city's ancient magnificence. On the sea side is an old ruin'd castle, and some remains of a small mole.

Friday, March 19. Leaving Beroot, we came in one third of an hour to a large plain extending from the sea to the mountains. At the beginning of the plain is a grove of pine trees of Faccardine's plantation. We guess'd it to be more than half a mile cross; and so pleasant, and inviting was its shade, that it was not without some regret that we pass'd it by. Continuing in this plain, we saw at a distance, on our left hand, a small village called Suckfoat. It belongs to the Druses, who possess at this day a long tract of mountains, as far as from Castravan to Carmel. Their present prince is Achmet, grandson to Faccardine; an old man and one who keeps up the custom of his ancestors, of turning day into night: an hereditary practice in his family, proceeding from a traditional perswasion amongst them, that princes can never sleep securely but by day, when men's actions and designs are best observ'd by their guards, and if need be, most easily prevented …

This city [*Tyre*], standing in the sea upon a peninsula, promises at a distance something very magnificent. But when you come to it, you find no similitude of that glory, for which it was so renown'd in ancient times, and which the prophet Ezekiel describes … On the north side it has an old Turkish ungarrison'd castle; besides which, you see nothing here, but a mere Babel of broken walls, pillars, vaults, &c. there being not so much as one entire house left. Its present inhabitants are only a few poor wretches, harbouring themselves in the vaults, and subsisting chiefly upon fishing; who seem to be preserv'd ill this place by Divine Providence, as a visible argument, how God has fulfill'd his word concerning Tyre, viz. That it should be *as the top of a rock, a place for fishers to dry their nets on*, Ezek 26:14.

[*On the party's return from the Holy Land*] … In one hour more we reach'd the other side of the valley, at the foot of Mount Anti-Libanus …

Friday, May 7. The next morning we went four hours almost perpetually upon deep snow; which being frozen, bore us and our horses; and then descending for about one hour, came to a fountain call'd, from the name of an adjacent village, Ayn il Hadede. By this time we were got into a milder and better region.

Here was the place where we were to strike out of the way, in order to go to Canobine and the Cedars. And some of us went upon this design, whilst the rest chose rather to go directly for Tripoli, to which we had not now above four hours. We took with us a guide, who pretended to be well acquainted with the way to Canobine; but he prov'd an ignorant director; and after he had led us about for several hours in intricate and untrodden mazes amongst the mountains, finding him perfectly at a loss, we were forc'd to forsake our intended visit for the present, and to steer directly for Tripoli; where we arriv'd late at night, and were again entertain'd by our worthy friends, Mr. consul Hastings and Mr. Fisher, with their wonted friendship and generosity.

Saturday, May 8. In the afternoon Mr. Consul Hastings carried us to see the castle of Tripoli. It is pleasantly situate on a hill, commanding the city; but has neither arms nor ammunition in it, and serves rather for a prison than a garrison. There was shut up in it at this time a poor christian prisoner, call'd Sheck Eunice, a Maronite. He was one that had formerly renounc'd his faith, and liv'd for many years in the Mahometan religion: but in his declining age, he both retracted his apostacy, and dyed to attone for it; for he was impal'd by order of the bassa [*pasha*] two days after we left Tripoli …

[*there follows a graphic description of the impalement process*]

જે

Hermits from Maifuq (Photograph by Gérard de Martimprey, 1893)

C-F Volney: *Travels* (1784)

Constantin-François de Chasseboeuf Volney was a French aristocrat, philosopher, Senator (under the First Empire), Academician, and traveller. Despite the dilettante tendencies of the day (displayed by Cornelius De Bruyn, for example), Volney dug deeper, staying in Syria long enough to learn Arabic before continuing his travels in the area; he later travelled to the United States before being arrested and expelled as a spy, returning to write a book about soil and climate in the young Republic. His commitment to the Enlightenment is evidenced by his choice of pen name (Volney is a contraction of Voltaire and Ferney, where Voltaire lived).

Between the Ansarians,[17] to the north, and the Druzes, to the south, we find an inconsiderable people long known under the name of *Maouarna* or *Maronites* …

They all live dispersed in the mountains, in villages, hamlets and even detached houses; which is never the case in the plains.

The whole nation consists of cultivators. Every man improves the little domain he possesses, or farms, with his own hands. Even the Shaiks live in the same manner, and they are only distinguished from the people by a bad Pelisse, a horse, and a few slight advantages in food and lodging: they all live frugally, without many enjoyments, but also with few wants, as they are little acquainted with the inventions of luxury. In general, the nation is poor, but no man wants necessaries; and if beggars are sometimes seen, they come rather from the sea-coast than from the country itself. Property is sacred among them as in Europe, nor do we see there those robberies and extortions so frequent with the Turks. Travellers may journey there, either by night or day, with a security unknown in any other part of the empire, and the stranger meets with hospitality, as among the Arabs; it must be owned, however, that the Maronites are less generous, and rather inclined to the vice of parsimony. Conformably to the doctrines of Christianity, they have only one wife, whom they espouse, frequently without having seen, and always, without having been much in her company. Contrary to the

17 A fiercely independent tribe living in the mountains of northern Lebanon and Syria, considered heretical by orthodox Sunni Muslims.

precepts of that same religion, however, they have admitted, or retained, the Arab custom of retaliation, and the nearest relative of a murdered person is bound to avenge him. From a habit formed on distrust, and the political state of that country, every one, whether Shaik, or peasant, walks continually armed with a fusil and poniards ...

In religious matters, the Maronites are dependent on Rome. Though they acknowledge the supremacy of the Pope, they continue, as heretofore, to elect a head, with the title of Batrak, or patriarch, of Antioch. Their priests marry, as in the first ages of the church; and their wives must be maidens, and not widows, nor can they marry a second time. They celebrate mass in Syriac, of which the greatest part of them comprehend not a word. The gospel, alone, is read aloud in Arabic, that it may be understood by the people.

Let us return to the religion of the Druzes ... They practice neither circumcision, nor prayers, nor fasting; they observe neither festivals, nor prohibitions. They drink wine, eat pork, and allow marriage between brothers and sisters, though not between fathers and children. From this we may conclude, with reason, that the Druzes have no religion; yet, one class of them must be excepted, whose religious customs are very peculiar. Those who compose it are to the rest of the nation what the initiated were to the profane; they assume the name of Okkals, which means spiritualists, and bestow on the vulgar the epithet of Djahel, or ignorant; they have various degrees of initiation, the highest orders of which require celibacy. These are distinguishable by the White Turban they affect to wear, as a symbol of their purity; and so proud are they of this supposed purity, that they think themselves sullied by even touching a profane person. Several degrees of perfection are mentioned, to which they arrive by successive trials ... In short, the proper and distinctive character of the Druzes, is, as far as I have said, a sort of republican spirit, which gives them more energy than any other subjects of the Turkish Government, and an indifference for religion, which forms a striking contrast with the zeal of the Mohammedans and Christians ... They may marry several wives, and repudiate them whenever they chuse; but, except by the Emir and a few men of eminence, that is rarely practiced ... The veil, worn by their women, is of itself a preservative against those desires which are the occasion of so many evils in society. No man knows the face of any other woman than his wife, his mother, his sister, and sisters-in-law ...

To the east of the country of the Druzes, in the deep valley [*Bekaa*] which separates their mountains from those of Damascus, we find another small nation, known in Syria by the name of Motoualis [*Shi'i Muslims*]. The characteristic distinction between them and the other inhabitants of Syria, is, that they, like all the Persians, are of the sect of Ali, while all the Turks follow that of Omar or Moaouia ... To this doctrine, which diametrically opposes the system of the Sonnites, the Motoualis add certain ceremonies which increase their mutual adversion. They curse Omar and Moaouia as rebels and usurpers; and celebrate Ali and Hosain as saints and martyrs. They begin their ablutions at the elbow, instead of at the end of the finger, as is customary with the Turks; they think themselves defiled by the touch of strangers, and, contrary to the general practice of the East, neither eat nor drink out of a vessel which has been used by a person not of their sect, nor will they even sit with such at the same table.

Till about the middle of this [*eighteenth*] century, they only possessed Balbek, their capital, and a few places in the valley, and Anti Lebanon, which seems to have been their original country ... After the year 1750, they established themselves among the heights of the Bekaa, and got footing in Lebanon, where they obtained lands belonging to the Maronites, almost as far as Besharrai ... At this period, not more than five hundred families of the Motoualis remained, who took refuge in Anti-Lebanon, and the Lebanon of the Maronites; and, driven as they are now from their native soil, it is probable they will be totally annihilated, and even in their name become extinct ...

The Pachalic of Tripoli comprehends the country which stretches along the Mediterranean, from Latakia to the Nahr-el-Kelb, and is bounded on the west by that torrent, and the chain of mountains which overlooks the Orontes ... Lebanon and the Kesrouan are inhabited entirely by the Maronites, and the sea-coast and cities, by Schismatic Greeks, and Latins, Turks, and descendants of the Arabs.

The Pacha of Tripoli enjoys all the privileges of his place ... [*He*] has always been desirous of personally governing the country of the Ansarians, and the Maronites; but these people having invariably opposed by force the entrance of the Turks into their mountains, he has been constrained to abandon the collection of tribute to under farmers, approved of by the inhabitants ... All the environs of Tripoli are laid out in orchards, where the nopal [*prickly pear*] grows spontaneously, and the white mulberry is cultivated for the silk-worm; and the pomegranate, the orange, and the lemon tree, for their fruit, which is of the greatest beauty. But these places, though delightful to the eye, are unhealthy. Every year, from July to September, epidemic fevers, like those of Skandaroon and Cyprus, rage here: these are owing to the artificial inundations with which the mulberry trees are watered ... Besides, as the city is open only to the west, the air does not circulate, and the spirits are in a constant state of oppression, which makes health at best a kind of convalescence ...

The port of Bairout, formed like the others on the coast, by a pier, is, like them, choaked up with sands and ruins. The town is surrounded by a wall, the soft and sandy stone of which may be pierced by a cannon ball, without breaking or crumbling ... We find likewise without the walls to the west, heaps of rubbish, and some shafts of columns, which indicate that Bairout has been formerly much larger than at present. The plain around it is entirely planted with white mulberry trees, which, unlike those of Tripoli, are young and flourishing; because, in the territories of the Druzes, there is no danger in renewing them. The silk, therefore, produced here, is of the very finest quality. As we descend from the mountains, no prospect can be more delightful to behold, from their summits or declivities, the rich carpet of verdure, formed by the tops of these useful trees in the distant bottom of the valley.

In summer, it is inconvenient to reside at Bairout; on account of the heat, and the warmth of the water; the town, however, is not unhealthy, though it is said to have been so formerly. It has ceased to be unhealthy since the Emir Fakr-el-Din planted a wood of fir trees,[18] which is still standing, a league to the southward of the town ...

---

18 The 'pine forest' (*hirsh al-snawbar*) was planted centuries before Fakhr ad-Din; Sandys and Maundrell also attributed it to him.

THE NINETEENTH CENTURY

This was a period of drastic change for Lebanon; even greater there than in Europe (where the base was more modern), or the rest of the Ottoman Middle East (where the base was even less developed, but the change less dramatic). From travellers' accounts we feel that the century began with Lebanon, like the rest of 'Turkey in Asia', a wild and woolly country where they described even their fellow-Christians as living in a semi-barbaric state of ignorance, dirt and sloth. Within fifty years, Lamartine could describe it as 'Eden'.

Even allowing for Romantic hyperbole, the country had changed, 'evolving' into something more like France, if not Eden. This was assisted evolution: with the decline of the Ottoman Empire – from a threat at the gates of Vienna, to the Sick Man of Europe – the European powers were able to extend their influence and presence, often spearheaded by cooperating with and protecting client minorities. The motives were undoubtedly mixed, both philanthropy and imperialism; but by the end of the century, there were 300 French schools in Lebanon, educating 30,000 boys and (another exception in the Middle East) girls. The teaching was mostly Catholic and much more old-fashioned than was the norm in France itself, but gave the pupils the tools to look outward and think critically and comparatively about their own countries. The ideas and principles of Revolutionary France (largely *dépassé* in Europe itself) and such foreign themes as self-determination and secularism were absorbed, stimulating a powerful if inchoate activity with several partly overlapping, partly contradictory motifs. These included, in varying proportions: Arab nationalism, the Arabic language, pan-Islamic movements, and some nascent nation-based or at least localised patriotic fervour. 'Arise, ye Arabs and awake!' was the rallying cry for the new spirit of pan-Arab nationalism; these are the words of Ibrahim al-Yaziji, a Christian. The modernizing schools sponsored by the Yaziji and Boustany families attracted sons and daughters of the elite from all confessions; printing and translation began in earnest; newspapers sprang up in Lebanon and Egypt; political societies were formed, repressed, and re-formed with increased intensity of purpose, and soon the Levant was a hotbed of ideas, linguistic renewal and national pride and aspirations.

By mid-century, Romanticism was in full surge, and most French writers and many other Europeans had to make, and record, their Levantine tour: Chateaubriand, Charles Kinglake, Gérard de Nerval, Lamartine, Flaubert, Gautier, Renan, and Pierre Loti. Some of them, like Lamartine, did some homework before sailing; others, like Nerval or Flaubert, did not burden the spontaneity of their impressions with an accumulation of facts. To be fair, Flaubert never thought of publishing his travel diary, which was found at his death and later published. Rather than admiring the landscape, he was reported to have been absorbed in planning *Madame Bovary*. Renan was at the other end of the spectrum, a great Catholic Orientalist who connected with the land and people, and not only Catholics, as well as with history in Lebanon. As he says, he left part of himself there (including his sister Henriette, who died during their long sojourn and is buried at Aamchit). And there were the odd – some very odd – Europeans who actually took up residence in the Levant: beginning as merchants and 'factors', they became acculturated families of hereditary honorary consuls of France, Greece or Norway. Others were misfits who somehow managed to charm or mystify the local population, for a time, such as Lady Hester Stanhope whose presence is felt in several of our extracts; or marry into their society and 'go native', like Colonel Charles Churchill, whose memoirs appear in the last section of the book.

The Duchess of Cleveland, *The Life and Letters of Lady Hester Stanhope* and Ian Bruce, *The Nun of Lebanon*

The grand-daughter of the first Earl of Chatham, as a girl Hester Stanhope was known as one of the best horsewomen of her day – especially for breaking the most intractable stallions. She became hostess to her uncle, the bachelor Pitt the Younger, until his death (he left her a pension for life), then found herself without a powerful patron or indeed an activity challenging enough for her exceptional energy and intelligence. The Continental Blockade unravelled about the same time as Napoleon's fateful invasion of Russia, and English gentlemen and gentlewomen were once again free to indulge in travel to Western Asia. Hester needed no coaxing, setting off on a journey which turned out to be that of a lifetime. Her first adventure was a romantic idyll with young Michael Bruce, who would go on to notoriety as a result of affairs with Caroline Lamb and, in Paris, with Louise Ney, Princesse de la Moskowa and wife of Marshal Ney. He also spent six months in prison for alleged complicity in the escape of the Marquis Lavalette, who had been condemned to death for helping Napoleon escape from the Island of Elba. His father disapproved of his liaison with Lady Hester (who shared Michael's admiration for Napoleon). In the cache of letters discovered and published by Michael's descendant Ian Bruce, she indeed comes off as a rather grasping older woman. In the end she sent the young wastrel back to his father, but only after she was promised £1000 a year ...

Then come the adventures in Syria, especially the famous entry into Palmyra described in another book in this series,[19] and finally the long sojourn in Mount Lebanon. She first took over a small convent, and then moved with her ever-growing suite to a larger one, in the mountains above Sidon. There, despite, or partly because of, a reputation for 'never receiving Europeans', she became an incontournable stop for European intellectuals and grandees on their grand tour of the now fashionable Orient. Her talent for mimicry produced delightful caricatures of Byron and Lamartine; the latter returns the compliment in his own Voyage en Orient. *Finally comes what appears to be a descent into poverty and something like madness ... or not? At any rate there is no denying the pathos of her last years, rejected by her own kind and increasingly deserted – and worse – by the natives, so that the lines from Pope she applied to herself in a late letter to Michael Bruce become all the more poignant:*

> *By foreign hands her[20] humble grave adorn'd,*
> *By strangers honour'd, and by strangers mourn'd!*

---

19 *Syria: through writers' eyes*, edited by Marius Kociejowski.
20 Pope: 'thy'.

Saide August 2nd 1812. H. S. to Craufurd Bruce

My Dear sir,

I write you a few hasty lines from this place to tell you that yr. Son is perfectly well notwithstanding the great heat, & to assure you that the plague never reaches the Mount Lebanon, where we shall be tomorrow. The King of the Druses has had a palace prepared for us, his message to me was this, it is yours for a day or a year, he has sent down 12 camels, 25 mules (his own riding mule for me) & four horses & 6 guards, besides men for the mules camels etc.

Darel Kamar Mount Lebanon August the 24th 1812
H. S. to Craufurd Bruce

Dear Sir ...

Above 40,000 Arabs are now at war with each other in these parts, therefore you may imagine the state of things in that quarter. But I trust we shall do very well, I have a Turkish Janissary who is the Devil, I have seldom seen a man with finer talents, & more capable for such a journey, my Greek boy also has fine cool courage! As for all the rest I would not give sixpence for them ... It would take me half a day to describe the mountain exactly, therefore in order to give you an idea of it, I shall simply tell you that except where this place stands, & the Prince's Palace, I have traveled for nine hours together & never found a place large enough to pitch a tent, except near one Village. The Vineyards are like stair cases, & every little flat place stuffed with mulberry trees for the silkworms, the roads are horrible, & the people savage & extraordinary, the women wearing a great tin trumpet on their heads & a viel [*sic*] suspended upon it, & seeming very proud of these frightful horns.

The Convent of Abra, Febry 28th 1814 H. S. to Michael Bruce

Yr. Letter arrived the 26th at night.

I cannot express my delight at seeing yr. hand writing dearest Love ...

I must now talk of my health, which is much mended within this last fortnight, & I toddle about upon a Ass, & enjoy my ride. I also have a good appetite for herb soup ... I mean to remain quietly here for another year as I think it wd. be imprudent to risk fatiguing myself or eating unwholesome food which I must do on bd. a Ship, just after my illness [*the Plague, contracted at Aleppo*] I was a monster larger at my knee joints than in the leg or thigh & my arm was enough to frighten anyone you cd. see the large and small bone & I looked altogether like a spectre, but I have picked up remarkably within these last few weeks, this air is delightful & a little beyond the convent one wood of olives & figs & every where a fine view, & a Spring of admirable water.

The Emir Becchir has been kindness itself to me, he sent on purpose to Damascus to have glass made for my windows, has given me oil that is like milk & his own favorite ass, in short I cannot express how kind & liberal he has been. He & the Shiek Becchir [*son of the Emir*] have given orders here on the Mountains that all is to be at my feet[.] the new Patriarch (for the first who lent me the convent is dead) is also all civil & has invited me to a convent 3 hours off, where there are 50 monks & if I go the bells in the Mountain are to ring.

The only commission I wish for in England is to remember the Emir Becchir he wanted a double barrold gun a strong Gun which wd. take a good deal of shot. I shall write to Rice to send a lamp of mine I think he will like a large red pocket book with scissors knives &c. wd. I think also please him. The Sheik Becchir ought to have something a pr. of pistols, or some Worcester China or Derbyshire China Goblets to drink Sherbert, a large jug to hold water of the same sort or a cut glass large Cup some coloured prints of horses & dogs in short something they have not seen which is not expensive, indeed perhaps if you go to Vienna you cd. find something there like China for example which might please them the more showey the better you know. Prints of Austrian & Prussian Soldiers & Hussars &c &c which are vastly cheap some bound in a large book with flourishes of gold on the back wd. please them much. The Prince of Wales Duke of York on horseback Ld. Wellington & so on wd. enable one to tell long stories & be objects of curiosity to them ... Adieu God in heaven bless & preserve you,

Yrs affectionately H. L. S.

Mount Lebanon, Jan. 8th, 1825 H. L. S. to Captain Yorke
Dear Captain Yorke,
The mountain which you so much admired is shortly likely to be a scene of bloodshed. All the Druse population has risen against the Emir Beshyr in favour of the Sheick Beshyr, who, they say, is supported by the Pacha of Damascus against the Pacha of Acre. The troops of the latter are encamped from the bridge all along the river, and he is expected to arrive to-morrow to head them ... It is said that another revolution is expected in the Metouali country, which is the range of mountains you saw above Sour [*Tyre*], and there is a road of communication between that mountain and the mountains here, in the direction of that high black mountain where I passed the summer. This report is given credit to, as the Emir Beshyr has ordered all the convents in that direction to remove everything valuable; it is supposed that these people will join the mountaineers here. I have had several civil messages from the camp from the Albanians, Hawaras, Sugmars, Delatis, &c., but you know that the officers cannot at times command troops, great part of which are banditti, but *all is written*, as I said before ...

Although I have never interfered in the political concerns of this country, and for many years have avoided all social intercourse with great men, the heads of parties, I could plainly see, by a sour silent discontent, that the state of things was not much to be relied upon. The revolution has now broken out, and the whole mountain is in a flame. The Pacha's troops are encamped two hours from me, and he is expected tomorrow. It is said he is in a violent passion. Whether his intention of heading his own troops is only a threat or his real intention I cannot pretend to say; only that preparations are made for his arrival. All the villages about me are deserted except one, which remains trembling between the troops on one side and the mountaineers on the other; but they say every place at Sayda is so full that they know not where to go; even the convents have been cleared of everything valuable, and the priests are ready to fly. My situation is not a very agreeable one – not that I fear danger (for I do not know what fear means), but from the great number of miserable people who have announced their intention of taking refuge here if they are driven

from the asylum they have chosen, presents me with the prospect of
starvation if this business lasts long, for these poor people are destitute
of everything … [*The Emir routed the forces of his son*]

Djoun, Mount Lebanon, May 30th, 1827
H. L. S. to Mr John Webb

A *Firmanlee* [outlaw] having taken refuge in the Mountain, under the
protection of the Emir Beshyr, contrived to pick a quarrel with my
water-carrier, who was quietly going about his business, and having
bribed some of the Emir's Jack Ketches, they beat him most
unmercifully. The Emir Beshyr and his chief people have likewise
been bribed by this man, who has plenty of money at his disposal.
They have all, therefore, taken the *Firmanlee*'s part, and acted in the
most atrocious way towards me. A short time since, the Emir thought
proper to publish in the villages that all my servants were instantly to
return to their homes, upon pain of losing their property or lives. I
gave them all their option. Most of them have remained firm, being
aware that this order is the most unjust, as well as the most ridiculous,
that ever was issued. Since that, he has threatened to seize and murder
them here, which he shall not do without taking my life too. Besides
this, he has given orders in all the villages that men, women and
children shall be cut in a thousand pieces who render me the smallest
service. My servants, of course, as you must imagine, cannot go out,
and the peasants of the villages cannot approach the house. Therefore
I am in no very pleasant situation, being deprived of the necessary
supplies in food, and, what is worse, water, for all the water here is
brought upon mules' backs up a great steep.

I should not be a thoroughbred Pitt if fear were known to me, or if
I could bow to a monster who could chain together the neck and feet
of a venerable, white-bearded, respectable man … For the space of
three years I have refused to have the smallest communication with
the emir. He sent me one of his grand envoys the other day – one of
those who were charged with the budget of lies sent to Mehemet Ali.
I refused to see him, or to read the letter of which he was the bearer.

⚘

Alphonse de Lamartine: *Travels in the East* (1832–3)

As always in the Levant, foreigners were given more consideration than they might have met with in their own countries. It was enough to be announced as a 'renowned poet of the Franks' to be admitted, like Lamartine, to the Prince of the Druzes, ruler of Mount Lebanon, the Emir Bashir II Shehab. Lamartine's account of the visit, where he observed – and only just avoided participating in – the princely preparations for a bath, is priceless, especially if you picture his 'mincing' manners as mimicked by Lady Hester Stanhope, related in Kinglake's account, below.

The captain of the brig has distinguished the tops of Mount Lebanon. He calls me to show them; I seek them in vain through the heated mist where his finger points. I can see nothing but the fog which the heat raises, and above, some clouds of a dull white. He insists; I look again, but in vain. All the sailors show me Lebanon, laughing; the captain does not understand how I do not see it like him. 'But where are you looking for it?' said he to me; 'you are looking too far; here, nearer, above our heads!' I raised my eyes towards the sky, and I perceived in reality the white and gilded crest of Sannin, which stretched in the firmament above us. The mist of the sea prevented me from seeing its base and sides. Its head alone appeared, glorious and serene in the blue of heaven. It conveyed one of the most magnificent and delightful impressions I have felt in my long travels.

There was the land to which all my immediate thoughts tended, as a man and as a traveller; there was the sacred land, the land to which I was going from such a distance to seek the recollections of primitive humanity; and then it was the land also where I was about to bring to repose, in a delicious climate, beneath the shade of oranges and palms, on the edges of snow-torrents, on fresh and verdant hills, all that I held dearest in the world – my wife and Julia. I did not doubt that a year or two passed under this lovely sky would strengthen the health of Julia, which for the last six months had sometimes given me gloomy forebodings. I saluted these mountains of Asia as an asylum where God led her to cure her; a silent and profound joy filled my heart; I could not draw my eyes from Lebanon …

Visit to the Emir Beschir

On the morrow, at four o'clock in the morning, M. de Parseval and I were on horseback descending the steep declivity which leads from her [*Lady Hester Stanhope's*] monastery to the deep valley of the torrent Belus; we cleared at a ford the waters exhausted by the summer heat, and we began to climb the high mountains of Lebanon which separate Digioun from Deir-el-Kammar, or the Convent of the Moon, the palace of the Emir Beschir, sovereign prince of the Druzes, and of all the mountains of Lebanon.

At the bottom of this immense valley, the hill of Dptedin [*Beit ad-Din*], on which the emir's palace is erected, took root and arose like an enormous tower, flanked with rocks covered with ivy, and shoots of waving verdure hanging from their fissures and indentations. This hill rose to a level with the precipice on which we ourselves were suspended; a narrow and groaning abyss separated us from it. On its summit the Moorish palace of the emir stretched majestically over all the table-land of Dptedin, with its square towers and battlements; long galleries rising one above the other, and presenting extended rows of projecting arcades, light as the trunks of the palms which crowned them with their aerial plumes; vast courts ranged by lofty steps from the top of the hill to the outward walls of the fortification. At the extremity of the largest of these courts, on which our eyes plunged from the height, on which we were placed, the irregular façade of the women's palace presented itself to us, ornamented with slender and graceful colonnades, which in irregular and unequal forms reached to the roof, and bore, like an umbrella, a light covering of painted wood, serving as a portico to the palace.

A marble staircase, decorated with balustrades sculptured in arabesque, led from this portico to the door of the women's palace; this door, inlaid with wood of various colours, with frames of marble, and surmounted with Arabic inscriptions, was surrounded by black slaves, magnificently attired, armed with silver-mounted pistols and with Damascus sabres glittering with gold and chasings; the large courts which faced the palace were likewise filled with a crowd of Servants, courtiers; priests, and soldiers, in all the varied and picturesque costumes which distinguish the five populations of Lebanon – the Druzes, Christians, Armenians, Greeks, Maronites, and Metualis.

Five or six hundred Arab horses were attached by the feet and head in cords which stretched across the courts, saddled, bridled, and covered with shining cloths of all colours; several groups of camels were lying, standing, or bent on the knee, to receive or discharge their loads; and on the most elevated terrace of the inner court some young pages were throwing the djerid, rushing with their horses upon each other, crouching down to evade the blow, returning at full speed upon their disarmed adversary, and going through with an admirable grace and vigour, all the rapid evolutions which this warlike sport requires. After having contemplated for some instants this Oriental scene, so full of novelty for us, we proceeded to the immense and massive gate of the first court of the palace guarded by Arabs, armed with muskets and long slight blades; similar to the stalks of long reeds. There we sent to the prince the letters which we had for him. A few moments afterwards, he despatched to us his first physician, M. Bertrand, a native of Syria, of a French family, who still preserved the language and recollection of his country. He conducted us to the apartments which the hospitality of the emir offered us, and the slaves led our suite and horses to another quarter of the palace ...

Our dinner, which was served on this table, consisted of a pilau, of a dish of sour milk which is mixed with oil, and some pieces of hashed mutton, which they heaped on boiled rice, and garnish with certain gourds like our cucumbers. This is, in fact, the most desirable and savoury food which one can eat in the East; for drink, pure water, which they drink in earthen jugs with long spouts, which are passed from hand to hand, and from which they make the water fall into the opened mouth, without the vase touching the lips. No knives, spoons, or forks; they eat with the hands – but the repeated ablutions render this custom less revolting for the Mussulmans.

Scarcely had we finished dinner, than the emir sent to tell us that he was waiting for us. We traversed an immense court, ornamented with fountains, and a piazza, formed of high slim columns rising from the ground, and supporting the roof of the palace. We were introduced into a very beautiful saloon, the pavement of which was marble, and the ceilings and walls painted with lively colours and elegant arabesques by artists from Constantinople. Waterspouts murmured in the corners of the apartment; and at the end, behind a colonnade, the inter-columniations of which were barred and glazed, an enormous tiger was seen sleeping with its head upon its paws. The half of the room was filled with secretaries in long robes, each bearing a silver ink-stand, pushed like a poniard into their belts; Arabs richly armed and clothed; negroes and mulattoes waiting the orders of their master; and some Egyptian officers, clad in European vests, and having on their heads the Greek bonnet of red cloth, with a long blue tuft hanging on the shoulders. The other part of the saloon was raised about a foot, and a large sofa, or divan of scarlet velvet ran round it.

The emir was squatted at a corner of this divan. He was a fine-looking old man, with a lively and penetrating eye, a fresh and ruddy complexion, and a flowing gray beard. A white robe, bound by a cashmere shawl as a belt, entirely covered him, and the glittering handle of a long and wide poniard issued from the folds of his robe as high as his breast, and bore a cluster of diamonds of the size of an orange. We saluted him in the manner of the country, first carrying our hand to the forehead, and then to the heart. He returned us our salutation with grace and a smile, and made us a sign to come near and seat ourselves beside him on the divan. An interpreter was on his knees between him and us. I commenced the conversation by expressing to him the pleasure which I experienced in visiting the interesting and beautiful country which he governed with so much firmness and wisdom; and I told him, amongst other things, that the highest eulogy I could pass on his administration was to find myself there; that the security of the roads, the richness of the cultivation, the order and peace reigning in the towns, were undoubted testimonies of the virtue and ability of the ruler. He thanked me, and put to me a multitude of questions on Europe, and especially on the policy of Europe in the contest between the Turks and Egyptians, which showed the interest with which he regarded that affair, as well as a knowledge and acquaintance with things very uncommon for an Eastern prince. Coffee and long pipes were brought, which were several times renewed, and the conversation continued for nearly an hour.

I was delighted with the sagacity, the information, and the noble and dignified manners of this old prince, and I arose, after a long conversation, to accompany him to his baths, which he resolved upon showing us himself: These baths consisted of five or six rooms, paved with marble flags, the arched roofs and walls being stuccoed and painted in water colours, with great taste and elegance, by Damascus artists. Jets of hot, tepid, and cold water sprang from the pave and spread their varied temperature through the rooms. The last was a vapour bath, where we could not remain a minute. Several handsome white slaves, with only a shawl of raw silk drawn over their limbs, held themselves in readiness in these rooms to exercise their functions as assistants in the bath. The prince proposed to us to take the bath with him; but we declined the honour, and we left him in the hands of his slaves, preparing to undress him ...

In the evening, after supper, the emir sent us some of his musicians and singers, who improvised Arabic verses in our honour. He has amongst his servants some Arabs solely devoted to this sort of ceremony [*zajal*]. They are exactly what the troubadours were in the castles of the middle ages, or the popular bards in Scotland. Standing behind the cushion of the emir, or of his sons, whilst at their repasts, they sing verses in praise of the masters whom they serve, or of the guests whom the emir wishes to honour. We got M. Bertrand to translate some of these poetic toasts; they were, in general, very insignificant, or their ideas were so far-fetched, that it would be impossible to put them into ideas or images appropriate to our European tongues. The following is the only thought possessing a little perspicacity which I find noted in my album: 'Your vessel has wings, but the courser of the Arab has wings also. His nostrils, when he flies over the mountains, imitate the noise of the wind in the sails of a ship. The motion caused by his rapid gallop to the hearts of the weak, is like the rolling of the waves; but it rejoices the heart of the Arab. May his back be for you a seat of honour, and may it often conduct you to the divan of the emir!'

At dessert, the wines of Cyprus and Lebanon were profusely circulated; the Christian Arabs, and the family of the Emir Beschir, which is Christian, or believes itself to be so, drink wine without scruple on occasions. Toasts were drunk to the success of Ibrahim, to the enfranchisement of Lebanon, and to the friendship between the Franks and Arabs. The prince proposed a toast to the ladies present at the fete; and his bard, being ordered by the prince to make verses for the occasion, sang in recitative, and at the full pitch of his voice, some of the following purport: 'Let us drink the juice of Eden, which makes drunk and rejoices the heart of slave and prince. It is the wine of those plants which Noah himself planted, when the dove, instead of the branch of olive, brought him from heaven a cutting of vine. By virtue of this wine the poet instantly becomes a prince, and the prince a poet. Let us drink it to the honour of those young and beautiful Franks who come from the country where every woman is a queen. The eyes of the women of Syria are soft, but they are veiled. In the eyes of the daughters of the West there is more intoxication than in the transparent cup which I drink. To drink wine and behold the visages of women are double sins for the Moslem; for the Arab they are double enjoyments and praises to God.'

The Greek, Syrian, and Arab cultivators who dwell in these houses at the foot of Lebanon have nothing savage or barbarous about them. Better educated than the peasants in our provinces, they all can read, and all understand two languages, Arabic and Greek; they are mild, laborious, peaceable, and decorous; occupied all the week in the labours of the field, or the working of silk, they refresh themselves on Sundays by assisting with their families in the long and showy rites of the Greek or Syriac creed; they return afterwards to their houses to enjoy a repast, somewhat more sumptuous than on ordinary days; the women and girls, adorned in their richest clothes, their hair plaited, and all strewed with orange-flowers, scarlet wall-flowers, and carnations, seat themselves on mats before the doors of their dwellings, with their friends and neighbours. It is impossible to describe with the pen the groups so redolent of the picturesque, from the richness of their costume, and their beauty, which these females then compose in the landscape …

In my boyhood I had often imagined to myself this terrestrial paradise, this Eden which all nations have in their remembrance, either as a charming dream, or as the tradition of a more holy epoch: I had followed Milton in his ravishing descriptions of the enchanting abode of our first parents; but here, as in all other things, nature far outstrips imagination. God has not permitted man to dream anything so beautiful as he has made. I had dreamed an Eden – I can say I have seen it.

Visit to Lady Hester

I crossed a court-yard, a garden, an open kiosque, with hangings of a geranium colour, then two or three dark passages, and I was at length introduced by a little negro child seven or eight years old, into the cabinet of Lady Hester. It was so extremely dark, that it was with difficulty I could distinguish her noble, grave, yet mild and majestic features, clad in an oriental costume. She rose from the divan, advanced, and offered me her hand. Lady Hester appears to be about fifty years of age … 'You have come a long way to see a hermit,' she said to me: 'you are welcome. I receive but few strangers, scarcely more than one or two a year; but your letter pleased me, and I wished

Lady Hester Stanhope

to know a person who, like me, loves God, nature, and solitude. Besides, something told me that our stars were friendly ... '

It appeared to me that the religious doctrines of Lady Hester consisted of an able though confused mixture of the different religions, in the midst of which she had condemned herself to live. Inscrutable as the Druses, of whose faith, perhaps, she alone in the world really knows the mystic secret; resigned as a Mussulman, and a fatalist, like him; expecting, with the Jew, the Messiah; and with the Christian professing the adoration of Christ, and practising his charitable morality. Add to this the fantastic colours and supernatural dreams of an imagination of oriental tint, and heated by solitude and meditation with the effect of some revelations, perhaps, of Arab astrologers – and you will have an idea of the sublime and strange compound which it is more easy to call madness than it is to analyse and comprehend it. No! Lady Hester is not mad: madness, which is written strongly in the eyes, is not expressed in her beautiful and amiable look ... If I were to pronounce, I would rather say that it is a studied – a voluntary madness – conscious of itself, and acting from peculiar motives ...

'Since destiny,' she said to me, 'has sent you hither, and such an astonishing sympathy between our stars permits me to confide to you what I would conceal from the profane world, come and you shall see, with your own eyes, a prodigy of nature, of which the destination is only known to me and my adepts ... ; the mare which is to carry the Messiah, and which is to be born ready saddled.' ... The mare had behind the shoulders a cavity so large and deep, and imitating so completely a Turkish saddle, that one might say, with truth, that she was foaled saddled, and but for the want of stirrups, one might mount her without requiring an artificial saddle ... Another mare, quite white, and in my opinion, infinitely more beautiful, partook, with the mare of the Messiah, in the respect and care of her ladyship. No one had ever mounted it either ... I fancied that Lady Stanhope reserved the white one for herself, to mount on the day on which she should make her entry, by the side of the Messiah, into reconquered Jerusalem.

ﻚ

Charles Kinglake: *Eothen* (1834)

Kinglake was an old Etonian who gave up the practice of law to travel. His account of his travels in the East ('eothen' means 'from the East'), published in 1844, won him immediate fame. He went on to write an 8-volume Invasion of the Crimea. *A terse style, keen powers of observation and wry sense of humour make* Eothen *a masterpiece of the genre.*

Beyrout on its land-side is hemmed in by mountains. There dwell the Druses.

Often enough I saw the ghostly images of the women with their exalted horns stalking through the streets; and I saw too, in travelling, the affrighted groups of the mountaineers as they fled before me, under the fear that my troop might be a company of Income-tax commissioners, or a press-gang enforcing the conscription for Mehemet Ali; but nearly all my knowledge of the people, except in regard to their mere costume and outward appearance, is drawn from books and despatches. To these last I have the honour to refer you.

I received hospitable welcome at Beyrout, from the Europeans as well as from the Syrian Christians; and I soon discovered that in all society the standing topic of interest was an Englishwoman (Lady Hester Stanhope) who lived at an old convent in the Lebanon range, at the distance of about a day's journey from the town. The lady's habit of refusing to see Europeans added the charm of mystery to a character which, even without that aid, was sufficiently distinguished to command attention.

Many years of Lady Hester's early womanhood had been passed with Lady Chatham, at Burton Pynsent ... You may suppose how deeply the quiet women in Somersetshire must have been interested, when they slowly learned, by vague and uncertain tidings, that the intrepid girl who had been used to break their vicious horses for them was reigning in sovereignty over the wandering tribes of Western Asia ...

I left Saide (the Sidon of ancient times) on my right, and an hour, I think, before sunset, began to ascend one of the many low hills of Lebanon. On the summit before me was a broad, grey mass of irregular building, which, from its position, as well as from the gloomy blankness of its walls, gave the idea of a neglected fortress; it had, in fact, been a convent of great size, and, like most of the religious houses in this part of the world, had been made strong enough for opposing an inert resistance to any mere casual band of assailants who might be unprovided with regular means of attack; this was the dwelling-place of Chatham's fiery grand-daughter.

The aspect of the first court I entered was such as to keep one in the idea of having to do with a fortress, rather than a mere peaceable dwelling-place. A number of fierce-looking and ill-clad Albanian soldiers were hanging about the place inert, and striving, as well as they could, to bear the curse of tranquillity; two or three of them were smoking their *tchibouques*, but the rest were lying torpidly upon the flat stones, like the bodies of departed brigands. I rode on to an inner part of the building, and at last, quitting my horses, was conducted through a doorway that led me at once from an open court into an apartment on the ground-floor. As I entered, an oriental figure in male costume approached me from the further end of the room, with many and profound bows; but the growing shades of evening prevented me from distinguishing the features of the personage who was receiving me with this solemn welcome. I had always, however, understood that Lady Hester Stanhope wore the male attire, and I began to utter in English the common civilities that seemed to be proper on the commencement of a visit by an uninspired mortal to a renowned prophetess; but the figure that I addressed only bowed so much the more, prostrating itself almost to the ground, but speaking to me never a word. I feebly strived not to be outdone in gestures of respect; but presently my bowing opponent saw the error under which I was acting, and suddenly convinced me, that at all events I was not yet in the presence of a superhuman being, by declaring that he was far from being 'Miladi,' and was, in fact, nothing more or less godlike than the poor doctor who had brought his mistress's letter to Beyrout.

Lady Hester, in the right spirit of hospitality, now sent and commanded me to repose for a while after the fatigues of the journey, and to dine. The cuisine was of the oriental kind – highly artificial, and, as I thought, very good. I rejoiced, too, in the wine of the Lebanon.

After dinner the doctor arrived with Miladi's compliments, and an intimation that she would be happy to receive me if I were so disposed. It had now grown dark, and the rain was falling heavily, so that I got rather wet in following my guide through the open courts that I had to pass in order to reach the presence-chamber. At last I was ushered into a small chamber, protected from the draughts of air passing through the doorway by a folding screen; passing this, I came alongside of a common European sofa. There sat the Lady Prophetess. She rose from her seat very formally – spoke to me a few words of welcome, pointed to a chair – one already placed exactly opposite to her sofa at a couple of yards' distance – and remained standing up to the full of her majestic height, perfectly still and motionless, until I had taken my appointed place: she then resumed her seat – not packing herself up according to the mode of the orientals, but allowing her feet to rest on the floor or the footstool; at the moment of seating herself she covered her lap with a mass of loose, white drapery. It occurred to me at the time that she did this in order to avoid the awkwardness of sitting in manifest trousers under the eye of a European; but I can hardly fancy now that, with her wilful nature, she would have brooked such a compromise as this.

The woman before me had exactly the person of a prophetess – not, indeed of the divine sibyl imagined by Domenichino, so sweetly distracted betwixt love and mystery, but of a good, business-like, practical prophetess, long used to the exercise of her sacred calling. I have been told by those who knew Lady Hester Stanhope in her youth, that any notion of a resemblance betwixt her and the great Chatham must have been fanciful; but at the time of my seeing her, the large commanding features of the gaunt woman, then sixty years old or more, certainly reminded me of the statesman that lay dying in the House of Lords, according to Copley's picture. Her face was of the most astonishing whiteness; she wore a very large turban made seemingly of pale cashmere shawls, and so disposed as to conceal the hair; her dress, from the chin down to the point at which it was concealed by the drapery in her lap, was a mass of white linen loosely folding – an ecclesiastical sort of affair …

A couple of black slave-girls came at a signal, and supplied their mistress, as well as myself, with lighted *tchibouques*, and coffee.

The custom of the East sanctions, and almost commands, some

moments of silence whilst you are inhaling the first few breaths of the fragrant pipe: the pause was broken, I think, by my lady, who addressed to me some inquiries respecting my mother, and particularly as to her marriage; but before I had communicated to her any great amount of family facts, the spirit of the prophetess kindled within her, and presently (though with all the skill of a woman of the world) she shuffled away the subject of poor dear Somersetshire, and bounded into the loftier spheres of thought ...

In truth, this half-ruined convent, guarded by the proud heart of an English gentlewoman, was the only spot throughout Syria and Palestine in which the will of Mehemet Ali and his fierce lieutenant was not the law. More than once had the Pasha of Egypt commanded that Abraham should have the Albanians[21] delivered up to him; but this white woman of the mountain (grown classical, not by books, but by very pride) answered only with a disdainful invitation to 'come and take them!' Whether it was that Abraham was acted upon by any superstitious dread of interfering with the prophetess (a notion not at all incompatible with his character as an able Oriental commander) or that he feared the ridicule of putting himself in collision with a gentlewoman, he certainly never ventured to attack the sanctuary; and so long as Chatham's grand-daughter breathed a breath of life, there was always this one hillock, and that, too, in the midst of a most populous district, which stood out, and kept its freedom. Mehemet Ali used to say, I am told, that the Englishwoman had given him more trouble than all the insurgent people of Syria and Palestine ...

Lady Hester was, in her youth, a capital mimic; and she showed me that not all the queenly dullness to which she had condemned herself – not all her fasting and solitude – had destroyed this terrible power. The first whom she crucified in my presence was poor Lord Byron. She had seen him, it appeared, I know not where, soon after his arrival

21 During a local political dispute, the local Pasha, Yusuf, had been deposed by his superiors, but the local garrison of infantry, mostly composed of Albanians known as 'delibash' (crazy-head) remained loyal to Yusuf (his son was their commander). True to form, Lady Hester went against the grain of authority by harbouring several fugitive delibashes.

in the East, and was vastly amused at his little affectations. He had picked up a few sentences of the Romaic, and with these he affected to give orders to his Greek servant in a *ton d'apameibomenos* ['*to him in answer*', *Homeric formula*] style. I can't tell whether Lady Hester's mimicry of the bard was at all close, but it was amusing: she attributed to him a curiously coxcomical lisp.[22]

Another person, whose style of speaking the lady took off very amusingly, was one who would scarcely object to suffer by the side of Lord Byron – I mean Lamartine. The peculiarity which attracted her ridicule was an over-refinement of manner. According to my lady's imitation of Lamartine (I have never seen him myself), he had none of the violent grimace of his countrymen, and not even their usual way of talking, but rather bore himself mincingly, like the humbler sort of English dandy …

Lady Hester's unholy claim to supremacy in the spiritual kingdom was, no doubt, the suggestion of fierce and inordinate pride most perilously akin to madness; but I am quite sure that the mind of the woman was too strong to be thoroughly overcome by even this potent feeling …

Lewis Cass: Visit to Lady Hester Stanhope (1838)

By the time Lewis Cass visited Lady Hester, three years before her death, she had read Lamartine's memoir of their meeting, and was not amused. Cass (1782–1866) was an American statesman, who early in his career led an expedition to discover the source of the Mississippi; he got the wrong lake but it was named after him anyway. He was Governor of the Michigan Territory and a vocal supporter of the forcible removal of Indian tribes from their homelands in the Eastern United States to the West; he is quoted[23] as saying:

22 Byron is reported to have been put off by her 'disposition to argufy with me', but noted a 'great disregard of received notions in her conversation as well as conduct' (*Works of Lord Byron* : ' Letters and Journals', London 1898, vol. i., pp. 302–3, letter of 10 October, 1810).

23 *North American Review* (1830).

'There can be no doubt … that the Creator intended the earth should be reclaimed from a state of nature and cultivated'. He also thought that states should have the right to decide whether or not to permit slavery, and ran unsuccessfully for president, in 1848, on that platform. During a prior six-year stint as Ambassador to France, he travelled to Syria and Lebanon in 1838. In the light of his merciless description of the 'decadence' and 'destitution' of most of Lebanon, 'now sterile and uncultivated, but once rich and productive', it is perhaps fortunate that he did not conceive any schemes for making it more productive.

She is an extraordinary woman, this Lady Hester Stanhope. Extra-ordinary in her character, in her appearance, in her opinions, and in the romantic incidents of her life. And here I am, seated in this ancient city of Tyre, to render you an account of the visit I have just made to her. How are the mighty fallen! How changed is this Turko-Egyptian-Arabic town, dirty and disgusting as it is, and filled with all manner of abominations, from the mighty Tyre of antiquity … It is, at present, a small place, situated on the shores of the Mediterranean, and upon an extensive plain, now sterile and uncultivated, but once rich and productive … The town contains about twenty-five hundred inhabitants, and it is the very picture of misery. The buildings are old, mean, and dilapidated; the streets, narrow, dirty, and crooked, and with all the usual disgusting appendages of a Turkish town. The inhabitants are in the last state of destitution. The Governor, or Mutselim, is a negro, who came out with his Egyptian troops to do us honor, and who gave us a salvo from a rusty piece of ordnance, calculated to terrify his friends rather than his enemies …

We went to the house of a person calling himself the American Consul, an Armenian Arab. The Consulates in this region are desirable situations, not for their emoluments, but because they confer valuable privileges and immunities upon the possessor. They are preceded in public by two persons, carrying long staves, with silver heads, and they enjoy an entire exemption from all impositions, and from the jurisdiction of the local authorities. After some refreshment and repose, for the day was a burning one, we proposed to return the visit of our Ethiopian friend; but we were told quite frankly, and without hesitation, by the Consul, that he was too much intoxicated to see us; and we sat still, waiting the happy moment of his Excellency's return to sobriety. So much for Eastern rulers.

Sidon is about twenty miles north of Tyre, in like manner upon the seacoast, and in an equal state of misery and decadence ... There must be something peculiar in the soil of this region, for to the eye nothing could promise greater sterility. The worst spot in the Alleghany mountain would seem to me to hold out greater encouragement to industry ...

When we reached her [*Lady Hester's*] house we found she had not risen, for among her peculiar habits is one which converts the day into night. She had, however, given orders for our hospitable reception, and requested we would dine, informing us that she would receive us about three o'clock in the afternoon. This, however, did not suit our arrangements, for one object we had to view in the journey, was to visit the Emir Beschir, the Prince of the Druses, who lives about seven

Lewis Cass

hours' ride beyond Lady Hester, in the midst of the Ridges of Lebanon. We, therefore, excused ourselves to her Ladyship for not waiting, promising to make our visit to the Emir that evening, and to return, so as to present ourselves again there by noon the next day ...

The same uninviting country met our view, until we crossed over some steep, rocky ridges, and struck a pretty stream, which discharges itself into the Mediterranean, between Sidon and Beiroot. It is the one in which the Emperor Barbarossa was drowned, while engaged on a crusade. We travelled up this stream to its source, and after dark reached the residence of the Emir, one of the most romantic spots in the world. This singular people, the Druses, occupy these mountains. They have preserved a species of independence, and are governed by their own princes ... The palace [*Beit ed-Din*] is by far the most magnificent building in Syria, and more than four times the size of our President's house. It is said the Emir keeps a thousand servants. During the journey of this day, we saw, for the first time, those horns alluded to in the scripture, which are worn by the women. They are at least fifteen inches long, and rise over the forehead, being covered by a veil – and most uncouth-looking objects they are.

We returned to Lady Hester Stanhope's at the hour indicated; and after a short time were introduced into her private apartment. She was sitting, dressed like an Arab, clothed in a robe, with a turban upon her head, and smoking a long pipe. She is tall and spare, with a worn and sickly complexion, and apparently about sixty-five years of age. I had heard from her physician, in Damascus, that she had been engaged early in life to Sir John Moore, and I looked for those traits which may have been supposed to have attracted the great captain. But the remains were not to be found ...

She has an unconquerable aversion to George the Fourth, and considers him the worst man who ever lived – except her neighbour, the Emir Beschir, who rather occupies the nadir in the circle of her affections ... I found she had so far lost the command of the English language, as to be driven occasionally to have recourse to the Arabic. She expressed much dissatisfaction at the accounts which some travellers have given of their interviews with her, and was particularly severe upon Mr Lamartine. Her strictures upon the work of this

Christian stalwarts

gentleman exhibited much feeling, and she considers his description of her dress, and manners, and conversation, as highly colored, and, in fact, distorted, and she qualified it by an epithet I feel no disposition to repeat ...

As may well be supposed, her peculiar opinions upon some subjects almost approached monomania. I imagine her long residence in the East has produced an effect upon her religious views, for there seems to be a *mélange*, in her conversation, of the doctrines of Christianity and of the dogmas of Islamism. She alluded, in pretty distinct terms, to a story resembling in its outline, the legendary tale of the Seven Sleepers of Ephesus, and which relates to certain persons now sleeping at Damascus, whose awakening, which is not far distant, is to be attended with some strange event ... Lady Hester has shown much friendship to our countrymen, and I think has received them whenever they have presented themselves, which she has not always done to British travellers ... We left her wishing her more happiness than I am afraid is in store for her.

Gérard de Nerval: *Voyage en Orient* (1843)

The poet Gérard de Nerval mixes fiction, observation and literary borrowings in his lively diary, in this selection describing his getting mixed up in an anticlimactic (and probably at least mostly authentic) affray between Druzes and Maronites.

That evening everyone was full of alarming news: panicking monks were coming down from neighbouring monasteries; there was talk of a high number of Druze fighters coming from their territory to infiltrate the mixed villages, previously disarmed by order of the Pasha in Beirut. The Kesrouan – part of the province of Tripoli – had been allowed to keep its weapons; so they felt they had to go help their defenceless brethren. To do so, they had to cross the Dog River at the border between the two territories; this meant serious conflict. The armed and impatient mountaineers thronged the village and the fields.

Horsemen rode to neighbouring areas, shouting old calls to war: 'Quickly, follow the call of God; quickly, to the fight.'

The Prince [*of the Maronites*] took me aside and said: 'I don't know what is going on; the reports might be overblown, but in any case we must get ready to help our neighbours. The help from the Pasha arrives always too late … . It might be safer for you to go to the convent in Antoura, or to go back to Beirut by sea.'

'No,' I begged; 'let me go with you … '

After walking four hours, we stopped near the convent of Mar-Hanna, where several people from the mountains came and joined us. The monks gave us lunch; according to them, it was better to wait: there was still no sign that the Druze had invaded the district. However, recent arrivals were of a different opinion and we decided to keep advancing. We left our horses to take a shortcut across the woods, and after some alarming noises about nightfall, we heard some gunshots echoing on the rocks … I went up to join the Prince, who was in state of high irritation … On seeing some Maronites going up to houses with burning pine branches, he ordered them back. The Maronites around him shouted: 'The Druze burned Christian property; today we are strong, we have to do the same to them' …

Meanwhile, only one old man wearing a white turban was found in all the houses, he was brought and I recognised him immediately: he had kindly invited me to rest at his home during my visit in Beit Meri. He was brought to the Christian village Sheikh, who was a bit embarrassed by the turmoil and who was trying – along with the Prince – to calm the agitation. The Druze elder kept his calm and told the Prince:

'Peace be with you Miran; what are you doing on our land?'

'Where are your brothers?' asked the Prince; 'they probably ran away when they saw us arriving.'

The old man replied, 'You know very well that is not their custom; but seeing there were only very few here against all your people, they took the women and children to safety. As for myself, I wanted to stay.'

'But we were told that you called on the Druzes from the mountains across the way, and that they came in large numbers.'

'You were deceived. You listened to bad people, foreigners who would have been quite happy for you to kill us, so that our brothers come and kill you in turn to avenge us.'

The old man had remained standing during this discussion. The Sheikh in whose house we were all staying seemed interested in his words and told him: 'Why are you acting as if you are a prisoner here? We were friends in the past; why don't you sit with us?'

'Because you are in my house,' answered the old man.

'Come now, let's forget all that,' said the Christian Sheikh. 'Do sit on this couch and we will have some coffee and a water pipe brought.'

'Don't you know that a Druze never accepts anything from a Turk – or their friends – for fear it might be the spoil of unjust taxes?' answered the old man.

'I am no friend of the Turks!'

'Didn't they appoint you Sheikh while it was I who was Sheikh during Ibrahim's time, when your people and mine lived in peace? Aren't you the one who went complaining to the Pasha because of a small quarrel, a burned house, a trivial incident among neighbours which we could have easily solved between us?'

The Sheikh shook his head without answering; but the Prince cut short this discussion and left the house holding the Druze's hand. 'You would drink coffee with me, I have never accepted anything from the Turks,' he told him, and ordered his servant to serve coffee in the shade of the trees.

'I was a friend of your father,' said the old man, 'and in those days, Druze and Maronites lived in peace.'

And they talked a long while of the times when the people of both religions were united during the rule of the Shihab family, a time when they were not left to the unpredictable outcome of battles.

They agreed that the Prince will take all his people back home and that the Druze will come back to their village without appealing for help from further away, and that the damages they had just suffered will be considered a retaliation for the burnt Christian house in the past.

In fact these people have the deepest understanding of each other, and never forget the bonds which used to unite them. They are stirred up by missionaries or monks, acting on behalf of European interests. They behave like old-time *condottieri*, who managed to have major battles without spilling blood. Whenever the monks preach war, the people have to take up arms; whenever the English missionaries make speeches (and pay bribes), they have to look fierce, but deep down they feel only doubt and discouragement. Each one is fully aware of the conflicting wishes and competing purposes of some European powers, which are compounded by the Turks' lack of foresight. In provoking fights in mixed villages, they think they are proving the need for a complete partition between two populations which were once united and had a common cause. The work being done nowadays in Lebanon under the pretence of pacification consists in exchanging the properties of the Druze in Christian areas for Christian property in the Druze ones. Then, they think, there will be no more civil disturbance, the reports of which are much exaggerated; there would be only two distinct populations, one which would probably be under Austrian protection and the other under the protection of England ...

Translated by A. Féghali Gorton

جﺦ

Gustave Flaubert: *Voyage en Orient* (1850)

The Levant seems to remind Flaubert of a vast set for a tragic opera. His travel notes, never intended for formal publication, nonetheless contain profuse local colour and choice vignettes, perhaps owing to their lack of post-voyage polishing.

Left Baalbek Tuesday about 10 a.m., leaving our white-bearded host who showers us with blessings for the forty piastres we give him. Headed straight for Deir el-Ahmar, taking three hours to cross the plain. Nothing special, except Mount Lebanon facing us: one part green and rather bulbous up to the middle of the mountain, then all grey. Dusky-faced women with white veils on their heads, cutting wheat in the dry flat grassland; all stop and stare at us with yearning and amazement, sickle in hand. At 1:30 we reach Deir el-Ahmar, after Max started off at a gallop and made all the baggage fall off two and a half of our mules. We pitch camp under a sort of lean-to held up by two columns, surrounded by poultry, dogs, donkeys and women. The latter are mostly ugly and dirty: their pointy tits dangle in and outside their dress, all grey with dust. An old ruffian with a full white beard and a big blue turban which reminded me of the High Priest's costume in *Norma*, leaning on his cane: a priest of this country, the local curate, so to speak ...

Thursday morning, walk to the plateau's edge, to a little hillock from which we could see Tripoli on the seashore at the plain's edge. We chat about the Maronites: he [*a young monk*] is reserved on the subject. Not long ago some English pastors wanted to spend the summer in Ehden; they had to flee before the Maronite sheikh's threats to burn their house. They tried again, same result. The matter finally brought before the Court of Beirut, which found in favour of the Maronites. The pastors went back to Tripoli. I asked my companion whether they – the monks – have any influence on the behaviour of the Maronites; 'none at all', says he. Maybe my question came too hard on the heels of the one about the pastors. Jealousy of the Maronite clergy with respect to the Latin brothers. The married ones especially ignorant: they have to go out to work by day, which earns them condescension and disdain.

We talk about the Druzes. The local sheikh tells me a few erroneous facts, which the prior corrects. According to the latter, this is what the Druze religion is all about (a few years ago, after an attack against one of their villages, some of their mystic books, written in a very ancient and very pure Arabic, were seized and sent to Paris): God created the Word, which created Good and Evil. The Word sometimes appears incarnate. At the present time, it is hidden, perhaps in the body of an animal or a sinner. It will reappear, sooner or later: if a truly great man appears, it will be Him. When Napoleon appeared in the East, the Druzes were convinced it was Him and rushed to meet him. Their religion is a sort of extremely exalted pantheism, mixed with a lot of Kabbal. They are closer to Christianity than to Islam, according to the Abbot, who it seemed to me has a high regard for their intelligence. Remarkable metaphysical spirit some of these Arabs have; he says he is often astonished by the subtlety of their theological debates.

Translated by T. J. Gorton

ﺨ

Ernest Renan: *Mission de Phénicie* (1864)

The French philologist, archaeologist, biographer of Jesus, historian of Christianity and professor, spent a year in the peaceful seaside village of Aamchit, just north of Byblos, living with his wife and sister Henriette in the home of a rich Christian merchant of the town. Henriette died during their stay and is buried in the family plot of Renan's host. Renan's love for Lebanon was deeply informed by his unconventional Catholic faith and ingrained French patriotism.

The cults in Mount Lebanon are as old as the world, and over the years have gone through several metamorphoses, borrowing elements from different sources; but in the first centuries of our era, they acquired a huge importance. Byblos and the area of Lebanon located above it became a holy land which drew pilgrims from many lands … A temple crowned the top of every mountain; the ruins indicate violent destruction, sometimes systematic in its virulence. The advent of Christianity in Syria was characterized by the destruction of numerous temples. The Lebanon made a powerful impression on the imagination. These mountains, a rare feature in these regions, are both majestic and benevolent: they are cheerful, blooming and perfumed Alps. The temples crowning them contributed to their beauty; a dangerous, deeply embedded paganism would fight to the end for its survival. Already, in the writings of the Hebrew prophets one finds on every page the horror of the cults, which were practised in the high places and under the green trees. In the imagination of the Christians, the Lebanon would be the last haven from Athalie and

Jezebel's crimes; so they systematically pulled down its crowning temples. Destroying the temples was considered a praiseworthy deed; thus we see the monks in Antioch and several pious people – Saint Maron, for instance – consider this their mission, criss-crossing the country in destructive fervour.

These holy sites all present certain similar features. A chapel has usually replaced the old temple; often it is easy to recognize in its dedication – whether for medical or other need – an echo of its original purpose. The simple and kind Maronite priests believe that this is the foundation stone of their church, and this is a fortunate error; for if they knew that these stones are in memory of pagan deities, they would have destroyed them, if nothing else but to prove their strange claim that the Lebanon has never been pagan. The altar is often the antique *bomos* with its inscription. Any stela, sculpture or other remnant of architectural decoration that might have escaped the destruction is placed on the altar, naively arranged without any aesthetic feeling for art.

The location of these temples is always extremely beautiful, the landscapes of Lebanon being particularly enchanting when seen from above. A centuries-old carob tree, woods, often of oak, and some oleanders shade these ruins. In the vicinity one sees wells, cisterns, pools, tombs cut in the rock, stone presses, millstones and troughs carved in the stone with others strewn around in an oak thicket. Chapels here are often more interesting than churches, since they escape the close scrutiny of the clergy: their naked walls still bear traces of older faith. Saint George and Saint Elias, their usual patrons, and the Prophet Jonas whose name one finds often on the coast, have in all likelihood taken the place of older deities. I am convinced that the interiors of many of these chapels with the kind of offerings, the way they are placed, the wishes one makes in them and the way one prays, hardly differ from the way it was sixteen hundred years ago. Often these cults – especially those pertaining to Saints George and Jonas – are common to both Christians and Moslems. Nowhere more than in this country could one say that here, humanity eternally prays in the same spots.

Translated by A. Féghali Gorton

Mark Twain: *Innocents Abroad* (1869)

Mark Twain provides, along with Lewis Cass (above), our other American view of Lebanon in the 19th century. The passage from Innocents Abroad *is vintage Twain, its humour quite good-natured, mocking his peers at least as much as the natives.*

We are in Syria, now, encamped in the mountains of Lebanon … As might have been expected, a notion got abroad in Syria and Egypt that the whole population of the Province of America (the Turks consider us a trifling little province in some unvisited corner of the world), were coming to the Holy Land – and so, when we got to Beirout yesterday, we found the place full of dragomen and their outfits …

[We] had nothing to do but look at the beautiful city of Beirout, with its bright, new houses nestled among a wilderness of green shrubbery spread abroad over an upland that sloped gently down to the sea; and also at the mountains of Lebanon that environ it; and likewise to bathe in the transparent blue water that rolled its billows about the ship (we did not know there were sharks there). We had also to range up and down through the town and look at the costumes. These are picturesque and fanciful, but not so varied as at Constantinople and Smyrna; the women of Beirout add an agony – in the two former cities the sex wear a thin veil which one can see through (and they often expose their ankles), but at Beirout they cover their entire faces with dark-colored or black veils, so that they look like mummies, and then expose their breasts to the public …

We are camped near Temnin-el-Foka – a name which the boys have simplified a good deal, for the sake of convenience in spelling. They call it Jacksonville. It sounds a little strangely, here in the Valley of Lebanon, but it has the merit of being easier to remember than the Arabic name …

Back yonder, an hour's journey from here, we passed through an Arab village of stone dry-goods boxes (they look like that), where Noah's tomb lies under lock and key … Noah's tomb is built of stone, and is covered with a long stone building. Bucksheesh let us in. The building had to be long, because the grave of the honored old navigator is two hundred and ten feet long itself! It is only about four feet high, though. He must have cast a shadow like a lightning-rod. The proof that this is the genuine spot where Noah was buried can only be doubted by uncommonly incredulous people. The evidence is pretty straight. Shem, the son of Noah, was present at the burial, and showed the place to his descendants, who transmitted the knowledge to their descendants, and the lineal descendants of these introduced themselves to us to-day. It was pleasant to make the acquaintance of members of so respectable a family. It was a thing to be proud of. It was the next thing to being acquainted with Noah himself. Noah's memorable voyage will always possess a living interest for me, henceforward.

At eleven o'clock, our eyes fell upon the walls and columns of Baalbec, a noble ruin whose history is a sealed book. It has stood there for thousands of years, the wonder and admiration of travelers; but who built it, or when it was built, are questions that may never be answered. One thing is very sure, though. Such grandeur of design, and such grace of execution, as one sees in the temples of Baalbec, have not been equaled or even approached in any work of men's hands that has been built within twenty centuries past. The great Temple of the Sun, the Temple of Jupiter, and several smaller temples, are clustered together in the midst of one of these miserable Syrian villages, and look strangely enough in such plebeian company ... But when you have gazed aloft till your eyes are weary, you glance at the great fragments of pillars among which you are standing, and find that they are eight feet through; and with them lie beautiful capitals apparently as large as a small cottage; and also single slabs of stone, superbly sculptured, that are four or five feet thick, and would completely cover the floor of any ordinary parlor.

The Temple of Jupiter is a smaller ruin than the one I have been speaking of, and yet is immense. It is in a tolerable state of preservation. One row of nine columns stands almost uninjured. They are sixty-five feet high and support a sort of porch or roof, which connects them with the roof of the building. This porch-roof is composed of tremendous slabs of stone, which are so finely sculptured on the under side that the work looks like a fresco from below. One or two of these slabs had fallen, and again I wondered if the gigantic masses of carved stone that lay about me were no larger than those above my head. Within the temple, the ornamentation was elaborate and colossal. What a wonder of architectural beauty and grandeur this edifice must have been when it was new! And what a noble picture it and its statelier companion, with the chaos of mighty fragments scattered about them, yet makes in the moonlight!

One might swear that all the John Smiths and George Wilkinsons, and all the other pitiful nobodies between Kingdom Come and Baalbec would inscribe their poor little names upon the walls of Baalbec's magnificent ruins, and would add the town, the county and the State they came from – and swearing thus, be infallibly correct. It is a pity some great ruin does not fall in and flatten out some of these reptiles, and scare their kind out of ever giving their names to fame upon any walls or monuments again, forever.

ﻙ

Pierre Loti: *Galilee* (1895)

For Pierre Loti, Lebanon came at the sad end of a pilgrimage to the Holy Land which he undertook 'devoid of hope, without faith'. After the exotic charm of Damascus and Palestine, Beirut repelled him with its 'banality', and even the – for once – untasted charms of a demure inn-keeper's daughter did not stave off anticlimactic end-of-journey depression. In case anyone thought that tourists spoiling the object of tourism was a recent phenomenon, they should read the Palestinian part of the journey and Loti's peevish fulmination at the Cook's Tours, polluting all the sites with their ubiquitous hearty presence and spoor in the form of 'discarded food-tins, fruit-peelings, and indescribable scraps of The Times ... '

Four hours riding along a straight and level road, our horses quite taken aback after all those steep tracks. Through vast prairies of barley and stones, totally devoid of trees. Between two mountain ranges:

Lebanon on the right, Anti-Lebanon on the left, both crowned and veined with snow. A bitter, cold wind lashes us mercilessly. Snow, snow on all sides, while down around the foot of the mountains we can see other veins of white – but those are fields of daisies ...

At midday, we stop at the entrance to an isolated village, in one of those 'khans' which serve as warehouses and inns, where the traveller finds a resting-place for the day, a hubble-bubble, and coffee. And so we take our meal, in the sun but sheltered from the icy wind off the snows, under a sort of lean-to daubed with whitewash; right next to the road where caravans pass, surrounded by the children, dogs, cats, and chickens of the household. We are served by a young Christian girl, her face unveiled.

Healthy and fresh, with that air of great well-being found in this valley: grey eyes, wide and open but very gentle, looking straight at you, at some length, and with a serene frankness. Her features are perfect, cheeks glowing with the golden health of youth; thick chestnut hair frizzy and rebellious under her white muslin scarf. Her pink indian-dress, of a European pattern from a decade back, is nonetheless charming and impeccably clean. It is a bit unbuttoned to reveal a long, full neck. That, despite her dress, she is woman of the Orient, is shown by the necklace of sequins and amber hanging down her breast, and by her eyebrows drawn out with henna.

She brings us modest country hubble-bubbles, of coarse glass and copper; but she took care to grace the water with the perfumed petals of red roses and orange-blossoms. She tries each pipe before presenting it to us, drawing on it to get the coals burning properly: totally unaware of how she enhances the charm of the mouth-piece by putting it in her mouth. An inn-keeper's daughter, after all: her beauty will be harvested by the first man to try ...

Towards evening, we rejoin, near Chtaura, the main road that leads from Damascus to Beirut. Around us, it is hardly the Orient any more: nondescript landscapes and houses, telegraph wires along a road where carriages and coaches pass ...

Midday. We have come down almost a thousand metres from the peaks, and it is high time to take a serious midday rest. The air is tepid, exquisitely limpid: a cheerful sun dries out our clothes and our horses' harness ... Down on the Mediterranean, off Beirut, we can distinguish objects which, from up here, look like small grey fish: European sailing-squadrons, fast steamers – iron visitors, more and more numerous, coming to unsettle the old Orient in its decline.

As the hubble-bubble hour comes round, we make it last as long as we can, not anxious to get back on our horses and throw ourselves into the banality of Beirut down below ... Our hubble-bubbles have burned themselves out, leaving behind the oriental odour of smoke mingling in the air with the violent scent of flowers.

Thus ends, this night, our pilgrimage – devoid of hope, without faith.

Translated by T. J. Gorton

TWENTIETH CENTURY

Travel in the Middle East was seriously disrupted at the beginning of the twentieth century, with the First World War, the final collapse of the long-moribund Ottoman Empire; then peace, and with it the redrawing of boundaries, creation of League of Nations Mandates, and crowning of new heads that followed. The end of the First World War brought a terrible famine to Lebanon, and the early 1920s saw a haemorrhage of men and families of diverse ethnic backgrounds seeking a better life in Michigan or Venezuela or Senegal. Lebanon and Syria found themselves under the tutelage of France, with Palestine and Transjordan administered by Britain. Lebanon's traditional (majority Christian and Druze) mountain heartland was enlarged by the French administration to include the coastal plain with its majority Muslim cities, Tripoli, Sidon and Tyre, as well as the Bekaa plain to the east. An unprecedented spirit of cooperation led the Muslim and Christian elites to militate for independence, which came in 1943 (with a push from Britain).

After the Second World War, Levantine travel writing comes into its own as both an inspiration and a guide to the contemporary traveller, and a modern literary genre. For Lebanon, the twentieth century up to 1975 provides a portrait of a society increasingly fissured and strained, a country with glorious natural and cultural advantages but increasingly deadly contradictions and inequality that would mean dire times and drastic changes for the little republic.

Sir James Frazer: *The Golden Bough* (1909)

Most of Frazer's Golden Bough, *which one could properly refer to as seminal, is written in an elegant but rarely florid style. His passage about the source of the River Adonis at Afka (ancient Aphaca), however, is positively lyrical, obviously a first-hand description of a visit to the spot where Tammuz/Adonis loved Aphrodite/Astarte and died. He is more expansive about the natural beauty than Lucian nearly two millennia before, but (perhaps characteristically), he is less explicitly critical of the annual flowing-with-*

blood that all observers commented on, and with which by the end of this book the assiduous reader will be excessively familiar.

The last king of Byblus bore the ancient name of Cinyras, and was beheaded by Pompey the Great for his tyrannous excesses. His legendary namesake Cinyras is said to have founded a sanctuary of Aphrodite, that is, of Astarte, at a place on the Mount Lebanon, distant a day's journey from the capital. The spot was probably Aphaca, at the source of the river Adonis, half-way between Byblus and Baalbec; for at Aphaca there was a famous grove and sanctuary of Astarte which Constantine destroyed on account of the flagitious character of the worship. The site of the temple has been discovered by modern travellers near the miserable village which still bears the name of Afka at the head of the wild, romantic, wooded gorge of the Adonis. The hamlet stands among groves of noble walnut-trees on the brink of the lyn.

A little way off the river rushes from a cavern at the foot of a mighty amphitheatre of towering cliffs to plunge in a series of cascades into the awful depths of the glen. The deeper it descends, the ranker and denser the vegetation, which, sprouting from the crannies and fissures of the rocks, spreads a green veil over the roaring or murmuring stream in the tremendous chasm below. There is something delicious, almost intoxicating in the freshness of these tumbling waters, in the sweetness and purity of the mountain air, in the vivid green of the vegetation. The temple, of which some massive hewn blocks and a fine column of Syenite granite still mark the site, occupied a terrace facing the source of the river and commanding a magnificent prospect. Across the foam and roar of the waterfalls you look up to the cavern and away to the top of the sublime precipices above. So lofty is the cliff that the goats which creep along its edges to browse on the bushes appear like ants to the spectator hundreds of feet below. Seaward the view is especially impressive when the sun floods the profound gorge with golden light, revealing all the fantastic buttresses and rounded towers of its mountain rampart, and falling softly on the varied green of the woods which clothe its depths.

In antiquity the whole of the lovely vale appears to have been dedicated to Adonis, and to this day it is haunted by his memory; for the heights which shut it in are crested at various points by ruined monuments of his worship, some of them overhanging dreadful abysses, down which it turns the head dizzy to look and see the eagles wheeling about their nests far below.

One such monument exists at Ghineh. The face of a great rock, above a roughly hewn recess, is here carved with figures of Adonis and Aphrodite. He is portrayed with spear in rest, awaiting the attack of a bear, while she is seated in an attitude of sorrow. Her grief-stricken figure may well be the mourning Aphrodite of the Lebanon described by Macrobius, and the recess in the rock is perhaps her lover's tomb. Every year, in the belief of his worshippers, Adonis was wounded to death on the mountains, and every year the face of nature was dyed red with his sacred blood. So year by year the Syrian damsels lamented his untimely fate, while the red anemone, his flower, bloomed among the cedars of Lebanon, and the river ran red to the sea, fringing the winding shores of the blue Mediterranean, whenever the wind set inshore, with a sinuous band of crimson.

ﻢ

Maurice Barrès: *A Levantine Investigation* (1914)

Maurice Barrès was already famous as a writer (and member of the Académie Française) and as a Boulangist propagandist when he travelled to the Levant just before the First World War (1914). Boulanger was a charismatic late-nineteenth-century general with mystical-reactionary-socialist-militarist ideas; he seems to have appealed to Barrès' Catholic ennui at the drab Republican politics of the Third Republic. In Lebanon, Barrès found an enchanted mountain that is less austere, but no less powerful than the hill in Lorraine he wrote about in La Colline enchantée. *He revelled in the landscape, but even more in the ostentatious Francophile Catholicism of the Lebanese Christians. His joy was somewhat damped by the perfidious presence of American missionaries clogging up the good works of the numerous French monastic and missionary orders he came to visit. Under the spell of the Holy Valley, he tells of the wishing-tree amid the ruined temples of Aphaca, where women mark their supplications by tying a scrap of cloth to a branch.*

This must indeed be strong medicine, for it is practised to the present day, by women of all religious groups.

First Sight of Beirut   Beirut gives such a sweet impression, the little whitish or greyish squares of its houses with their gently pointed roofs, the red tiles so harmonious amid the greenery. I shall never forget this heat, this humidity, the mist that seems to wrap around us … I am breathing the odour of Asia …

I am not confining myself to the great premises of the Saint Joseph University. Each day, from morning until night, I criss-cross Beirut: to the Brothers of Christian Doctrine, the Daughters of Charity, the Sisters of Nazareth, and those of Saint Joseph; or to the French Lay Mission, or to the Jews. That is to say, everywhere one is safe from the enemy, the American Protestants.

The danger is that we are bringing up a young generation of misfits: uprooted, idle, discontented, always shooting off in the direction of political, social, and religious reforms. The graduate is enough of a trouble-maker in the West, full of hatred for a society that fails to provide him with a position commensurate with his expectations. In the Islamic World he becomes a Young Turk, Young Egyptian or Young Tunisian …

A young man came to see me, and said: 'I am the son and grandson of official dragomans. My grandfather met Lamartine and Saulcy; we have a number of letters from them. How do you find our country?'

'Very beautiful indeed.'

'Beautiful?!', he exclaimed, horrified.

I led him to the window and pointed to Lebanon, Mount Sannin covered with snow, those peaks reaching up towards the infinity of Heaven. 'It is impossible to live here,' he said. 'You wish to come to Paris?' 'All the young people of this country would like to go there … '

At the end of the meal, a charming boy was brought in, the son of Mr Tobia [*of Aamchit, where Renan wrote and where his sister Henriette is buried*]. Off we go to see the house where Renan lived, and meet the boy's father who remembers well having met him. We chat as we walk, the boy and I. 'Your country is so beautiful: I cannot recall ever having seen a more beautiful one.'

'Ah!', he said. 'When Monsieur Vedrines [*French aviator*] passed by, up in the sky [*ciel*], he slowed down his flight as he passed over here.' I was greatly moved by what he had said: how proud this charming little chap is of his country, and how happily he associates the idea of heaven [*ciel*] with the idea of France!

Translated by T. J. Gorton

❧

T. E. Lawrence: *Seven Pillars of Wisdom* (1935)

One of the witnesses to the aftermath, suitably horrified by the French and British Mandates and what he saw as general betrayal of wartime promises to Arab allies, was of course T.E. Lawrence. For him, Lebanon was too frenchified to be of much interest, hence his acid little vignette of Beirut just after the war.

Beyrout was altogether new. It would have been bastard French in feeling as in language but for its Greek harbour and American college. Public opinion in it was that of the Greek merchants, fat men living by exchange; for Beyrout itself produced nothing. The next strongest component was the class of returned emigrants, happy on invested savings in the town of Syria which most resembled that Washington Avenue where they had made good. Beyrout was the door of Syria, a chromatic Levantine screen through which cheap or shop-soiled foreign influences entered; it represented Syria as much as Soho the Home Counties.

Yet Beyrout, because of its geographical position, because of its schools, and the freedom engendered by intercourse with foreigners, had contained before the war a nucleus of people, talking, writing, thinking like the doctrinaire Cyclopaedists who paved the way for revolution in France. For their sake, and for its wealth, and its exceeding loud and ready voice, Beyrout was to be reckoned with.

❧

Robin Fedden: *Syria and Lebanon* (1965)

Robin Fedden grew up in France (from which he drew inspiration for Chantemesle, *an evocation of his boyhood there). After Cambridge, he found work as a diplomat (in Athens), an English teacher (in Cairo, with Lawrence Durrell), and a vocation as a thoughtful travel writer. His* Crusader Castles *supplements Lawrence's youthful book as required reading before a tour of the Levantine coast. To him goes the privilege of preparing us, at least, for a visit to Baalbek.*

Noah is reported to have settled with his flocks and herds in the Bk'aa valley. It was a wise choice if the patriarch had a taste for landscape and its atmosphere. There can be few valleys more beautiful. Most people get their first view of it where the Beirut–Damascus road crawls over a pass in the Lebanon Mountains. Between the snow-capped ranges on either side, it lies as smooth as velvet, a pastoral invitation. The valley runs so evenly up to the abrupt mountains, and the minute branch-valleys insinuate themselves so closely into the mountain flanks, that the total effect is one of natural upholstery. The width of rich alluvial earth is fitted into its rocky frame with pleasing precision.

The mountains that overlook the Bk'aa are very different from those on the Mediterranean side of the Lebanon. There the heights are exclamatory and picturesque, dramatic gorges carve and cut them, and peaks rise jagged, tier on tier. They are worn and fretted by millennia of north-west wind and storm. Above the Bk'aa the mountains impress rather differently; they are quiet, sculptural and solemn. They watch rather than speak. In early spring their snows reach the valley, and where the snow melts crocuses push up. The soaked earth is a rich russet, across which creeps a film of green – at first imperceptible but growing daily brighter – the shoots of the Bk'aa corn. By midsummer the valley is burnt all shades of yellow-brown, carries thistles, sere-grasses and indomitable wild hollyhocks, but wherever a spring breaks from the mountainside or water flows, the expanse blotches into a dark stain of green with birds, prospering vines and the grateful shade of trees. But to say so much, or so little, of the Bk'aa gives no idea of its quality. The traveller will often ask himself why the valley is exceptional, why, each time he sees it, the same feelings of wonder, almost of awe, should be evoked. Proportion must have something to do with its effects. If golden numbers and ideal ratios exist, they must enter into the composition of this landscape, so perfectly are the width of the valley and the height of the mountains proportioned to each other. The guidebooks call the Bk'aa a plain; it might alternatively be called a mountain valley. In fact, it is either too wide or too narrow to fit these descriptions. Escaping both the sprawling vagueness of a plain and the cupped closeness of a mountain valley, it is the miraculous complement to the hills that frame it, at the same time boundless and intimate, great and small.

Differing methods of travel change the impact of a landscape; what is enthralling by car may become intolerable on foot. Slow progress calls for variety of scene. Thus Gertrude Bell plodding the length of the Bk'aa on horseback found it a 'most dreary valley'. For once one may be grateful for a car. The miracle of form and colour has no time to pall. The road from Beirut drops into the valley at Chtaura, a green and fertile oasis seized by indefatigable Jesuits some eighty years ago from swarms of malarial mosquitoes. The hillside above the village is now strung with vineyards where they grow a palatable *vin rosé*, and bottle an *eau de vie de marc* which seems smooth on the edge of the Syrian desert. From Chtaura the valley runs due north between its mountain ranges, snow-covered, corn-covered, or tanned as the desert, according to season. The light changes with the hour, creating gulfs of shadow on the mountain flanks and crowning their white summits with a brief *Abendglüh*. Driving north, one hardly realises that the valley is slowly climbing, and it is almost with surprise that its watershed is reached. There, where the valley at its wildest and loneliest slips over an almost imperceptible divide to fall away into the wide plain of Homs, the Orontes rises.

Its rising is worthy of so famous a river; one that was the backbone of the Seleucid empire, that created Antioch, and saw upon its banks some few miles north at Kadesh the destruction of the Hittite power. At the foot of the Lebanon mountains its waters, clear and cold and deep, flood in silence from beneath a ledge of rock. They hesitate for a moment in a pool, shadowed by a gigantic plane-tree, and then hurry down a curling ravine followed by a thread of tamarisks and twisted willows. The ravine softens into a coomb as it works its way from the last mountain and spurs into the plain, and the river between rapids and boulders flattens into long rippling glides and deeper pools. There are trout here that run large. Fishing in this deserted Syrian coomb seems dream-like, familiar yet unreal. When one has fished the evening rise until a fly is no longer visible and there is only a white glimmer on the water, the black mountain shapes appear to grow larger to overhang the river and to threaten. It seems presumptuous to follow a leisurely Anglo-Saxon pursuit in this ancient landscape.

This is the moment, as the moon rises, to climb from the river to that weird monument, the Tower of Hermel. Capping a rise of ground in the midst of a desolate expanse, it surveys the valley for miles around. Though by day the resort of shepherds who seek the shade, when the sun has set it is deserted. As you walk round it, staring up in the moonlight, you have the impression of breaking many centuries' isolation, of imposing an unwelcome human contact on a thing which knew utterly different types of men, and that long ago. A pyramid surmounts its massive stonework, and carved upon its square tower are deer and weapons, a wounded bear that dies pierced with lances, and wolves that drag down a gigantic bull. No inscription dates this enigmatic memorial, and in spite of the use of the Ionian order, it has little classical about it. It is not altogether unlike the ancient 'spindles' of Amrit and the effect on the traveller is much the same: an impression of contact with a civilization altogether strange, and because not understood both fascinating and disturbing. The most probable supposition is that it was built in the first or second centuries BC by some local princeling who had made himself independent in the interval of chaos before the Romans came. One may even play with the idea that its dramatic quality is linked with the date of its birth, and that it was the last purely Semitic monument to be erected in western Syria. When these stones went up in the Bk'aa, Rome was at hand, and Syria, about to acquire that all-embracing civilization, was never again to be her primitive Semitic self.

It is in the Bk'aa valley, half-way between Chtaura and the Tower of Hermel, that one grasps perhaps better than anywhere else in

Syria[24] the force and energy of the civilization which the Romans brought. One of the springs that rises at the foot of the Anti-Lebanon creates the oasis that has been famous for nearly two thousand years as the site of the Temple of Baalbek. Baalbek itself, as the name shows – the Baal of the Bk'aa – was an ancient religious site, but the vast ruins that remain today are a legacy of Roman rule. They were mainly raised in the second and third centuries AD when Baalbek had become the Graeco-Roman town of Heliopolis, and the surrounding fields were owned by the descendants of those veterans whom Augustus settled there when he made a colony of the place. In typically elastic Graeco-Roman fashion, the newcomers took over the old gods and gave them new names and a classic veneer. A triad of gods, analogous to the triads favoured by the Phoenicians, presided over the sanctuaries. To the Heliopolitan Jupiter, doing duty for the Semitic Hadad, to Venus cloaking the Atargatis, and to Mercury, perhaps disguising Adonis, the three major temples were raised. Jupiter was worshipped in the Great Temple, Venus in the so-called Temple of Bacchus, while Mercury's shrine, which has long disappeared, lay perhaps in the gardens to the south-west. The tremendous wealth and popularity which the sanctuaries enjoyed, the ruins still reveal. They are vast and give an impression of undertakings on a scale paralleled only in the temples of Upper Egypt.

The stones of the trilithon – perhaps the largest cut blocks in existence – are famous, but the giant proportions of the place are perhaps even better typified by the stone slabs with which the Temple of Bacchus was once roofed: each of these stone 'tiles' has an area of thirty square feet. The temple itself, though known as the 'Little Temple' to distinguish it from the greater Temple of Jupiter nearby, was larger than the Parthenon. Great wealth, careful organization and a popular cult, could alone have achieved such monuments. They are colossal, and remain so in spite of the inroads of earthquakes, emperors and collectors. Constantine and Theodosius, with Christian fervour, started the destruction, and hardly more than a century ago,

24 'Syria' in the geographical sense, including modern Syria, Lebanon, Israel/ Palestine and part of Eastern Turkey.

Lamartine, with a modesty exceptional for the times, made off with a mere camel-load of good things. Destruction continued until a German archaeological expedition rescued the site in 1900.

There is little point in adding another description of what has before so often and so enthusiastically been described, yet it is worth noting that the effect of the Temple of Baalbek is by no means purely

Beirut in 1967, with the columns of the Roman Law School in the background

architectural. The temples are more impressive than the architecture strictly warrants, because the landscape, this amazing Bk'aa valley, sets them off. Weathered stone against blue distances, Corinthian columns against snow-covered mountains, such things are an essential part of Baalbek. Largely conceived and monumental, buildings and valley suit one another; they are in proportion. The best place and time to appreciate the temple and its setting are at sunset from the terrace of the ruined tower in the south-west corner where a small fountain bubbles away to itself and the whole valley is unfolded. In winter the oasis is a network of bare branches finely etched in sharp air, and the trunks of the walnut-trees stand out purple-grey against the reddish soil. In summer it is a sea of green; lush, bird-filled and shady. Beyond are the mountains whose snows never melt. Perpetually changing their tone and colour, they always modify and condition the feeling and atmosphere of Baalbek itself. The interaction of nature and art which adds so much to the temples is equally striking in the Great Mosque. Situated some distance to the northeast of the *propylea* it is easily overlooked but well worth visiting. Built from the spoil of the Roman sanctuaries, probably in the Mameluke period, and now itself ruined, its position gives it particular charm. Its remains have been incorporated into the rural economy of the oasis: corn grows between the pillars of its triple colonnade and fruit trees overshadow the Corinthian capitals ...

⚓

Colin Thubron: *The Hills of Adonis* (1968) (from Chapter 6)

Colin Thubron needs no introduction, nor his sinuous, hypnotic prose any presentation. The Levant must have been one of his first loves, for in two years (1967-8) he produced his first two books, two masterpieces: Mirror to Damascus, *and* The Hills of Adonis. *We admit to being greedy in quoting from two chapters of the latter, with every expectation that the reader will forgive us. In the first, he gives a rare account of the southern (Druze) mountains around Jezzine. Going inside a monastery to drink Benedictine and commiserate with one of the lost souls he finds (or attracts?) along his way, he gives us, as he so often does, not just the wish that we had been there, but the feeling that we were, that we are now revisiting a still-vivid memory rather than reading someone else's journey.*

Jezzine is typical of the pretty towns and villages of the Mountain, built out of limestone and roofed with pink European tiles. Down its ravine two waterfalls glisten for a hundred and thirty feet before their rivers run together in a flower-filled valley. Its people are Maronites – Christian mountaineers – and are well known for their work in cutlery, which they decorate cheerfully with inlaid bone.

Here the mountain history begins: vestiges of families grown to power through courage and intrigue, who sometimes ruled the Lebanon independent of the Ottomans, building forts and palaces in the hills for their brief years. At Jezzine the emir Fakr ed Din took refuge in a gorge and defied the Turks with scarcely a friend beside him. Years before, his father had been trapped by the Ottomans in the redoubt of Niha-Toron not far away, and had died of poison or starvation; and the twelve-year-old prince was smuggled by his mother to a Christian family in Kesrouan, where he passed his boyhood secretly. But he grew up in his father's religion – as a Druse, the most wayward of the sects of Islam. Before he came of age he acquired command of a district, and fifteen years later became the first sole ruler of Lebanon. He was so small, it was said, that if an egg dropped from his pocket it would not break …

Thinking three centuries ahead of his time, he envisaged a 'Greater Lebanon', free from Turkey and orientated westward. Under his rule the Roman Catholic missions first entered the Mountain, and his ports became depots for European merchants – Florentine, Venetian and French – where Lebanese silks, olive oil and cereals were exported with profit. So Fakr ed Din was able to pay an army of forty thousand mercenaries and refortify the decayed march castles of the Crusaders. He bought European artillery, furnished patrols for his roads, and financed spies and his own faction in the court at Constantinople…

When his star fell he took refuge in the fortified galleries of Niha-Toron, where his father had died thirty-six years before; but the source of his water-supply was betrayed to the Turks, who poisoned it by slaughtering animals there. So one night he fled to Jezzine and was guided to a cave along a path against the mountain. Here the Turks, by mining beneath the grotto and smoking out its defenders, at last captured Fakr ed Din. Two years later, as a prisoner in Constantinople, he was strangled by mutes, and it was said that a Christian cross was found among his clothes.

The farmers of Jezzine told me that the grotto was inaccessible now, and infested by snakes. But I found it in the cliffs above a tangled hill, far from their orchards. The rock-cut path which the emir took, though crumbling and so low that one must often crawl, still reaches the entrance. It is scarcely more than three feet square, and overgrown, like a natural cave; but inside I saw that grooves had been cut in the passageway, where four successive doors had sealed it.

A black snake melted into darkness like a spirit. From the gallery a shaft led upwards and cobwebs hung from the soft limestone ceilings like acrobats' netting; there may have been a snail staircase once, but the Turks had burnt everything, and I wedged my feet among the crevices to climb into the upper gallery. The rampart closing its entrance had broken down, so that the sun shone on a floor bright with watercress and in its jagged breach the mountains stood, tragically beautiful.

Into the rock-face behind had been cut a corridor where my torch-beam awoke long, glistening streams. It was as if the emir had hoped to hew his way to the other side of the mountain, but after a hundred yards I reached the end, where the walls had been idly gashed, then suddenly abandoned.

I took a road from Jezzine which soon became a track, past hills of umbrella pines, smooth as mushrooms. The Jezzine and Barouk rivers met in an oasis of light. Here and there were farmhouses of handsome stone, broken in among cistus, victims of the 1956 earthquake which shook the valley of habitation. And near the water's confluence stood an Arab bridge, whose lower stones might have been Roman cut; and four granite columns were sunk to their necks in the ground.

This was the ancient city of Borri, now an orchard of bitter oranges, falling ungathered. Borri is scarcely mentioned by ancient chroniclers, but gave its name to the Bostrenus river, which forms there. It must always have occupied a position of beauty and usefulness, for through it the route from Sidon bent north to Damascus into a valley secretive with hills; and another may have linked it to the road passing out of Tyre over Hermon, or joined the highway paved by Trajan from the Red Sea. On either side the rivers flow down into its stillness, and a Roman road reaches it through pine-woods in the northwest.

The granite columns, very large for so small a town, could only have been raised for a god, and the Jezzine river nearby has rubbed away its banks and uncovered the base of the temple. It appears to have been heavily made: the tribute of a merchant city with money in lieu of taste. Probably it was dedicated to Eshmun, whom the Romans linked with Aesculapius, for the river on which it stood, 'the graceful Bostrenus', was itself held sacred to him and finds the sea near his temple at Sidon.

I started along its valley by the last of the Wadi Barouk, and noticing Roman stones beneath my feet, looked down into the river. There under the green water shone the streets and pavements of the ancient city, level and straight as they were first laid. In that miasmal light the fragments moved and glittered, as if the city quickened into life; from its smoothed foundations the roofs and porticoes grew through water toward the sky, scraping the river's surface: a whole city. Here the farmers planted vines and olives, and merchants came, bringing perfumes and Cappadocian horses, cassia and the Adonis cult. And the river, which has rediscovered this, is easing out its stones and rolling them, one by one, toward the sea.

❧

Ralph and Molly Izzard: *Smelling the Breezes*

This English family, their stay in Lebanon done (he was the Daily Mail *correspondent), had the wonderful idea of touring it from top to bottom, with their four small children, two donkeys and a local guide. In 1957 this certainly sounded less bizarre than it might today, and if their book is much less of a literary experience than Fedden or Thubron, their descriptions of the spontaneous hospitality they met with everywhere, of scenes like the one of an old man using an ox to thresh corn, indicate that they were touring through the end of an era.*

Our last night at Laklouk was enlivened in a manner we had not anticipated. After supper Elias and Miles set off on Big Stick [*their donkey*] to buy cigarettes. Hardly had they disappeared into the darkness than the whole district seemed to rock with a series of dynamite and hand-grenade explosions, while from all around came the cracking of rifle and pistol shots. Going quickly to the door and peering out, we were astonished to see that every cottage had its bonfire burning brightly, and across the valley we could hear the voices of the inhabitants calling happily to each other. Much mystified, we waited anxiously for Big Stick's return. It would be unfortunate, we felt, if another feud had broken out in the district and Miles and Elias were to ride into the line of fire. But the bonfires and fusillades continued and the joyous voices, which hardly seemed the atmosphere of doom and disaster. After a while we heard the donkey returning, with Elias as mystified as any of us.

He and Miles had nearly fallen off at the first explosions, so startled had they been. We stayed up some time watching the bonfires blazing from all corners of the plateau, while the shots echoed in the bright, starry sky, and finally went to sleep with the noise of the explosions still ringing in our ears.

Next day we were up early, ready to pack and go. From the cowherd Boulos we learned the reason for last night's excitement. The news had just reached the district that Hamid Frangie, the Opposition nominee for the next Presidential elections, had obtained from President Nasser the release from prison of one Sheikh Georges Beg Yussef, a landowner of the district. Georges Beg Yussef had been sentenced in Cairo to life imprisonment for hashish-smuggling; he had been arrested while boarding an aircraft in Cairo. Marked bank-notes planted by agents of the Narcotics Bureau served to convict him. Fourteen months of his sentence had been served when Hamid Frangie's intercession obtained him his release. The whole district was in a ferment of excitement and all along our route that day we heard people talking happily of the news. The popularity of this release seemed to augur a strong vote for Frangie among the Christian farmers of this district.

We left Laklouk with the feeling that, had we lingered any longer, we should never have stirred ourselves away from it ...

At last the tarmac ended and a white stone road replaced it. We were now winding down the steep sides of a gorge and below us we could see the roofs of a village half hidden in fruit trees and piles of chaff beside the circular threshing-floor. A stream fell in a cascade down the face of a cliff and ran down the narrow valley under a stone bridge, shaded by huge walnut trees. The descent of the gorge had been hot and tiring and we were grateful for the shade which enveloped us as soon as we entered Tannourine. The village straggled down the side of the stream, shut in on three sides by tall cliffs, but open seaward for a dazzling glimpse down the valley of a wide sky and distant fall of cloud-wreathed escarpment. We were greeted by several women and taken to a house for coffee and repose, while Elias sought about for a suitable camp site. At last one was found for us, a charming situation beneath two large walnut trees, comparatively secluded. The stream ran gently beside us, like a Scottish burn, falling over rocks and forming little pools.

A fresh spring bubbled up by the roots of one of the trees, supplying us with drinking water. Even in the heat of the day the place was fresh and cool, for the stream was edged with planes and poplars and ran through quiet groves of apricot and olive trees. The villagers were very friendly and showered us with gifts – a basket of apricots, bunches of fresh chick-peas which are eaten raw, a basin full of mulberries. 'Me big friend this fruit,' exclaimed Elias joyfully, as a withered old man poured them out before us and watched with a smile while we scooped them into our mouths. Another old man was threshing corn on the other side of the stream; we could see his brown ox patiently circling the yellow threshing-floor, while his driver dozed on the chair fixed to the flint-studded sledge which is used to separate the grain from the ear. There was an old stone mill a little downstream from us, the water led in by a rough stone channel, and falling out in a thin stream. Here the pools were deep enough for the children to swim in, and they spent the afternoon scrambling over the rocks and sending leaf boats down on long, adventurous journeys to the distant sea.

We were surprised to notice a large hashish plant growing in a patch of potatoes and from casual conversation with the villagers learned that they were all admirers of the hashish smuggler, Georges

Beg Yussef. In fact, they were hoping and expecting him to pay a triumphal visit to their village so that they could offer their congratulations to him. This probably explained the *gendarmerie* jeep which we noticed patrolling at intervals along the road, full of heavily armed gendarmes. 'That's nothing,' said our hosts; 'we had a celebration last night when we heard the news and let off some rifle-shots, but they don't know whose rifles they were, and they can't do anything about it.' Relations between the village and the *gendarmerie* appeared to be warily cordial, neither side wishing to provoke the other. It was a fruit-growing village, sending down late apricots to the coastal markets, but it supplemented its income by the cultivation of hashish. Prices, however, were bad this year, and a cause for concern. A plant was worth only three *lira* now, showing a fifty per cent drop on last year's prices. Like the apple growers of Lebanon, the hashish growers are also feeling the economic squeeze applied by Egypt, but, unlike the apple growers, they are not entirely dependent on one crop.

Hashish is mostly grown as a very profitable sideline, a cash crop that brings a quick return for very little outlay. Egypt is the principal customer, as hashish is a drug used to counteract the impotence caused by bilharzia, said to afflict eighty per cent of the Nile-valley population in some degree or other. The Egyptian buyers this year had cut the price drastically and the peasants were faced with a considerable drop in profits, but as the hashish traffic is largely illegal in Lebanon, it was not a matter they could very well raise through their parliamentary deputies. As far as we could understand from our hosts, the growing of hashish is not actually illegal, though we had heard of cases of crops being destroyed on the ground. Presumably in such out-of-the-way districts it is difficult to enforce any regulations which may exist, so what cannot be stopped is tolerated. The toleration extends to the harvesting and threshing of the crop, which is done in a windowless, air-tight room draped in sheets, in the grower's house. The plants are cut at the end of summer, when the green leaves are beginning to turn yellow. They are laid in rows on the floor of the dark room to complete the drying process, then they are gently beaten. The light dust resulting from this threshing clings to the sheets and is scraped off. The first threshing represents prime-quality hashish, for which the highest price is paid; subsequent threshing produces a coarser powder, for which there is a corresponding lowering of price. As long as the hashish remains in the grower's house, he is relatively immune from police action; it is only when the sealed-up packets of the drug, usually the size of a cigarette tin, are moved down to the coast that the police net comes into action. Stoppings and searchings on the main roads, running gun-fights, secret motorboat runs are all commonplace incidents in the smuggler-versus-excise-men intrigue which occupies a large part of the attentions of the Lebanese coastal patrols. There are check points along all the coast roads and it is nothing to see a whole busload of people being turned out on the roadside, while the excise men and gendarmerie search the vehicle.

The buying is done by agents who come up early in the season to estimate the crop and fix the price. When the hashish is ready for collection, a runner starts off on the dangerous job of getting it down to the collection centre. This is when the authorities try to intercept the traffic, and it is their wits against those of the smuggler and his agents. The big smugglers never leave town, and are men with considerable commercial interests; the carriers are armed and often shoot it out rather than surrender to a police-trap. Graft and corruption both play their part in this variation of the classic cops-and-robbers theme and famous smugglers have a sort of Robin Hood glamour in the remote mountain areas.

The peasants and mountaineers who grow the crop can see no reason why they should discontinue this profitable source of income. They never use it themselves, and wrap their faces carefully in their headcloths when they are threshing the dried plants, to avoid intoxication. Possibly an old man smokes it occasionally in his hubble-bubble pipe, we were told, if he is very old and ill, but that is unusual. Certainly we never saw any being used and were never offered any, though it is easy enough to obtain hashish-filled cigarettes in any bar or coffeeshop in the seedier quarters of Beirut.

Cedars

THREE

Identities

Ethno-cultural generalisations are treacherous things, but a glance at the history of Lebanon already suggests four constants: political pragmatism, cultural eclecticism, commercial dynamism and fierce attachment to clan or tribe, locally and narrowly defined. From the interaction of these constants comes the charm – and the tragedy – of Lebanon, alternately resplendent and benighted. Where and how such constants originate is certainly debatable, if one accepts their existence; in the case of Lebanon, the long centuries of Ottoman rule would seem to be the first place to look.

The Ottoman Empire gave every modern country in the Levant its dominant cultural flavour. For nearly half a millennium, the seaboard and its hinterland from Egypt to Greece, all the country from the Mediterranean to Persia, through Jerusalem and Damascus to Baghdad and south to the great Arabian desert, was part of a Muslim Empire run from Istanbul. Names like 'Syria' and 'Iraq' and 'Palestine' were used, but referred to geographical expanses, not political or cultural boundaries. If you asked a random person what he was, he would say: 'I am a Sunni Muslim from Aleppo', or 'a Greek Orthodox from Sidon', or 'a Chaldean from Mosul', or 'a Cairene, Muslim by the grace of God' (the list could go on and on). But what he would *never* answer, is 'I am a Syrian', or 'a Lebanese', or 'an Iraqi'.

True to this tradition, the modern Lebanese identifies himself first through his religion, and then through a specific locality ('a Druze from Deir al-Qamar', 'a Maronite from Souq el-Gharb', 'a Sunni from Tripoli', 'a Shi'a from Jebel 'Amil'). This sort of dual label speaks volumes to someone who understands the codes. But it does not tell the full story. The Maronite from Ehden may be on blood-feud terms with the one from Bsharri; the Shi'a from the far South may be the sworn political enemy of the one from Baalbek or Byblos. So there is a further shibboleth which differentiates subgroups with an already severely fragmented ethnicity: the *za'im*, 'leader' or 'capo'. There are further sub-groups, such as the traditionally pious among the Shi'a as opposed to those who publicly espouse 'modernity'.

When two Lebanese meet, the initial ritual is to situate the other person in terms of religion and outlook:

> It is difficult to be an atheist in Lebanon, or rather, it is impossible to refuse a religious identity … In Lebanon, the question 'Where are you from?' is a not-so-subtle way of trying to identify a person's sect.
> – You are American?
> – I have American citizenship, but I was born in Lebanon.
> – Your Arabic is 'heavy'.
> – Yes, I was raised in the United States and have lived there most of my life. And my mother is Armenian.
> – [Laughs] Yeah … So you are more American than Lebanese. Where in Lebanon are you from?
> – My father is from Hamat, and my mother is from Anjar.
> – Right, you said she was Armenian. Where exactly is Hamat? Somewhere in the North?
> – Yes, it's north of Beirut, just past the tunnel near Batroun.
> – So you're Christian?
> – My father's family is Orthodox Christian.[25]

It takes discipline, a sort of suspension of disbelief, to unravel all these knots and find the spirituality that underlies the religious affiliations of the Lebanese. But it is there. You can see and hear it on their feast days and in their prayers, and, perhaps most tellingly, in their funeral services.

25 Deeb, *Enchanted Modern*, pp. 10-11.

VOICES OF FAITH: RELIGIOUS IDENTITY

We begin this section with texts from three of the principal communities of Lebanon: Druze, Maronite Christians, and Shi'i Muslims. It may seem surprising that there are no extracts from Sunni Muslims. They are of course one of the most ancient and influential communities in the country, but as their faith is that of the majority of the countries and people of the Middle East, we have not identified any texts that are characteristically *Lebanese* to include in this section.

The former Jewish community is sadly absent; the small but thriving colonies mentioned by Josephus had grown to about 6,000 people by the time of Lebanese independence, supporting sixteen synagogues; this held more or less steady through the creation of Israel and the 1967 War, but, beginning with the Israeli invasion and siege of Beirut in 1982, and accelerating with the Islamist attacks on the main synagogue and individual Jews in the mid-1980s, those who could leave did so. Today only a few dozen very elderly Jews are reportedly left, mostly in Beirut.

The Druze

Much hostile – partisan, or simply ignorant – nonsense has been written about the Druzes over the centuries, as some of our European travellers' accounts testify all too eloquently. This is partly because of the tenet of secrecy, of 'not divulging divine knowledge to those who do not deserve it'. Our excerpt from Volney in the previous section is typical: not entirely wrong on all points, but illustrating how misleading a little knowledge can be. Understanding the complex spiritual philosophy of self-knowledge and the Unity of God that is at the core of their faith, officially Muslim and Isma'ili Shi'i, is a major undertaking; we have included one short extract on reincarnation, a key doctrine of the Druze, as well as a short prayer that one would have thought any Christian, Muslim or Jew, and perhaps others, could relate to. If so this may give one some inkling of why the Druze refer to themselves as muwahhidun, 'unifiers'. This unorthodox group has significant political and cultural importance in Lebanon. For political (in Lebanon, confessional) power-sharing the Druze are counted as Muslims, and in some respects they observe the outward tenets of Islam. However, they are secretive about their beliefs and practices and most Sunni Muslims do not regard them as 'orthodox' Muslims. Despite relatively small numbers, they are an active component of Lebanon's unique population mix, and have played a key role in Lebanese history.

Sami Makarem, *The Druze Faith*

Sami Makarem writes about his faith in an officially authorized account that is the best summary of the history and beliefs of the Druze.

Why Reincarnation?

Since man originated as a spark from the divine Will and since the divine Will is eternal, so is man's reality, i.e., his soul. In his reality he shares reality with the divine Will, and in his bodily structure he shares corporeality with the physical world. He belongs to both worlds. Since the terrestrial world originated from the non-physical world, we see that both aspects of man, his soul and his body, came out of one origin, which in turn originated from the One. Soul and body therefore complement each other. The body is the medium through which man's reality actualises itself. So man must keep his body in a manner befitting its purpose. Anything which harms the body impairs its effectiveness as a medium. That is why the use of any stimulant or depressant, such as alcohol, nicotine etc. is proscribed. In fact over-indulgence in food or any other usually beneficial thing is also forbidden. Inflicting harm on one's own body or on others is condemned.

If the soul and the body are complementary and if the body is mortal, what will happen to the soul when it loses its medium?

After corporeal death the reality of man persists in a new human body so that this soul may continue its destiny by being in man's constant experience. Hence, as soon as the soul of a human being leaves its body then it acquires a new one. This new human body would also serve as a medium for this soul to actualise its being and participate in the progress of man towards knowledge and happiness, a progress which started with the origination of man. A soul can only progress in knowledge by means of a medium through which it can acquire this knowledge. Likewise it can only regress in ignorance, and be self centered, and consequently live in discord and contrariety, by means of a body whose selfish indulgence deflects it from its natural course. Thus, to the Druzes, the soul can only have a human body ...

To the Druzes, if the soul acquired a nonhuman form, then this form would defeat its purpose of being a medium through which man's reality is actualised. If, on the other hand, the soul were to be deprived of a physical medium, then it would cease by definition to be man's reality – the purpose of which is to be actualised and, consequently, to reach happiness. It is only in the physical world that happiness and distress can be felt.

In one of his epistles, al-Muqtana Baha'uddin[26] tells those who hold that the soul can survive without a human body:

> O you who are distracted, how can he who is deprived of corporeal means obtain knowledge? O you who are heedless, how can he who abandoned his sensual faculty reach ignorance? And O you who are perplexed, how can the souls exist by themselves? And how can they settle in their origin, and yet have a life and procure their pleasures?

> [Druze] Prayer to be Recited in the Morning
> O God, I enter the morning in need of Thee,
> Powerless and unable to avoid what I dislike,
> And incapable of accomplishing what I want,
> Except with Thy help.
> O God, I enter the morning pledged for what I have done.
> Everything is in Thy hand.
> I am most in need of Thee,
> And Thou art most independent of any being.
> Make not, O God, my enemies to gloat over me,
> Protect my friends from any misfortune,
> And me from the misfortunes of unbelief.

26 Ali ibn Ahmad, who was appointed to take charge of the nascent Druze Movement in 1020, just before the disappearance ('occultation') of the Caliph and Imam al-Hakim bi-Amrillah.

Let me not be concerned with worldly endeavour.
I pray that on the Judgment Day I will have been
Worthy of Thy sanction through Thy mercy.
O God, Thou art the most merciful of the merciful.

❧

Jaber El-Atrache: 'The Divinity of al-Hakim', from *On the Druze Religion*

The short excerpt from Jaber El-Atrache gives a brief explanation of the dogma relating to the tenth-century AD Fatimid Caliph al-Hakim bi-Amrillah, who occupies a central place in Druze theology as well as that of other Shi'i-influenced sects like the Ismailis.

'The Caliph al-Hakim had the personified God within him'. This is the dogma; Hamza and his colleagues explain this idea by means of the philosophical concept of 'apparition' (*at-tajalli*), which must be carefully distinguished from 'incarnation' (*at-tajassud*).

Al-Hakim, they teach, appeared to us in human form: God appeared in a form, but did not become flesh and blood. He made use of a form in order to appear to mankind; but that form had no intrinsic existence because no soul had previously inhabited it, and because God made use of it for a single purpose, to make Himself visible. Thus such a body cannot be touched by physical suffering. Hamza defines this concept as follows:

> He made visible the 'veil' under which He was hidden, and the 'place' from which he spoke to us, so that we might adore Him in the 'form' of a sentient, visible being.

The body of al-Hakim thus had no real existence: it was a mere dwelling-place destined to receive the God Personified.

The conclusions that follow from the above are that al-Hakim was not born of woman, and that he did not die. History, in fact, tells us very little about him: historians recount the most contradictory theories about the birth and death of al-Hakim

Maronite

As the reader will have gathered, the Maronites get a lot of attention in the writings of early European travel writers, who were surprised to find Oriental Catholics speaking Arabic, conducting the liturgy in a mixture of Arabic and Syriac (Aramaic) and worshipping on feast-days under the cedars. Their origins can be traced back to a fourth-century monk from Antioch; they took refuge on Mount Lebanon during ecclesiastical quarrels and persecutions from the sixth to the tenth centuries. By the eleventh century they were officially and finally affiliated to the Roman Catholic Church, though the independence of the Maronite Patriarch (of Antioch, but residing north of Beirut) is recognised, and the church retains unusual particularities in addition to the liturgy, such as the absence of celibacy for the lower orders of the clergy.

ﻢ

Paul Daher, *A Cedar of Lebanon*

The Maronite Saint Yusuf Makhlouf was born in the highest village in Lebanon, Bika'kafra, in 1825. An ecclesiastical calling led the young man to take holy orders, becoming a monk at the monastery of Annaya, and then following a still more austere path, that of the hermit. His reputation for saintliness drew many pilgrims and people in need of physical or other healing, and he soon became famous throughout the region for the miraculous cures that followed such visits. In the extract from *A Cedar of Lebanon*, a twentieth-century book by a Maronite prelate about the life, death, and miracles of the (then) saint-to-be, the piety of the Christians of the mountain is clearly illustrated, and one can sense behind it something of the popular awe for the holy hermit that one heard described in the earliest travel writers.

Brother Elias Mehrini paid a visit at midnight to the Blessed Sacrament in the church where Father Charbel's body lay in state on the night immediately following his death. As he prayed he beheld a light which, radiating from the tabernacle, came to pray over the Father's body, then, rising, returned to the tabernacle.

On the night immediately after the burial many villagers who lived in the houses facing the monastery saw a great ray of light rising and descending by turns over Father Charbel's tomb. And the phenomenon recurred for forty-five nights. A country witness, George Emmanuel testified before the patriarchal commission: 'An extraordinary glow appeared above the cemetery, which all we villagers saw from our houses opposite the convent.'

Another witness, Miladeh, widow of Tannous Chehadeh, deposed: 'The body was exhumed because of the appearance of the light, many times repeated. I, myself, saw it three times. The monks to whom we reported the fact would not believe us. But the superior of the convent, Father Antony Al Michmichani, came to our house opposite the monastery and satisfied himself of the appearance of the light. After which the body was exhumed.'

Non-Christians also saw this light. Let us quote an extract from the evidence of Saba Bou Moussa in this connection:

'It happened that the regional prefect, Mahmoud Hehmadeh (a Mahommedan) was with some of his men searching for a criminal he believed to be in hiding in Annaya. On the night on which they were in the neighbourhood of the convent, they saw a light appear at first faintly, then shining and flashing very brightly on the east of the chapel. By the time they came close to the monastery the light had faded. They woke up the superior, Father Antony Al Michmichani, and told him of it. He said to them "As a fact, for some weeks now, many people see this light shining over the tomb of Father Charbel." "I swear," the Moslem prefect answered, "that at the first opportunity I will go myself to notify His Beatitude the patriarch of the fact." ' …

The superior, Father Antony Al Michmichani, asked permission from the superior general of the Order and of His Beatitude, the patriarch, Elias Hoyek, to open the tomb and transfer the precious remains of the monk Charbel to a special grave.

Permission having been granted, the tomb was opened on the 15th April, 1899, in the presence of the superior of the convent, of monks and laity, including ten witnesses who had been present at the burial of Father Charbel four months before in the same cemetery … the body when cleared of the mildew with which it was covered was found intact in all its members, tender, flexible, supple in every joint. The skin retained its freshness, the muscles their suppleness; not a hair of his beard, nor a lock from his head had fallen out; the outline of the iron chain the hermit wore round his waist was clearly visible.

'The hands,' testifies Father Joseph Younez who is still living at Annaya, 'were folded on the breast, clasping the cross; the body was tender, fresh, supple; on the face and hands was a sort of white mildew resembling fine cotton. When Saba Bou Moussa wiped off this mildew, the face and hands looked like those of a man asleep. Blood that was quite red mingled with water trickled from his side.'

Father Elias Abi-Ramia, an eye-witness and also still living, relates:

'The body was supple, tender, exuding fresh blood, without any trace of corruption, as if one had just buried it that instant.'

Recently, with the authorisation of Rome, the tomb of Father Charbel was opened on the 7th August, 1952, fifty-four years after his death. I myself saw the body, intact as ever and always exuding this strange blood-like liquid, with which the coffin, the priestly vestments and adornments were literally soaked. On being removed from the coffin it was placed in a sitting position and the priestly vestments were removed. Short hair covered the head, the sinews were visible, and the skin was dark brown in colour. The body was reclothed. Afterwards it was replaced in the new coffin, made of cedar-wood and glass. On this same occasion I was even allowed to kiss the hand of Father Charbel and take it between mine, the flesh felt supple, almost breathing and lukewarm.

One had no fear or sensation such as one usually experiences on touching a corpse. Countless crowds, an ecclesiastical commission, a medical jury, twelve archbishops and bishops, His Eminence Cardinal Tappouni, ministers, the wife of the President of the Lebanese republic, people of every nationality, all saw and witnessed to the state of the body's preservation on this occasion …

Shi'i

Shi'i Muslims probably constitute the largest single population group in Lebanon, perhaps close to 40% of the total (one can only guess, in the absence of a census). Their origins date back to the dynastic and doctrinal conflicts of the century following the death of the Prophet Muhammad ('shi'i' derives from 'shi'at 'Ali', the 'party of 'Ali', the Prophet's son-in-law). Today only Iran and Iraq are majority Shi'i states, though (in the Arab world) there are significant minorities in Bahrain, Kuwait, and Lebanon, and smaller numbers in Syria, Saudi Arabia and Oman. The Lebanese Shi'i have lived for centuries on the coast and on certain parts of the mountains, notably in the south (Jebel 'Amil), though there are Shi'i villages in the Shouf and above Byblos. They were somewhat neglected during the adoption of power-sharing formulas at independence and even more recently, creating tensions both with the Maronites and with Sunni Muslims. In recent years, Iran has supported militant Shi'i in Lebanon, and provided funds and arms which have enabled the creation of a powerful militia and political party (Hizbullah). This party has a considerable degree of political control and military presence in Shi'i majority regions (especially in southern Lebanon), and has acquired significant popular support through the provision of social projects and services.

Lara Deeb, *An Enchanted Modern*

The high point of the year for Shi'i Muslims, in Lebanon as elsewhere, is the 10th day of the month of Muharram, when the 'Ashura celebrates the martyrdom of the Imam Husayn at the Battle of Kerbala in 61 AH (680 AD). The mood is of intense grief and shared suffering; the battle and the death of the Imam and his followers is re-enacted in graphic detail, and followed with great emotion by the crowd, who having attended a majlis or 'assembly' consisting of homilies and speeches, then forms a procession (masira) through the streets. In the traditional masira, the men strike themselves rhythmically with knives and swords as they walk, drawing blood and sometimes doing themselves serious injury; this striking is called latam or, metaphorically, 'hitting Haydar'. There is a lively debate within the Shi'i community as to whether these traditional practices should be continued; there is also tension between the ancient, purely spiritual aspect of the occasion, and the contemporary identification with revolutionary ideals. Lara Deeb, a Lebanese-American anthropologist, has studied these tensions in her book An Enchanted Modern, *where she gives us a vivid description of two recent Lebanese masiras, one traditional and quietist, but (to an outsider) violent; and one 'authenticated' or alternative and revolutionary, and curiously peaceful.*

A Traditional Masira: Ten Muharram in Nabatieh (2000)

The sunrise call to prayer woke us early. Soon after, the shaykh's voice exploded into every corner of town. Facilitated by loudspeakers, he began the day's lamentation. By 7:30 a.m. we could hear the crowd beginning to gather outside. All I could see from the balcony was a sea of black – spectators waiting for the day's events to begin. They had carefully left the road framing the town center clear for groups of mourners to pass. People claimed spots on balconies, ledges, and rooftops, and a group of young men climbed the mosque at the corner of the square. Those whose homes overlook the center opened their doors to guests, serving coffee and food throughout the day.

The sea of black was dotted here and there with white and red – the men who were 'hitting Haydar.' They began in the early hours of the morning and continued through the end of the reenactment. A group of between six and twenty men or boys would move quickly along the road, blood flowing from self-inflicted wounds on their heads and staining their white shins or bare chests draped with white cloth (representing shrouds) a bright red.

Throughout the morning, group after group passed beneath the balcony, almost at a jog. Their chants were punctuated by the sounds of their hands hitting their heads and the stomps of their feet. One or two sometimes held the razor blades or knives that had been used to cut a small incision at each man's hairline (though I was told that these cuts were usually made by a town butcher or barber). As each hit his wound in rhythm with the group, their blood flowed down their faces and chests …

The majority of those 'hitting Haydar' were youth, though there were boys as young as ten or twelve and older men as well. Younger boys seemed to be out earlier in the day, before the sun became too hot and the crowd too large. Some fathers carried their young sons – some who looked as young as two or three years old – on their shoulders, the children hitting their uncut heads along with the others in the group. A few men had cut their sons' heads lightly and were helping them to gently tap the cuts so a little blood would flow.

None of the children were crying. I was told that these were usually children who had been ill, and whose parents had vowed that they would 'hit Haydar' if God helped them recover.

By the time the reenactment began, everywhere, including the balcony where I stood, was packed with spectators and mourners ... Even during the reenactment, every so often a group 'hitting Haydar' or, more rarely, a car draped in Hizbullah flags with an elegy blaring from its speakers, passed by. By noon there were streams of blood in the street, and groups of men and boys walking around with their faces and chests soaked red and bandages wrapped around their foreheads.

The most obvious change that has occurred in *masira*s concerns the style of *latam* that men perform. As the Shi'i Islamic movement grew in popularity, the shedding of blood during *latam* was criticized as unIslamic because it involves purposely injuring oneself. Eventually, following the lead of Iran, Lebanese Shi'i clerics issued *fatwas* condemning the practice, and Hizbullah banned it outright in the mid-1990s. This was accompanied by calls for those who feel the need to shed their blood during Ashura to do so for the community good, by instead donating blood to local bloodbanks ...

A sharp contrast to traditional *masira*s and *latam* is presented by Hizbullah's *masira*s, that take place each year in several areas of Lebanon, including al-Dahiyya, Nabatieh, and Baalbek in the Beqaa.

An Authenticated Masira: Ten Muharram in Al-Dahiyya (2001)

People sat on every available inch of curb and ground, listening attentively to the narration being broadcast from the tent's speakers. We found a spot under the overpass near the women's entrance to the tent ...

There were children everywhere, babies in strollers and kids running around or trying to wipe away their mothers' tears. They too were dressed in black, some with t-shirts or headbands that said 'oh Husayn' or 'oh Abbas.'

Many little girls – including a friend's five-year-old daughter – wore *hijab*s or *'abaya*s even if they were too young to normally wear them. When the *majlis* ended, everyone walked towards the upper road to join the *masira*. Thanks to our Hizbullah press passes, Aziza and I were able to skirt crowd control and take a shortcut down to the highway so that we could watch the entire *masira* from the beginning.

The *masira* was highly organized. It began with four huge portraits of Khomeini, Khamenei, Nasrallah, and Musa al-Sadr.[27] These were followed by many groups of boys, scouts, youth, and men, organized by increasing age.

They were either dressed uniformly as scouts or entirely in black, 'Husayn' written on their colored arm- or headbands. Each group marched in three neat rows behind a microphone-bearing leader, who initiated *nudba*s [elegies] and chants, and ensured that everyone performed *latam* in perfect unison. This *latam* did not involve blood. Instead, those performing it swung both arms downwards, then up, then out away from their bodies, and finally in to strike their chests with their hands. It was done to a four-count rhythm so that on every fourth beat the sound of hands striking chests resonated loudly, providing a percussive accompaniment. The organized groups were followed by a large group of men marching in solidarity, some hitting their chests lightly, and by a group of shaykhs and sayyids, surrounded by security, walking quietly.

Then the women's part of the *masira* began, with colored panels of Ashura scenes. These were followed by female scouts and students, again in orderly rows organized by age, all dressed in full *'abaya*s. The girls chanted in response to a leader or sang *nudba*s but did not perform *latam*. One group wore *fish*s – full face veils – and were chained together, representing the women who were taken captive by

27 Ayatollah Ruhollah Khomeini, the 'spiritual guide' of the 1979 Iranian Revolution; Sayyid Ali Khamenei, the current 'Supreme Leader' of the Islamic Republic of Iran; Sheikh Hasan Nasrallah, leader of Hizbullah; and Muqtada al-Sadr, the Iraqi Shi'ite leader.

Phoenician glass

Yazid's men. Some marchers carried photographs of young Resistance martyrs, assumed to be their relatives. Again, the organized women were followed by a large group of female supporters walking en masse, not necessarily wearing 'abayas but all muhajjaba. Many pushed young children in carriages. As the masira arrived at the field designated as its end point, men went to one side and women to the other. Nasrallah [Hassan Nasrallah, leader of Hizbollah] spoke, then everyone prayed together behind him ...

Making glass near Byblos, 1972

THE QUESTION OF LEBANON:
POLITICAL IDENTITY

On 31 December, 1946, the last foreign armies completed their
withdrawal from Lebanon during the Presidency
of H.E. Bishara el-Khoury, President of the Republic
Stela at the mouth of the Dog River

The Cedar-covered mountains and monastery-studded valleys, the
ports – once Phoenician, now Ottoman or 'Turkish' to the European
travellers whose accounts have dominated previous sections of this
book – must now be left behind for the less evocative field of politics.
In order to make any sense of what Lebanon is today, we must first
consider its political evolution during the long decline and final agony
of the Ottoman Empire; and the European intervention that created
the modern nation-state. Our travellers, so engrossed in the exotic
and amusing detail, the shocking or flattering anecdote, were neither
qualified nor interested to provide an enlightened commentary on
such issues.

The Ottomans controlled their sprawling empire by allowing each
religious-ethnic group to administer itself for civil purposes, a system
known as '*millets*' – after the Turkish pronunciation of the Arabic
word for 'sect' – with foreign and defence affairs reserved for the
Ottoman rulers and their local deputies. In the Near East, they used
administrative divisions largely inherited from the Mamlukes, and
which served the same basic purpose: to discourage any idea of local
factionalism through an artificial drawing of boundaries, dividing to
rule. Thus Tripoli and its hinterland were separated from Sidon and
Tyre, while Beirut was a sub-division of the *Vilayet* of Damascus; the
Mountain had a special status, under a governor who – in later
Ottoman times – was a Christian, but never a local one (an Armenian
from Istanbul, for example).

The First World War brought to a head the long-festering 'Eastern
Question' (basically, how to divide the spoils of the disintegrating
Ottoman empire), in Lebanon as elsewhere in the Levant. The French

Mandate, accepted with enthusiasm by a probable majority of the inhabitants of Lebanon, and with sullen reluctance by the rest, had to be imposed by armed force in Syria. The Twenties and Thirties were peaceful, and in fact the Second World War enabled the Lebanese to press for independence, which they were grudgingly granted by the Free French in 1943, and actually achieved a year later.

In 1943 the various Lebanese elites agreed an unwritten 'National Pact' based on the principles that Lebanon should be independent; that it had an 'Arab character' (*wajh 'arabi*); and that the key jobs in government would be shared proportionally among the minorities, with the Presidency going to a Maronite. The Prime Minister would be a Sunni, and the Speaker of the parliament a Shia Muslim. The seats in Parliament would be distributed 60:40 in favour of the Christians. This was an arrangement based on bargaining power, not a democratic result based on demography or suffrage. If it roughly corresponded to what was thought (in the absence of a census) to be the overall ratio of two deeply fragmented sections of the population, it begged several key questions – such as whether to classify the Druze as Muslim.

The ratio of the population, thanks to emigration and different demographic trends, has by all accounts changed significantly since 1943, to the disadvantage of the Christians. In 1990 the parliamentary ratio was updated to 50:50. How much the ratio has in fact altered, and how this and other factors have affected the relative position of the different groups since the crucible of the 1975-90 Civil War, is impossible to say with any precision; but the country remains under a government where parliamentary election lists and seats, Cabinet portfolios and the top jobs in the State are allocated according to religious affiliation at birth.

Lebanon is, more than many countries, a Question, the way the Ottoman Empire itself was – that is, when it was not a Problem or a Crisis. This section presents the visions of three writers who were at least partly Lebanese, and one Frenchman. These are not literature.

K. T. Khairallah: *The Liberated Arab Areas: Open Letter to the League of Nations* (1919)

This plea for independence for the Arab Region at the end of the First World War was sent to the League of Nations by K. T. Khairallah. A Christian Lebanese, he had taken refuge in Paris after falling afoul of the Ottoman authorities through pro-independence pamphleteering. The majority of the Lebanese population, of all backgrounds, had supported the independence movement that resulted in the 1916 hanging of twelve patriots in what is still known as Martyrs' Square. There was wide popular disappointment in the imposition of League of Nations mandates; the 'martyrs' were accused, with some justification, of aiding the Entente Powers against the Ottomans, who had of course joined the war on the side of the Central Powers.

Paris, 24th November 1919

To the Most Honourable Sir James-Eric Drumond, K.C.M.G.C.B.
   First Secretary of the League of Nations.

Most Honourable Sir,
I am taking the liberty of sending you some documents and considerations concerning the Arab areas that have been liberated from the Ottoman Empire … The current situation as it is evolving in Iraq, Syria, and Lebanon is poorly understood.

This situation, Most Honourable Sir, is intrinsically, and in more than one respect, worthy of your attention and of that of the public.

The intense suffering of the populations in the Arab World must be one of the most unfortunate episodes of the World War: physical and psychological torture, banishments, mass executions, prison, famine, epidemics: the full gamut. To mention specific examples: Lebanon has lost half its population through famine; Medina, which used to have a population of sixty thousand, now has barely a few thousand; in Beirut and Damascus, 21 leading Arab figures were hanged on the same scaffold in a single day.

On the other hand, the Arab army that fought so valiantly, under the orders of General Allenby – in Palestine and in Syria – was made up of volunteers coming from the various Arab regions.

There is, nonetheless, one consideration which takes precedence over all others. This land which is currently up for grabs, is an eminently venerable one, the cradle of civilisation; civilised human-kind cannot, without ingratitude, fail to respect the place of its origin. It is here that man first was conscious of being Man. It is here that the great philosophical and religious ideas were born, the ones that make up the universal heritage of the human race …

It is true that since then, darkness has descended on these memorable countries: Babylon, Nineveh and Palmyra are in ruins; Byblos, Tyre and Sidon are insignificant towns; Damascus and Baghdad are dim reflections of what were capital cities of the Caliphs. But amongst these ruins, in the middle of this general dilapidation, a new spirit is rising. This new spirit is looking to the civilised world to grant it the right to life.

The modern era has already seen dramatic resurrections: Athens has recovered its place in the sun, along with its freedom; Rome has witnessed new celebrations in its Capitol.

Why then must Tyre and Byblos, Damascus and Baghdad stay enslaved?

The direct heirs of those past civilisations are here. They are fully conscious of the nobility and grandeur of the legacy which they have received from the past, and they request – they demand – of the civilised world the formidable honour, the burdensome task of bringing back to life this antique land, which witnessed the glory of their ancestors, to endow it with a new life and a new civilisation.

Translated by T. J. Gorton

ـه

Pierre La Mazière: *Off to Syria* (1928)

One Frenchman, at least, was sensitive to the frustration of many of the people of Syria and Lebanon at seeing their support for the Entente war effort rewarded with a modernised form of colonial rule. Pierre La Mazière makes a startlingly contemporary-sounding plea for the French to get out of their Syro-Lebanese quagmire, illustrating the difficulties, cultural and geographical, inherent in governing from a distance.

At the bank where I presented myself in order to obtain a letter of credit, I was given a document addressed to Mr. X, Beirut, 'Turkey in Asia'. I immediately felt less ashamed of my own ignorance. How can this be! We accepted the Mandate for Syria [*and Lebanon*] six years ago; for six years we have been sending High-Commissioners, administrators, all kinds of bureaucrats ... and nobody, or nearly, knows even where it is located, what is going on there, what we are doing there, or what we hope to accomplish; and one of the main French organisations has not even realised that it has been detached from the ex-Ottoman Empire: 'Beirut, Turkey-in-Asia'!!!

For our curiosity to be piqued, for us to take interest in that faraway land, there has to be a catastrophe; some general has to endure a defeat on behalf of our flag; some of our sons have to be slaughtered. Then, we wake up and take interest ...

Many – too many – of the French who were sent out here acted as though they were in a conquered land. Well, they were not, and their behaviour which might just possibly have been justified if it were, was entirely inexcusable here. Gouraud was a great soldier, a handsome figure of a man, but the least prepared, least qualified person one could imagine to play the rôle of High-Commissioner: a rôle which requires so many talents which are incompatible with a military mindset. And so he landed at Beirut, full of preconceived ideas – and the mentality of a Crusader ...

This haphazard fragmentation of a country, and most especially the creation of the State of Greater Lebanon, is one of the causes – the main one, the gravest one – of the conflict that has erupted between the Mandatory Power and its Syrian pupils ...

We have spilt enough of our blood, spent enough of our millions on this adventure. Let us leave the Syrians and Lebanese to their fate, or rather to whoever would take over responsibility for them.

And let us go home.

Translated by T. J. Gorton

Michel Chiha: *Lebanon Today* (1942)

This is a thoroughly Cartesian discussion of the immediate post-Independence political situation in the 1940s, from an essay by intellectual, political theorist and writer Michel Chiha.

Politically, Lebanon is not a country given to rash behaviour or revolutions. It is a country whose traditions must protect it from violence. Every shock that it undergoes destroys to some degree what time has accomplished ... With us, a slow but far-reaching evolution is always to be preferred to a revolution.

Lebanon is a crossroads-country, a sort of public square; it must build a strong edifice of laws on the foundation of its traditions, strengthening the Lebanese family by every possible means, teaching our children to let the spiritual take precedence over the temporal, and to prize freedom more than wealth ...

Every time during the last twenty years that we have convened an assembly of which the basic objective was *to strengthen our desire to live together*, a forum where we could deliberate together matters relevant to the common weal (putting aside sectarian interest for a moment): Maronites, Sunnis, Shia, Druze, Greek Orthodox, Melkites and the rest, we have all done everything possible to discredit and spoil that parliament or assembly ...

In 1861, then in 1864, the Great Powers (with generous and liberating France in the lead) tried yet again to sort us out, instructing their ambassadors to work out a plan for the future organisation of Lebanon (a Lebanon that was less complex than that of today), it was up to six individuals, representing six heads of state of which the most democratic was the Queen of England, to come up with the idea of an elected parliament, one that represented its communities ...

We would be unworthy of respect if we forgot that Tyre existed two thousand years before the foundation of Rome ... the centuries have passed over our trials and tribulations. Those who conquered us, and their conquests, have disappeared; we remain ...

Translated by T. J. Gorton

A. H. Hourani: *Syria and Lebanon, a Political Essay*

From Albert Hourani we borrow a dispassionate discussion of the position of the minorities who together make up Lebanon's population. Hourani was professor of Middle Eastern studies at Oxford and author of The History of the Arab Peoples: *perhaps the most comprehensive single book on the vast subject, detached without being dreary, dispassionate without being bloodless. After the war, he came to feel that 'Syria and Lebanon: a Political Essay' was rather dated, especially as regards wartime relations between Britain and France; but that is not the angle that interests us. The excerpt we have chosen sets forth a clear and largely still applicable description of Who's Who among Lebanon's minorities and their modern interrelationship. We hope he would not have minded.*

Lebanon and the Minorities

The Lebanese Republic of to-day was formed after the First World War, by the addition to the pre-war autonomous Sanjaq of Lebanon, which consisted mainly of Mount Lebanon itself, of certain towns and outlying districts. In the former, the population is almost entirely Christian (mainly Maronite) and Druze. The additions included the coastal towns of Tripoli, Beirut, Saida (Sidon) and Sur (Tyre), and the districts of the Biqa' in the east and Jebel Amil in the south. In the towns the population is largely Sunni Moslem, although there are also numerous Shi'is, Greek Catholics and Orthodox and Armenians (mainly in Beirut). In the Biqa' and Jebel Amil the Shi'i Moslems are predominant, but here again there are large Greek Orthodox and Catholic and other communities.

In Mount Lebanon the majority is Christian, but the Druze community is large and strong enough to have played at least an equal and sometimes a greater part in the history of the Mountain. Thus the sectarian composition of Mount Lebanon is very different from that of the rest of the Mandated Territories. To a great extent also its history has diverged from that of other parts of geographical Syria. This has given rise to a specific Lebanese tradition. It is a tradition of asylum: remnants of sects and tribes, driven for one reason or another from the plains of the interior, have found refuge in the previously almost impenetrable valleys of Lebanon, where they could worship and live unmolested from outside. The various communities which have established themselves there have usually respected one another's beliefs and ways. There have been tension and suspicion between them, but in normal times they have lived peaceably together. It is true that for generations Lebanon was torn by internal strife, but it was the strife of factions and families. It was only for a short time during the nineteenth century that it took the form of a religious war, and even then the fundamental causes were social and political rather than religious.

The Lebanese tradition was also one of autonomy. Caliphs, Crusading rulers and Ottoman Sultans alike refrained from demanding more from Lebanon than tribute and the formal recognition of their suzerainty. They left the internal affairs of the Mountain to the care of local dynasts, more often than not members of local landowning families. Often Lebanon was partitioned between more than one of these dynasts; but on occasion a ruler succeeded in uniting the whole Mountain and even in extending his sway beyond it. His rule over the Lebanese, however, was never absolute …

There are some who do not regard Lebanon as possessing a special mission. For them the Lebanese are simply a branch of the Arab people, distinguished from the other branches by nothing of political significance; their destiny is indistinguishable from that of the Arab people as a whole.

Others do not go quite so far. They admit that history and tradition give Lebanon a slightly different character from the other Arab regions; but they do not regard this difference as forming the basis of a special mission or destiny in the present. It is nothing but a relic of a past age, an obstacle to· be overcome before the Lebanese can fulfil their true function, which in the view of this as of the first group is to become a full part of the Arab people.

A third group believes in a special function for Lebanon, but a restricted one. It is to continue to provide an asylum for those whose religious loyalties or racial origins make it difficult for them to live in neighbouring regions. This, although a noble conception, is also a limited one: first because it can only be actualized under perpetual foreign protection or guarantee, since the hills and valleys of Lebanon no longer render her immune from interference; and secondly, because it offers to the communities who seek refuge in her no ideal except to be left alone and to live on the margin of history, and no common aim except that of defence.

A more positive conception is that of those Christians who realize that Lebanon's being largely Christian and her being more advanced than the surrounding countries impose upon her peculiar and positive duties. There are some who maintain that Lebanon should become fully a part of the Western Christian world and that she should not be politically or in any other way a part of the Arab world, although she must retain close and friendly relations with that world.

For them the ideal in the political as in other spheres is that Lebanon should be self-subsistent, but if that is impossible they would wish her to be dependent upon a Christian European State rather than be part of a Moslem Arab State.

Finally there are some who wish Lebanon to remain Christian without at the same time ceasing to be Arab. The specific duty of the Lebanese is a duty at the same time to the Christian West and to the Arabs: it is to serve as a centre from which Christian and in general Western influences can radiate to Arab Asia. If they are to perform this duty, the Lebanese must form an integral part of the Arab world, politically as in other ways, but receive a special position and special treatment inside that world. They also need the help of some Western State or institution which will take in them an interest other than purely political and self-regarding, though they must avoid becoming the clients of a Western State in a way which will alienate them from the rest of the Arab people.

The differences between these five conceptions are not closely related with the differences between the sects. Roughly however, and with considerable reservations, it may be said that the first two views are held by many of the younger generation of the Druzes and Greek Orthodox Christians, but by fewer of the Maronites; the third view by those, to whatever sect they belong, who are deeply suspicious of the Sunni Moslems and at the same time conscious of their own weakness.

The fourth and fifth views are of course held only by Christians: the fourth by many of the Maronites, the fifth by those who have been moved by the nationalist sentiment without trying to make it a substitute for religious belief ...

A Druze Fiancée from the Mountain (Adrien Bonfils, 1880)

PEOPLE OF THE BOOK: LITERARY IDENTITY

Il y a des jardins qui n'ont plus de pays
Et qui sont seuls avec l'eau

Georges Schehadé

'People of the Book' is the usual translation of '*ahl al-kitab*', the Islamic term used to describe Christians and Jews. But the inhabitants of what was Phoenicia have a good claim on such a description: our word 'Bible' derives indirectly from Byblos, and in Herodotus and in Meleager's epitaph one senses the Ancients' respect for the sharp traders who took time off from business to teach Greece to write.

By the Arab conquest, however, Phoenicia was no more, Lebanon not yet born: a dissenting Byzantine province, then a Persian satrapy, then a collection of fiefs fought over by Crusaders, Assassins and the Arab-Kurdish-Turkish armies of Saladin. Then, briefly, a Mamluke province, and finally an administrative sub-district of periodically reconfigured *vilayet*s as the long Ottoman night set in. When Europe was having its Renaissance, the Levant was in the throes of the "*asr al-inhitat*", the 'Age of Decadence'. Classical culture was no longer accessible as Greek and Latin were forgotten, and there was no regional urban centre of learning or literature in Arabic (Aleppo under the Hamdanids came closest, briefly, in the tenth and eleventh centuries AD). Literature was mostly archaic and laboured poetry, the slightly ridiculous nostalgia of town-dwellers for an Arabian Arcadia they had never experienced, if indeed anyone had.

Interesting post-Classical prose is extremely rare between the Classical Period of Arabic literature (to about 1100 AD) and the nineteenth century, when the language and culture of the Arabs was revived from a long coma by the tireless efforts of a group of Lebanese and Syrians such as Ibrahim al-Yazigi, Butrus al-Bustany and others. Centred in Beirut, this became a movement leading to the *Nahda* ('rebirth') of the language, making it possible to establish the basis for a modern education system in Arabic, including the first proper dictionary and grammar of the language since the Middle Ages, and an encyclopedia that is still in use. The first wave of this Arab

Renaissance came in the form of translations of European literature; in Egypt, the presses left behind by Napoleon's army were rehabilitated around 1830, but Lebanon (which had its printing press since 1697) was the undoubted cradle of reinvigorated Arabic culture.

Lebanon of Memory: Popular Poetry and Nostalgic Prose

The First World War was traumatic for the Lebanese more because of the horrific famine it caused than as a result of military operations. The ensuing inter-war decades were a time of relative peace and prosperity, one of those occasional idyllic interludes. The Middle East theatre of the Second World War also largely passed it by, other than a passing unpleasantness between the Vichy faithful and the Free French. The transition to Independence in 1943–4 was relatively smooth, basically amounting to the creation of a condominium of power among representatives of the various communities. It is from those three or four decades that we have chosen texts to illustrate the Lebanon that some people living today still remember, one that still exists here and there and from time to time, and with luck may come again to replace the notes of war and destruction that have become sadly synonymous with Lebanon.

This is a Lebanon where mixed villages such as Beit Meri, and mixed areas such as the Shouf, provided examples of harmonious coexistence, *convivencia* – in Arabic, *ta'ayush*. Muslims attended the Université St-Joseph founded by the Jesuits, Christians of various sects mixed with everyone else at the American University, and one could be forgiven for hoping that the sectarian bitterness of the past was – of the past.

There is a rich folklore that is the common patrimony of the people of the Mountain whatever their faith, in their stories, legends, riddles, jokes and, especially, the *zajal*. This means literally 'ditty' and derives ultimately from a long tradition of orally-composed colloquial poetry first known to have existed under that name in al-Andalus, in the streets and courts of Cordoba in the twelfth century AD. In Lebanon it is mainly a mountain thing, but not a sectarian one; during long *zajal* evenings or parties, the best poets of the genre would spar, improvising songs on a theme which was announced to them with very little time for preparation. The 'literary' *zajal* also exists, a poem composed in reflection rather than in the heat of extemporaneous composition.

Some of the *zajal*-poets were famous all over the country, like Shahrour al-Wadi, the 'Nightingale of the Valley' whose *zajals* are still recited, especially in his native Shouf. In this ethnically mixed area, which produced a number of the best poets, the *zajal* remains an example of the harmonious and playful intermingling of people from all of Lebanon's ethnic groups. The keynotes are nostalgia, description of nature, and pride: boasting, whether of one's own skill as a *zajal*-poet, or about Lebanon and its mountain. They are devilishly difficult to translate, as their musical lilt and catchy rhyme are as important as the literal meaning of their lyrics. One sometimes hears the same particularly catchy line or hemistich repeated, so that the audience can sing along, which also allows the extemporising poet some thinking-time. The selection includes excerpts from what are usually rather long compositions; these make most sense when read as taunts to a rival or responses to a rival's taunt. They are invariably sung to the accompaniment of a tambourine.

Poetry: *Zajals* and Sung Popular Poetry

This extract is from a zajal-contest that brought together the famous Shahrour el-Wadi, Ali el-Haj, Shaikh Shahin Hobeish, Ramez al-Bustani, Yusuf Abdallah al-Kahale and others: two Maronites, a Shi'i, a Sunni, a Greek Orthodox and a Druze. Shahrour begins with the traditional praise of the place where the event is staged, here Jounieh at the foot of the Kesrouan hills:

Shahrour:
Lovely Kesrouan, where could I find hills to rival you –
Even if I tramped the whole world over, place by place? …
What heart could fail to flutter – at least a little – at your sight?
You sent forth your sons to destiny, their minds
A cradle for mankind, bringing life and fire and vision;
They use the sword as deftly as the pen,
And their palms are a spring of plenty and of grace,

But their foes feel their deadly lances' point …
On horseback, they put the knights of yore to shame;
When they leap gracefully into the saddle,
Their hooves clattering on the wings of night,
Sparking in the air both thunder and lightning
And showering the earth with the blood of enemies …
Shaikh Shahin:
Listen, O brother, to what I have to say:
If you want to go hunting, then hunt with the best
You have been singing well, and very well at that:
But it takes more than one to make a round number!
Shahrour:
O Shaikh Shahin, the number's not the point,
Don't let the numbers game get your goat;
A zero on the right is more than rounding up,
But with you the zero is placed on the left!
Ali el-Haj addresses Shaikh Shahin:
It looks like the Son of Hobeish [*Shahin*] is rather lame,
But if one is patient, the dawn must come at last;
Anyone else who came along would fare the same as him,
Though it must be bitter to be stuck in a corner!
Shahrour to the Shaikh:
O Shaikh, don't let your glory's lamp flicker and go out,
As you try your luck with the mothers of both bride and groom;
It's a shame for you to be stuck in that corner,
When your place is centre-stage, most honoured place of all!
The Shaikh to Shahrour ['nightingale' in Arabic]:
Now Shahrour, don't get prickly and envious to boot,
The falcon ['*shahin*' *in Arabic*] is used to killing birds:
So don't be so impressed with the size of your two wings,
Wherever you are coming from, it's me the king of birds!

This is from a literary *zajal* attributed to As'ad Saba:

The Emigrant's Song
O God please take me home to Lebanon
So I can kiss its holy soil

And feel its valley breezes on my eyes;
Lie down on its green grass, and fall asleep.
My heart no sooner thinks upon the Cedars,
Or on the clustered graves of kith and kin,
Before I feel the tears begin to flow –
Beads trickling down my cheeks, one by one.
There, where the orchard and the river meet,
In that green village which I call my own …
Oh Lebanon! Wherever I go, I see before my eyes
The graven letters of your name –
Oh God, don't come to close those eyes
Before I truly see it once again!

The following is not a *zajal*, but a traditional song sung by the women at a Christian mountain wedding, to the bride; a long-drawn-out 'ooha!' begins every line:

Oooha! Young and lovely bride, sitting stately as a queen,
With those eyes that would fire saintly Joseph with desire;
The ripest bunch of grapes, ready to be picked:
A man who fails to marry you will wish that he was dead!
Li Li Li Li Li!

Oooha! The first suitor for your hand offered as his prize
Two hundred mares, feisty, never foaled;
The second suitor offered two hundred bay purebloods;
But the one she chose pushed the others to the side,
And said: 'This is my bride, I'll fight for her if I must!'
Li Li Li Li Li!

This is an *'ataba*, a sort of plaintive Lebanese version of *fado*; the form has roots in Beduin songs.

Oof, oooooooooof …
My love walked out on me, forsook me just like that –
When being close to him had healed my wasted body;
Oh judge of love, take my advice, your verdict should be fair:
Is it no crime to wound the blameless ones you love?

[*refrain*]
Oh night of woe, won't you tell the world my misery?

Rejection's cast me down into a deep, dark tomb
And all I can do is pray, and beg you to relent;
After the burning pain of loneliness, who knows?
Just seeing you might yet bring happiness.

Oh night …

Oh my heart, if you could but sprout angels' wings
And fold me in them, close to you for evermore –
Like a turtle-dove, had she but wings like those,
Who'd take me flying with her, far away.

Oh night …

Translated by T. J. Gorton

Prose: Amin al-Rihany, 'The Village' (from *Qalb Lubnan*, 'Heart of Lebanon')

Amin al-Rihany was born in 1876 in Freike, Lebanon, and has been called the 'father of Arab-American literature'. He was influenced by Shakespeare and Walt Whitman on the Western side, Abu al-'Ala al-Ma'arri and Omar Khayyam to the East. It would be more accurate to say that he was both a Western writer – an expatriate Lebanese who lived off and on in America – and a Levantine who was equally steeped in the Arabic literary tradition. He died in 1940 after falling from a bicycle. His The Heart of Lebanon *reveals his deep attachment to his native land, though by quite early on he was identified as a 'philosopher' even by his boyhood friends …*

It was as though the inhabitants of Beit Shabab had been inspired by a local writer – or sorcerer – to reject the usual appellations 'town' or 'hamlet' or 'burg', and called their town a 'village'. Or, more properly, '*the* Village', Village with an capital 'V', an honour accorded even by the folk of neighbouring villages such as Dik al-Mahdi or Shawiya. If one of them was going to – or coming from – Beit Shabab, he would say: 'I'm off to the Village', or 'I've just come from the Village' …

Shi'ite villagers from Ras Baalbek
(Photograph by Gérard de Martimprey, 1896)

Back then, that is twenty years ago, the Village was flourishing, prosperous as its artisans. Bells were cast there, the 'national' cloth ('*dima*') was woven there, there were potters, and silkworm cocoons nestled in her workshops. She had her smith, and her carpenter, and masons, along with the weavers and potters; some of these were famous in the area, all over the Metn and elsewhere up and down Mount Lebanon.

How gorgeous the first view of this Village is, as you walk over from the direction of Freike, or to those who first catch sight of it as they come down from Bikfaya to the west. She fills the breast of the mountain with her houses and gardens, with her workshops and churches: surrounded by pine groves, crowned with vines. Her many springs mean water is abundant. Wood-smoke rises up from the workshop-chimneys, and diffuses its subtle fragrance through the gardens.

Sublime for her beauty, down-to-earth for her buildings, ... charming with the contrast of white stone and heavenly red roofs, everywhere invaded by trees: mulberry, towering poplars, walnuts and willows.

If you drive through her, you go through three squares, following each other along the tortuously winding tarmac road beetling over steep cliffs. Now at the first square, you will meet the Church of Our Lady, Our Lady of the Walnut. If you are pious, ask her for safety and keep climbing along the spiralling highway, fearlessly trusting in God.

Even if you are not a believer in Virgins or Saints or churches consecrated thereto (but do notice how very many churches there are in the Village), however, or especially in that case, you will do well to follow the alleyways with their steps, and penetrate into the heart of the town, and climb up above the workshops and factories.

These are the alleyways Brother Hanna and I followed ... We went aimlessly along one of the side-streets, and were so glad we did. The first place we stopped was a weaver's house, and at the loom, facing us, was a young Huri of Paradise, busily weaving with both hands and feet. She held the wooden frame with one hand, and the shuttle-cord in the other; her bare feet were pumping the pedals up and down as though she were practising a dance. She was the weaver-girl, the unquiet motor of the loom. It was not so much her voice that captivated us – a voice like a tambourine-bell – but the song she was singing, a plaintive "*ataba*'. When we stopped in front of the open door, she stopped both song and work and invited us to come in. There was another woman there, sitting on a cushion in front of the loom, turning the spindle with her right hand, guiding the thread with her left hand as it wound around the spool her companion was using with the shuttle.

The lady stood up, the damsel rose from her loom, and they welcomed us. We soon learned, after importuning them with questions, that the young girl was newly married to the manager of a silk factory, and the woman who was helping spool her spindle was her mother-in-law. We also found out that there were in the Village more than a thousand looms for weaving *dima* [*cotton cloth, used among other things for making men's jackets*], some run by women and some by men, with brothers and sisters, husbands and wives helping, and sometimes whole families pitching in.

This is seen as honourable, independent work: you work the home loom at the hours you please, two or ten or twenty hours a day … Before the Great War, there used to be at least one, and sometimes two or three looms in every house in Beit Shabab, producing as much local cloth as there was silk production, which found its way all over the Mount Lebanon, to Syria and beyond – to Egypt, and Cyprus, and Turkey.

Weaving in Lebanon was hard-hit during the World War and after it, and the textile industry nearly died out. Mass-produced European textiles dealt it one blow, while another came from emigration: over a third of the population of Beit Shabab went abroad. Then there was the change in attitude, with women turning away from weaving, living on remittances sent by their men-folk in Africa …

Even the art of making bells has succumbed to Africa: skills that were handed down the generations since olden times. And who in Lebanon or Syria knows how to cast bells like they used to in Beit Shabab? The bell *is* its ringing, its voice; and there is a magic in the voice of church-bells all over Mount Lebanon; they have many different rings, each shaped by the artful hand of their makers: some great peals, echoing far away, some delicate and soft, with every shade and nuance in between. The sound of church-bells, around sunset, rung by hand in the courtyards of monasteries, on the tops of mountains, carried by the breeze, echoing through the valleys …

And then there is the silk industry. Do you know about those little worms on whose account all those mulberry trees are planted, houses are constructed, all for the tiny capsule with the precious silk thread inside? … and the spinners, male and female; did you ever hear them chanting prayers while they work, at the close of day, sitting over their jars and boxes, unwinding and reeling up the silken thread? The one with the finest voice lets hers rise above the rest, imploring the Virgin: '*Kyrie Eleison. Christe Eleison.* Oh Queen of Virgins, Queen of all the Angels!' and the refrain is taken up by fifty or a hundred other voices: 'Intercede for us … '

There is another craft that is still alive, even if its production is nothing like it used to be. That is the making of pottery; if seductive Africa has lured away many of those who manned the thirty kilns that used to exist in Beit Shabab, there are still a few left. One belongs to my old school friend the Hajj Abu Yasu'. We learned the alphabet together, read the first Psalm of David to the young deacon, under the walnut-tree in the lower courtyard. That was while my father was still living in Beit Shabab, during the 1880s, when he ran a silk-factory there. I think you will remember the saying, 'teach me to read, I'll be your slave'; this deacon had a lot of slaves by the time God called him home. I was merciful with the deacon, but my friend Abu Yasu' was not. Some of the pupils used to say about the deacon, 'he's a waste of *sabtiyyeh*', the latter being a loaf of bread we carried from home to give to the teacher on Saturday [*sabt*]. The Hajj Abu Yasu' still says that about him, that he was a 'waste of *sabtiyyeh*'; and all because he never managed to kindle the spark of learning for him as he did for others – me, for example.

Translated by T. J. Gorton

Khalid Ziyade: *yawm al-jum'a, yawm al-ahad* ('Friday, Sunday')

Khalid Ziyade, a professor at the Lebanese University, has written widely on the life and traditions of his native city, Tripoli. His is a story of mostly peaceful relations between Lebanon's religiously-defined communities, or millets. Friday, Sunday – *the twin holy days, and holidays, in the school week at that time – is told from the point of view of the young Muslim schoolboy the author was. We see him exploring the strange customs of his new Christian neighbours, feeling like an anthropologist in the rain forest, discovering difference and strangeness; then transcending all that, ignoring labels like Christian and Muslim, urban dwellers and country folk. There is a nostalgia for a time that would soon end, but also a message of hope; for if peaceful coexistence can happen once, it can again.*

In my primary school experience, there was one teacher who was not from our neighbourhood, or even our city; on top of everything, he was Christian. That was his principal qualification as our French teacher in the upper form – the final year before moving on to high school. The pupils in the upper forms wore black jackets, while their French teacher wore a grey jacket or a dark blue one. We lower-form pupils wore black tunics like all other schoolchildren in the city.

After 1960, a new crop of teachers came to our school, when the policy began to allow hiring younger teachers, in their twenties. These were less tyrannical – that is, less cruel, our vocabulary – than the previous, older ones who treated us so severely. About a third of the new crop were Christians; one of them caught our eye because he wore a coloured shirt rather than a dark jacket; he was nearer to the students than to the other teachers in both age and behaviour. Another of them always wore a black jacket and a white shirt with a funny collar such as we had never seen before. We finally figured out, after much surreptitious enquiry, that he was a Christian man of the cloth. The one with the funny collar was exceedingly kind; but we astonished him on the first day. At two-thirty sharp, as soon as the muezzin's call blared forth from the Taham Mosque next to the school, every single pupil rose, raised their fingers and began to mumble the noon prayer. That was our way of asserting to this teacher our identity, our difference from him. The few Christian teachers had to accept this halting of school business during the noon prayer or the evening prayer during the afternoon session of the school day. But the pupils never did such a thing when the teacher was one from their city and their sect.

When I was in the fourth year of middle primary school I was moved to a different school. This was in the middle of the modern part of the city, not far from the house my family had moved to. But the move was more dramatic in terms of time, than of distance. Our old neighbourhood had shared its walls with the history of the Ottoman Empire. The new one dated to the Mandate, and took its final shape during the fifties. It was peopled by immigrants from the countryside around Tripoli, Christian in the majority, until the beginning of the sixties. At first I had the impression that we were living in a Christian neighbourhood, as though it were an extension of the Nazarethan Quarter [*the historic Christian quarter*]; but it was not, being in reality one of the mixed neighbourhoods which made their appearance at about that time. Mixed, that is, between Muslims and Christians, but also between people from the country and city folk; and in fact it was more complex even than that. Our neighbour in the apartment facing ours was a Christian of Palestinian origin, while the grocer (the only one in the neighbourhood) was Greek, and lived in the building across from ours. On the other corner was a family who were thought to be French, and there were families from Syria; but most of the Christians living there were from the nearby countryside.

After a while, my mother was sporadically invited to visit her neighbour-ladies; but she always had the impression that our 'real' neighbours were those we had left behind in our old neighbourhood. We imagined that our stay there was a temporary one. I avoided making friends with any of the local boys; but I did keep an eye on the girls, and used to chat from one balcony to another with the daughters of the Greek grocer.

The character our new neighbourhood had in the sixties was itself gradually displaced. But before the subsequent changes began to make themselves felt, I had time to carry out a thorough investigation of life in the new neighbourhood, to observe it in some detail. For me, the place was like a laboratory for anthropological observation of the lifestyle of the Christians from the countryside. I discovered the Sunday traditions, when the men put on their new clothes to sit around the house, or give a hand with the barbecue at lunch time. I discovered the feasts of Christmas, of New Year's, and Easter, as though they had no prior existence; I observed their funerals and their celebrations. The funerals I found deeply frightening, with all the black, and the rituals and the priests walking in the front of the procession. And especially because the funerals were mixed occasions, with men and women and young people carrying wreaths. But what impressed me most of all was the appearance of the women: they went around talking to men outside of their homes, without shame. Then there was the lady who lived in the ground-floor flat near the Greek grocer's shop, who used to drink coffee in the morning or early evening, sitting in the small garden-space in front of her home, in the company of her snow-white daughters. She would chat with the neighbours as they passed, and invite them in for a cup of coffee. I used to wonder with great perplexity about the significance of this daily ritual which induced a lady to go outside of her own house. There were no secrets between neighbours, but an intimacy like that between siblings; as for us, we were never admitted into any such intimacy, with its overtones of country familiarity.

This was a time of mixing and happiness, and my new school was much less frightening than the old one; it too was a mixed place, and for the first time I began to make Christian friends at school. Not to mention the teachers, who taught us geography and French and natural sciences ... In my first year there, my bench-mate was a Christian boy; about a quarter of the pupils were Christians. From the second year onwards, there was an influx of more Christians, coming up from the private and missionary schools. They were better than us in French. Our generation, more than previous ones, benefited from this mixing which reached its high point about that time. There would be a Catholic from Zahle, a Druze from the Shouf, and a Shi'i, in addition to all the Maronites from the country and the Orthodox from the city-centre. Our [Islamic] religion teacher was amazed to see all these [Christian] boys get up and promptly leave the classroom the first time he walked in.

I saw the secondary school as a place for socialising, not for anthropological research. There were quarrels between classmates, but benign ones, of no concern. Some – especially those from outside the city – tried to conceal their prior identity, their roots in other areas, their local accents … Religious holidays were vacations from school, and the students followed their religious traditions and practices in the family milieu, not on the school premises. There were no religious or theological discussions. Friendship mixed us, and we mixed together in the movements and causes which moved the youth of the day. The Christian boys in the class would compete in following the whims of fashion and western music; we, for the most part, were more conservative. But the distinction was not, in actual fact, along religious lines, but depended on whether one was more attached to the conservative values of one's religious background, or to the more modernising influence of fashion. And those who were more attached to tradition – whether Muslim or Christian – were the butts of our jibes and sarcasm.

Translated by T. J. Gorton

Exiles

Lebanon has always been a net exporter of its sons and daughters. Partly through demographic pressure, in this 'mountainous land whose soil was less fertile than its women'.[28] But restlessness, the wanderlust that pushed Phoenician seamen to sail westwards around Africa in 600 BC – a thousand years before the Portuguese – and the urge to improve economically rather than to accept the way things are, must have contributed to this perennial net outflow. Today, it sustains Arabic-language newspapers in Brazil and *zajal*-singing contests in Toronto. The paradigm of the expatriate Lebanese has him emigrating young to '*al-nu-yark*', making a tidy fortune, returning to the village twice: once to find a bride and again to die. Emigrants who returned with intellectual capital and inspiration, who kept a foothold in both native and adopted cultures, are numerous and played a key role in the revival of letters and ideas in the nineteenth and early twentieth century.

28 Hitti, *History of Lebanon*, p. 473

Beirut from the Mountain, 2008

Gibran Kahlil Gibran

Lebanon's most famous modern writer is an unlikely hybrid of indigenous mountain-bred mysticism and Manhattan. Mount Lebanon has always inspired people to prophecy, or prophetic delusions: some of the 'real' prophets of Antiquity; later on, resident outsiders like Hester Stanhope, who could (and did) go on for hours on end in what sounded like a trance of messianic madness; or children of the mountain like Khalil – or Kahlil as he spelt it in America – Gibran. Gibran is undoubtedly the most famous local practitioner of the genre. The pure voice, undeniable sincerity and threads and gleams of insight here and there in *The Prophet* and his other works outweigh the bits that will strike one as maudlin if approached in too down-to-earth a mindset. Like sweet wine, it is best taken in small quantities and without great thirst.

Gibran spent formative years in exile in New York City, where he learnt English. The brutal ways of the New World and its frantic indifference, stark contrast to his native Bsharré. He wrote his early works in Arabic: *Broken Wings* and *A Smile and a Tear*, but from *The Prophet* onwards he mostly wrote in English. He is not a stylist, having had little formal schooling other than the Bible with which he was reportedly taught to read. His writing is deeply influenced by the pellucid, hushed tones of the Psalms. If not style, it is certainly a distinctive voice. Gibran left the royalties to his writings to his native village, where they became just another asset for the unruly mountaineers to squabble and feud over; if they ever read their famous son's book, it did not affect them much.

The Prophet   ALMUSTAFA, the chosen and the beloved, who was a dawn unto his own day, had waited twelve years in the city of Orphalese for the ship that was to return and bear him back to the isle of his birth.

And in the twelfth year, on the seventh day of Ielool, the month of reaping, he climbed the hill without the city walls and looked seaward; and he beheld the ship coming with the mist.

Then the gates of his heart were flung open, and his joy flew far over the sea. And he closed his eyes and prayed in the silences of his soul …

There are no graves here.
These mountains and plains are a cradle and a stepping-stone.
Whenever you pass by the field where you have laid your
    ancestors look well thereupon, and you shall see
    yourselves and your children dancing hand in hand.
Verily you often make merry without knowing …

But as he descended the hill, a sadness came upon him, and he
    thought in his heart:
How shall I go in peace and without sorrow? Nay, not
    without a wound in the spirit shall I leave this city …

And some of you have called me aloof, and drunk with my
    own aloneness.
And you have said, 'He holds council with the trees of the
    forest, but not with men.
He sits alone on hill-tops and looks down upon our city.'
True it is that I have climbed the hills and walked in remote
    places.
How could I have seen you save from a great height or a great
    distance?
How can one be indeed near unless he be far?

The Broken Wings

Silent Sorrow   You others may rejoice as you recall the images of your first youth, your joy only mixed with sadness at its passing; but I recall them as a prisoner remembers the walls of his cell, or the weight of his shackles. You may call those years which separate childhood from youth a golden age, free from cares and anxieties, when you soared above all worry and bother as a bee flies over a swamp on its way to a luxuriant garden. For me, the years of my first youth were nothing but sorrows, hidden and silent, dwelling within my heart and torturing it, growing within it as it grew. I could find no escape to the world of knowledge until love entered my heart, opening its doors and illuminating its darkest corners. Love freed my tongue and it spoke; touched my eyes and they wept; it opened my throat, and it swelled and moaned.

You others may remember the fields and gardens and village squares and streets that watched your childish games, and listened to the whispers of your innocence. I too remember that beautiful spot in North Lebanon, and every time I turn my eyes away from these my surroundings, I can see those valleys full of awesome enchantment, and those mountains rising gloriously towards Heaven. Every time I shut my ears to the din and bustle of this place, I hear the murmur of those brooks and the rustle of those branches. But even as I remember the beauty of all those things, and long for them, my longing is like the yearning of a weaned child for its mother's arms. Those memories torture my bound and fettered soul, causing it to suffer as the caged falcon suffers on seeing a flock of his free brethren soaring through the vast openness of the sky. Those memories filled my breast with painful hope, and bitter thought, and with fingers of perplexity they wove round my heart a net of confusion and despair.

Whenever I went out into the countryside, I returned with a heavy heart, not knowing why. Whenever I looked out at the sunset, the clouds coloured by the sun's rays, or heard the song of the nightingale or the gurgling of the spring, I felt sad and depressed, my sadness only deepened by my ignorance of its cause.

They say that lack of learning makes a man empty, and that emptiness brings peace. That may be true for those who are dead when they are born, and live out their lives like cold cadavers on the surface of the earth. But blind ignorance afflicting the awakening of feelings and emotions is more terrible than the abyss, bitterer than death. A sensitive youth who feels much, but knows little, is the most wretched creature under the sun, for he is under the power of two contrary and violent forces. One is a hidden, invisible force, whisking him up into the clouds, revealing to him the beauty of creation through a fog of dreams; and another, palpable force, which chains him to the earth, clouding his eyes with dust and leaving him lost and frightened of the deathly darkness.

Such was my life up to the age of eighteen. When I look back on that year, it is like a mountain-peak soaring above all my past life, for that is the year I first awoke to this world, and saw the ways of mankind, the meadows of man's delights and the worrisome toil of his existence, the caverns of his rules and dead conventions.

In that year I was born to this world a second time, for if a man has not known melancholy, has not been riveted by despair – and then found love along the path of his dreams, his life will remain a blank page in the book of life.

In that year I saw the angels of Heaven looking at me from behind the eyelashes of a beautiful woman. I saw lurking in her all the devils of Hell, making a commotion in the heart of a sinful man; and the man who has not seen the angels nor the devils in the good and bad of life is condemned to share his life with an ignorant heart, devoid of all feeling.

The Hand of Fate

I was in Beirut in the spring of that year full of marvels. April had covered the earth with greenery and flowers, so that even in the city gardens it was as though the earth was whispering its secrets to Heaven. The almond and apple-trees were garlanded in fragrant white, peeking out between the houses like houris in their wedding-dresses, sent forth by Nature to be brides for the youthful poets and dreamers of the world.

Spring is beautiful everywhere, but in Lebanon it is most beautiful of all. Spring is an unfathomable divine spirit that flits quickly over the earth, but when it comes to Lebanon it slows its pace, looking back and talking with the spirits of kings and prophets hovering in the void, singing along with the eternal Song of Solomon, chanting with the Cedars the hymns to ancient glory.

Beirut in the spring is more beautiful than in any other season, cleansed of winter's mud and summer's dust, between the past rains and the coming heat like a young girl who suns herself on the river-bank, letting her body dry after bathing in the spring …

Translated by T. J. Gorton

Amin Maalouf: *The Rock of Tanios*

Amin Maalouf, an expatriate Lebanese writer who writes in French, is perhaps best known for Leo Africanus and other historical novels set in the distant past. Most of his books have an imaginary or at least clearly non-Lebanese setting. He did write one novel set in more recent times, and in his native village: The Rock of Tanios. *This won him the Goncourt Prize in 1993, perhaps more for its clever story-within-a-story than for the depth of characterisation. It begins with a description of the relationship between a Christian mountain sheikh or village-headman and the ordinary people.*

In those days the heavens were so low that no man dared draw himself up to his full height. However, there was life, there were desires and festivities. And if one could never expect the best in this world, one hoped every day to escape the worst.

The whole village belonged at that time to one feudal lord. He was the heir to a long line of sheikhs, but when anyone speaks today of 'the time of the Sheikh', without further precision, there is no doubt who is meant, the reference is to the one in whose shadow Lamia lived …

'Women!' old Gebrayel said to me, and his predatory eyes lit up in his hawk-like face. 'Women! The Sheikh coveted them all, and he seduced one every evening!'

As far as the last part of this sentence was concerned, this was pure fabrication. But for the rest, which after all is the essential, it does indeed seem that the Sheikh, following the example of his ancestors, and so many other lords, in every latitude, had the firm conviction that all the women in his domain belonged to him. Like the houses, the land, the mulberry-trees and the vines. The men, too, for that matter. And that, any day, at his convenience, he could make the most of his rights.

One must not, for all that, imagine him prowling about the village like a satyr in search of his prey, with his henchmen acting as procurers. No, that is not the way things were. However imperious his desire might be, he never for a moment relinquished a certain dignity, never would he have dreamed of slipping furtively through a secret door, like a thief, to take advantage of a husband's absence. It was on his own premises that he officiated, so to speak.

Just as every man had to go, at least once a month, 'to see the Sheikh's hand', so all the women had to put in a day's work at the castle, to help in the daily or seasonal labours, that was their way of showing their allegiance. Some of them demonstrated particular talents, an unrivalled way of pounding the meat in the mortar, or kneading the dough for the bread. And when a feast had to be prepared, all skills were needed at once. A form of forced labour in brief; but shared between dozens, hundreds of women, it became less onerous.

I have perhaps let it be understood that the men's contribution was limited to the morning hand-kissing. That was not the way things were in fact. They were required to be responsible for the wood and the many repairs to the Sheikh's estate, restoring any crumbling terraces, not forgetting the ultimate duty of all the males – war. But in peacetime, the castle was a hive of women bustling about, chatting and also enjoying themselves. And sometimes, at siesta-time, when the whole village sank into a dimly-lit torpor, one or other of the women would stray between corridors and bedchambers to surface two hours later in the midst of whispers.

Some of them fell in with these games willingly, flattered at being courted, desired. The Sheikh had a fine presence, and they knew moreover that, far from throwing himself at the first female face he saw, he appreciated charm and intelligence. They still repeat in the village this saying of his, 'Only a donkey would sleep with a she-donkey!' Insatiable, yes, but difficult to please. That is how he is still seen today, and that is probably exactly how his contemporaries, his subjects, saw him. So, many of the women were anxious at least to be noticed, this reassured them about their charms. Even if it meant subsequently letting themselves be led astray – or not. A dangerous game, I agree; but at the time when their beauty was budding, then flowering, could they, before it faded, give up all wish to attract?

And yet, in spite of what old Gebrayel says, most of them would have nothing to do with these compromising affairs which had no future. The only part they would play in these amorous diversions was to side-step the advances, and it seems likely that the Master managed to accept defeat when his 'opponent' proved too cunning. And, what was more important – far-sighted, since, as soon as the object of his desire found herself alone with the Sheikh, she could not reject him without humiliating him, which no village-woman would have had the nerve to do. They had to exercise their skill earlier, in fact by avoiding finding themselves in this embarrassing situation. They had to think up a variety of ruses. Some of them, when it was their turn to come to the castle, arrived with an infant in their arms, their own or that of a neighbour. Others brought along their sister or mother, certain that, in this way, they would not be harassed. Another plan, to escape the Master's attentions, was to sit right next to his young wife, the Sheikha, and not leave her side all day.

The Sheikh had not married until he was nearly forty, and even then it had been necessary to force his hand. The Patriarch of his community had received so many complaints against the incorrigible seducer that he had decided to use his influence to put an end to this scandalous situation. And he thought he had found the ideal solution: to marry him to the daughter of an even more powerful feudal chief, the Lord of the Great Lord, in the hope that in this way, out of regard for his spouse, and even more to avoid annoying his father-in-law, the Master of Kfaryabda would be obliged to behave himself.

No sooner was the first year over than the Sheikha had already given birth to a son, who was christened Raad. However, despite his satisfaction at having an heir, the man quickly resumed his depraved habits, neglecting his spouse during her pregnancy and even more after the confinement …

In the castle she feigned indifference or proud irony and drowned her sorrows by indulging her sweet tooth. Sitting for hours on end in the same place, in the little saloon next to her bedchamber, she sported by way of headdress an old-fashioned *tantour* – a sort of tall silver tube, planted vertically in her hair, on which was draped a silken veil, an outfit so complicated that she took care not to remove it even when she went to bed. 'Which,' Gebrayel remarked, 'was scarcely conducive to regaining the Sheikh's favours. Any more than her corpulence, either. She was said always to have within reach a basket full of sweetmeats over which the serving-women and visitors kept permanent watch, for fear it become empty. And the chatelaine gorged herself like a pig.' She was not the only woman to suffer, but it was among the men that the Sheikh's excesses aroused the most resentment. If some of them pretended to believe that the thing happened only to other men's wives, mothers, sisters and daughters, all lived constantly in fear of seeing their honour tarnished. The village ceaselessly buzzed with women's names, every jealousy, every revenge was expressed by this means. Quarrels sometimes broke out, on futile grounds, which revealed the suppressed rage of various individuals.

People watched each other, spied on each other. A woman had only to dress with a touch of coquetry when she was leaving for the castle for her to be suspected of setting her cap at the Sheikh. And immediately, she was judged guilty, more guilty than the latter, for whom they offered the excuse that 'that was the way he was made'. It is true that there was one infallible procedure available to those women anxious to avoid any adventure: this was to present themselves before the Master looking hideous, dressed like scarecrows, deformed …

However, there are some women who cannot manage to hide their beauty. Or perhaps it is their Creator who feels loath to see it hidden; but, Lord! how many passions around them!

One such woman lived in my village at that time. This was Lamia, in fact. The Lamia of the old saying …

Translated by Dorothy S. Blair

FOUR

Wars

Pity the nation divided into fragments, each
fragment deeming itself a nation
GIBRAN KAHLIL GIBRAN

Choose your neighbour before your house
LEBANESE PROVERB

You might think that in such surroundings, humans would live in harmony, enjoying the contemplation of natural beauty, the fruits of the land and the satisfaction of their own gentle labours. But no. This last section is all about war, or rather wars, as Lebanon seems to undergo them with almost predictable regularity, each convulsion followed by a generation or so of peace: peace idyllic enough that a new generation grows up without memory of war, without the defences that such memory ought, in theory at least, to provide. The most recent war, with its uncertain aftermath, lasted longer than a generation, creating a whole crop of young adults who never knew the country the older ones among us boringly – and painfully – remind them we knew and loved and enjoyed.

To end this book on such a note would be depressing, and certainly wrong. But can one really be sure that Lebanon is now 'post-War', with a well-deserved respite around the corner? Not if July and August 2006, were anything to go by: a particularly violent summer which very few people would have predicted even a week before it began. At least nowadays the major military operations for control of territory seem to be done with, and the kidnapping of foreign civilians long since discarded as a negotiating tactic or money-maker. The conflict that remains is a more political one, with – for the first time in many years – all parties competing for dominance of the existing state structure. To the extent that this competition is mostly peaceful, it should be seen, cautiously, as a hopeful development.

More than one book could be filled with the battles, sieges and massacres that have taken place on this small patch of ground. Alexander's famous siege of Tyre would belong in the chronological middle between the Egyptian Middle Kingdom and the summer of 2006. We begin therefore with the mid-nineteenth century; by then, the events we read of revolve around the issues, sects, ethnic boundaries and often families one finds in today's news.

NINETEENTH CENTURY TO THE SIX-DAY WAR

Colonel Charles Churchill: *The Druzes and the Maronites* (1862)

Colonel Charles Churchill had illustrious ancestors, military, artistic and political: he was an illegitimate descendant of the Marlborough family, as well as of Nance Oldfield, the eighteenth-century actress and renowned beauty, and of Robert Walpole. After a time in Damascus as part of the western wing of the Great Game (when he fell out with his colleagues and the Turkish authorities alike), he married a local girl and retired to Lebanon. There he integrated into the elite circles of both Druze and Maronites (his two daughters married into the princely Shihab family), and wrote highly personal accounts of life on Mount Lebanon, especially during the 1860 Druze–Maronite civil war, which he blamed on the Turkish troops and pashas whom he despised. One especially interesting passage describes the attempts by the European Powers to bring those responsible to justice through an International Commission, which held dozens of meetings but came to nothing.

On the 30th of August, 1859, a serious affray took place between the Druzes and the Maronites in the village of Bate-mirri, three hours distant, in the mountain, from Beyrout. The original cause was a quarrel between a Druze and a Christian boy. The father of the latter, afterwards with three other Maronites, reproached the father of the Druze boy, and insisted that he should chastise his son. The Druze informed his relations, who, greatly excited, sent for reinforcements of Druzes from neighbouring villages, and the following morning assembled together and demanded an apology for the insult. The Maronites were about to accede to the request, when some of the Druzes fired off their muskets as a bravado. The former, mistaking this for a challenge, rushed to arms, and fired a general volley on the Druzes, following it up by a vigorous attack. The Druzes were driven out of the village with great loss. The next day, a Sunday, the Druzes rallied; a desperate encounter, which lasted all the day, ensued between the two sects, and the Christians were in their turn defeated. On the whole, however, the Druzes had lost in killed twenty-eight more than the Christians, who on this occasion had displayed unusual bravery.

The Turkish authorities were evidently taken by surprise. An officer was immediately sent to the village, who secured the principal offenders on both sides, and effected an apparent reconciliation. The Druzes, nevertheless, in other parts of the mountain, had taken the affray as a signal for civil war. Writhing under their unexpected defeat and heavy loss, they had already, under the guidance of one of their sheiks, commenced burning some Christian villages, when Kurchid Pasha, informed of the serious aspect which matters had assumed, rode up to a central position on the Damascus road, accompanied by a few soldiers, to stop the further progression of the evil. He there summoned the chiefs of both parties to his presence, and peremptorily enjoined them to keep the peace. Order was at once re-established. But the Druzes who had committed the outrages above mentioned were neither punished nor arrested. The power of the Turks over the mountaineers to enforce obedience to their commands, was thus clearly demonstrated. Here had been no necessity for artillery, or cavalry, or thousands of troops to separate the combatants. Civil war, at that moment, did not suit their purpose. They willed that hostilities should cease – and they ceased.

All who knew the temper of the rival sects, and the passions by which they were animated, saw that civil war between them, notwithstanding its temporary suspension, was from henceforward merely a question of time ... A fortnight later, a general agitation prevailed throughout the Druze districts of the Lebanon. Isolated Christians, sometimes even parties of Christians, were attacked and assassinated by the Druzes, on the high roads, which were more or less intercepted in every direction. Seized with consternation and alarm, whole families of Christians now abandoned their villages and sought refuge in such central places as Zachlé and Deir-el-Kamar ... There could now be no further doubt as to the nature of the Druze aggression, and the Christians of the Lebanon, in self-defence, took up the gauntlet of defiance. On the 27th of May, the men of Zachlé advanced, 3000 strong, to attack the Druze village of Aindara. They were encountered by 600 Druzes led on by their sheiks, on the

Damascus road, when the first regular conflict between the two sects took place. The battle raged all day and ended in the complete discomfiture of the Christians, who retreated in the utmost confusion. The Druzes rapidly followed up their success, and spread into the neighbouring district of the Metten, where they were equally successful, and burnt down some Christian villages. Throughout the remainder of the civil war, which lasted altogether about a month, this district was the scene of constant encounter between the hostile parties, with alternate success, until all its villages, amounting to more than sixty, had been destroyed ...

On the 28th of May, the insurgent Maronites of the Kesrouan, fearing for the fate of their co-religionists in the village of Baabda and Hadet, the residence of the Shehab emirs, an hour's distance from Beyrout, sent a body of three hundred men to protect them ... On the morning of the 30th of May, the Druzes, by a preconcerted understanding with the Turks, and even acting by signal, descended from the heights immediately over the above mentioned, and now abandoned villages, and commenced a furious onslaught ... The Christians, men, women and children, fled in the utmost consternation. One hundred Turkish soldiers had been previously placed in such a position as to support the Druzes, in case, by any chance, of a reverse, and these now joined the latter in following up the fugitives. The Turkish irregular cavalry also joined vigorously in the pursuit, cutting down every Christian they overtook, and robbing and plundering the women whom the Druzes had left unmolested. The Turks began the work of incendiarism long before the Druzes arrived ... The loss of the Christians, in life, had not been considerable; but the amount of property destroyed was immense ...

The European consuls-general, seeing the Lebanon thus plunged into all the horrors of a civil war, and justly alarmed by the strange conduct of Kurshid Pasha, proceeded in a body to his camp on the 1st of June, and made such representations as they thought most likely to awaken him to a sense of his duty ...

From the very commencement of the hostilities, the mob leaders of the Maronites in the Kesrouan, and even bishops, had dispatched letters couched in the most inflated and bombastic terms to the great

Christian centres amongst the Druzes, calling upon them to rise fearlessly on their oppressors, and promising their immediate assistance ... The Maronites had embroidered the Cross on the sleeves of their right arms. They were 50,000 strong, united by one common sentiment, and could afford to distribute their numbers. On a given day 10,000 would march on such a point, 8000 on another, 5000 on another ... But the promised relief never came, and, in the hour of need, they found themselves left to struggle as best they could.

[*There followed massacres of Christians in Druze-controlled territory at Hasbaya, Rachaya, Zahlé, and Deir el-Qamar*] The principal native Christian families, and even the tradesmen and lower orders, left daily by thousands, in any ships they could obtain, for Alexandria, Scyra and Athens. Boats were stationed ready to take off the European residents at a moment's notice. Nothing could convince the Christian population of Beyrout, but that the fate of their brethren at Deir-el-Kamar, Hasbeya and Rascheya, awaited them, at the hands of the Turks, their authorities and their troops ... More fatal sign than any, Kurchid Pasha had issued orders to two Turkish regiments to hold themselves in readiness to march into the Kesrouan *to protect the Maronites*! From the moment this ominous fact became known, the European consuls-general felt there was not another moment to be lost. They had seen the nature of that *protection* ...

The following representation was accordingly drawn up. 'It is with the greatest regret that we, the consuls-general of England, Austria, France, Prussia and Russia, are obliged to state that pillage, massacres and devastation, continue in such a measure as to merit our highest disapprobation ... our governments cannot look with indifference on the continuation of such a state of things.' ...

ৎ

Desmond Stewart: *Turmoil in Beirut* (1958)

Desmond Stewart moved from Iraq to Beirut just in time for the 1958 troubles, which were caused by the constitutional crisis afflicting the presidency of Camille Chamoun. Chamoun had refused demands to break off relations with Britain and France, or to discuss involvement by Lebanon in the union between Egypt and Syria that had been announced – as the United Arab Republic – in February of that year. The country spent several months in a tense and sometimes violent deadlock. The July revolution in Iraq that resulted in the deaths of King Faysal and others and the coming to power of a nationalist Arab regime caught the attention of America. Eisenhower responded to a request for assistance from President Chamoun by sending in the Marines. Stewart's sympathies were all with the revolutionaries in Iraq and the protesters in Beirut, but his piece for all its bias is one of the rare accounts of this crisis. This includes some grimly prophetic analysis of Western policy in the Middle East and an amusing cameo appearance by Kim Philby, whose own cover as Observer *correspondent was still intact at that time.*

Sunday, May 18th [1958]   Swimming, as though there was nothing in the world but the brilliant sea, and with the hazy peaceful mountains rising above what looks still an idyllic small town of the Levant. Adnan and his friends do quick runs and then dive one after another into the sea. Under the awning, the local youth, plus a number of Armenians, drink Pepsi-Cola, and from their deep-set balconies some American marines look down, rather wistfully.

To try and revive the illusion of normality, and to exploit the day, as the curfew comes so soon, we have lunch at Lucullus. It is crowded, the food is as good as ever. But people look nervously towards the great glass windows, on a level with the fronds of the palms in the Avenue des Français, through which the sea glints. People notice suddenly how like a greenhouse the restaurant is, and there have been more bombs. So throughout the talkative meal there are sudden islands of silence.

Two days ago Adnan guided me and Kim Philby into Basta. Adnan seems suddenly known there. Everyone we passed, with sporting gun or rifle, shakes his hand, greets him, and accepts us, on his authority. Though very short, he has authority. He continually asks me in Arabic if Philby is impressed by what he sees, by the spirit of the people, and carried away by his own intoxication with this spirit he says: 'Tomorrow I am not going to the bank. I am on strike.' Philby is impressed by the spirit.

Monday, May 19th   Today again to Basta, as the city enters its second week of total strike. Only a few shops at Bab Idris were open this morning, and just as I reached Saeb's fortress, through a street more defended than before, a bomb in the vegetable market went off and shut the town. The shops are like sea anemones, they close at the first touch. Inside the fortress, the same atmosphere of intellectuals answering the phones and preparing statements, and of burly young workers raising their machine-guns at the buzz of a cicada.

From the window [*of the house of former Prime Minister and leader of the opposition, Saeb Salam*] which commands the whole roofscape of Beirut right down to the sea with the queueing ships, we can see the partisans in the small front garden, almost a carnival atmosphere: boys in beach shirts lying on the grass. Men with big moustaches shout up to us, others barge into the salon on some urgent mission, their guns under their arms. And all the while Mrs Salaam and other women of the family sit and talk, or wander off into other parts of the house.

There is great confidence, partly as a result of yesterday's Russian warning to America, and Saeb's own declaration that the Americans must not intervene in the internal affairs of Lebanon. America had issued a statement to the effect that arms deliveries would be stepped up, and that the United States must be ready to help Lebanon, if Lebanon asked for help. All this against a confused political situation, in which only Chamoun's resignation could bring about a quick solution. (I think capitulation by the Opposition is unthinkable. They already control most of the country north of Tripoli, much of the Bekaa Valley and Sidon and Tyre. In the Chouf mountains to the south-west of Beirut, Jumblatt has complete control, now that the partisans of the picturesque but ridiculous Majid Arslan have beaten a retreat back to the airport.) But [*Lebanese President Camille*] Chamoun's resignation seems unlikely. He is personally pigheaded, and is being backed by the Western powers. Every day from my balcony I see the American ambassador pass below in a big black car, with outriders on motor-cycles, on his way to the President's Palace. So the suppressed excitement in Basta is linked with a certain anxiety about how long all this will last. But it is not all strain. Ordinary life goes on as well. From the little balcony behind Saeb's study, I can see people sitting in their doorways, perhaps more watchful than normal, but with the usual hubble-bubbles. And women are just being women, washing clothes, beating carpets on the roofs …

Afterwards In the West the bare typewriting of the agency cables caused alarm. The deaths of a few people [*in Iraq*] were magnified into a general massacre; Mr Cabot Lodge mourned a living but arrested Fadhil Jamali, and the *Daily Telegraph* lamented the Queen Mother of Iraq in whose funeral procession I had myself walked more than seven years before. The men who had come to power were assumed to be communists and anti-west fanatics. And the oil which had made Iraq precious and the Hashemites invaluable was assumed as lost. (Yet a moment's thought might have assured a reasonable man that whatever its new regime, Iraq's wealth of oil would have to be sold to be of any use to the Iraqis.) Under the panic of this loss, and a smokescreen of the supposed massacres, the statesmen of the West showed how little they had learnt from the mistakes of recent years.

The panic movement of Americans into Lebanon, and British into Jordan, secured the West in possession of a bathing beach and a desert, while alienating still further Iraq and Egypt. It identified western policy with an unpopular monarch and a discredited oligarch. The British intervention was merely stupid, harmful to British reputation and interests, but not actively mischievous: to pose as protector of an unpopular king against a majority of his subjects could not do much harm to the Hashemite monarchy, which was already harmed beyond repairing; for Hussein personally there was a possibility of exile. But the American intervention in Lebanon, prompted by panic over Iraq, was mischievous as well as stupid. The patriarch had asked: 'Do the Americans want to put a placard, "Anti-Arab", on every Christian in the Middle East?' That placard was in effect the American gift to Lebanon. Only the wisdom of such men as the Patriarch himself, and General Chehab, could tear that placard off. But the Americans themselves had intervened in a sectarian dispute, on the side of a Christian who did not disguise his dislike for Moslems, or his hatred for the greatest Arab leader of the day. No move, incidentally, could have done more good to Nasser.

*

Colin Thubron: *The Hills of Adonis* (1968)

Colin Thubron happened to be travelling in Eastern Lebanon when the six-Day War broke out, and gives us a firsthand, grassroots impression of how the Lebanese – Christians and Muslims – and Syrians he met reacted to the first euphoria, quickly replaced by bitter disbelief.

The land was dying, as the ancients said it died; the sun had worn the valleys brown and drunk the streams. I walked with relief toward the mountains, dreaming of the sea which was beyond, and of Byblos. From the furrows a single column grew, and here and there a Roman had marked on a rock the boundaries of his land, at a time when it was more fertile: 'C. Coraco', 'Utinia Cornelia'. It is said that there are places of sacrifice on the Banaat hill which juts into the western valley, but I could not find them although the wind blows through a shattered temple and rolls the blocks along its slopes.

My track petered out among foothills where the villagers of Chlifa had wired it against the people of Yammouneh, with whom they have an old feud. These are independent hills, crossed with many invisible boundaries, where grazing rights have been disputed for centuries in blood and a shepherd from afar can tell a man's village from the way he walks. But nobody was to be seen along the oak-spotted glens.

I found the road which the Romans paved between their cities at Yammouneh and Baalbec. In the plains the farmers have spread the fields above it, but through the solitary valley it wound with a cobbled brightness by empty, defensive passes beyond which the mountains rose in a low plume of clouds. Cream-coloured sheep-hounds reared savagely from vantage-points in the rocks, and I saw a fortress-village, the hashish crop young in its fields, and men with guns walking on the crags.

Along the track the flowers were dying, leaving the maquis brutal, with a host of shrubs whose airy, ciliate stems waved and rasped across the stones: juniper trees, cistus and many spiny, aromatic plants, with arbutus whose wood is used for flutes; and here and there anemones had wilted and dropped their petals one by one, Adonis already dying.

The Roman road curled under shadows, where the hills had a

strong, unfinished look. I almost trod on a tortoise, thinking him a rock, and he waved his arms at me, opening his red mouth as if to cry. At last the High Lebanon rose cold and steep as a wall, the village of Yammouneh in the valley against it, and a river shone blindingly where the sun struck it in a scimitar. My feet sent tiny pebbles rolling down the track, and I was surprised, looking at the far village, that it was silent and the fields empty, the whole valley in suspension …

The water which tumbles from the hill is called 'the Spring of Forty Martyrs', for the villagers claim that it starts to flow every ninth of March on the Feast of the Forty Martyrs, and dries up on the last day of July. There is a temple here, formless in the pastel quiet of trees and water, made of heavy Roman blocks and dedicated to Astarte, whose holy lake it is; for Phoenician legend says that she fled here from the monster Typhon and changed herself into a fish …

I approached the Christian hamlet of Ainata and knew from a distance that something had happened. The street was filled with men and boys, who stared at me so bemused that I had almost passed before a burly man stopped me. 'You realize there's a war on? Egypt, Syria and Jordan attacked Israel an hour ago. Lebanon is in it too.'*

They crowded round me without smiling or enmity, but with a kind of stifled pity which frightened me.

'You must avoid Moslem villages,' said the man. 'They will be mad now. They might kill you. They say the English are the allies of Israel. In each place you come to, look for this' – he pointed to the church belfry – 'and you know you will be safe. If you see a minaret, go the other way.'

'I'll walk over the mountains,' I said. I pointed where a track, engineered by the French army, stretched up the valley face and vanished under whiteness high above. 'Over there it's Christian country.'

'But there's nothing but snow,' the man said. 'Fifty kilometres before the nearest village. It may be impassable. Nobody has come over yet this year.'

---

* In fact it was Israel who had attacked, shortly before eight o'clock that morning, 5th June 1967.

I said that I would try it, not believing that the snow, even after the hard winter, could still smother the track. And I felt relief as I looked up at its beauty – the spine of Lebanon – for it is easier to risk nature, whose hazards are innocent, than the hostility of man.

So I started up the track until the Beqaa valley was grand and remote below, and a cartload of nomads, moving to some upper pasture, caught up with me and hoisted me onto their folded black tents with chickens, umbrellas and corn-headed children. They were Christians, and tried to sell me a jewelled cross which a beautiful girl kept in a scarf; and one of the men offered to buy my boots …

Into the noon silence, from an invisible height, came a whining like mosquitoes. A few minutes later something exploded faintly in the valley, and to the south sounded a hollow, passionate thumping as if someone were beating a drum beyond Hermon. But all these notes – the guns from the Syrian heights and the dying of an Israeli aeroplane – fell with an unreal and miraculous clarity on the mountain wind. And by late afternoon I was astride the High Lebanon; to the east lay the Moslem valleys, the foothills hiding Syria and imagined deserts, while to the west, wave upon wave, the Christian mountains rose through blueness like atolls on a hazy sea.

Soon I could see the Old Grove of cedars, more than four hundred, but pitifully small at the head of the valley, and came down to a shop and a locked hotel. I found shelter with a gang of Syrian road-menders in a bare building nearby. An old man slept on a board in one corner of a room and was startled to awake and find me lying on the floor beside him. He cooked a cauldron of beans and we sat in the fading light, eating them in silence: the first day of war. Later twenty or thirty young men came in, but the reports issuing from Radio Cairo were making the downing of Israeli planes seem like a royal grouse-shoot, and they were jubilant and forgot to resent me.

'Egypt has shot down sixty-eight planes, Jordan twenty, Syria eleven, Lebanon four!' Martial music followed the messages. Then the voice would speak again and the roadmen would cheer and shake my shoulder good-naturedly as I tried to sleep.

'News! Egypt has now shot down seventy, Jordan twenty-one, Syria eleven, Lebanon four!'

I asked them to switch to the BBC and they did; for a moment there was only crackling.

'They are machine-gunning the BBC,' someone said.

Then from the circle of swarthy faces the notes of Big Ben rose one by one with an exotic majesty. The Overseas Service. I interpreted: 'Israel claims to have pressed back Egypt in the Gaza strip ... ' Faces fell. But mostly the news was so vague as not to be news. All was conjectural or contradictory. The roadmenders shrugged and switched to Beirut which gave instructions for black-out and for action when bombs were falling in the streets ...

At dusk I heard distant aeroplanes and listened to the Syrians shuttering their windows. It was night when I came back to the rooms and forgetting which was mine, groped along passages, striking matches where the men sprawled close together and moaned at the light. I noticed my rucksack in the corner of a room now crowded, and the old man awoke and offered me his board, but the tiled floor was as soft. I opened a shutter, the place being without light, and lay for a long time looking at the sky, and wondering how many people had been killed that day.

The next morning I found a lorry going to Tripolis and a bus for Beirut. Helicopters were dropping leaflets on the city, and a muffled rifle-fire sounded from the American embassy where students were attacking troops. A note from the British embassy awaited me: 'British subjects in Syria, Lebanon, Iraq and on the East Bank of Jordan are advised that in view of the tense situation they should make preparations to leave at short notice.' The note was twelve days old.

In the little hotel I began to understand what it must have been like for the besieged in a castle. Hostility, imagined and genuine, surrounded us. Faces which had smiled were now turned away or pretended not to see: the little slights of war. It is the dilemma of Lebanon that she is almost equally divided between Christian and Moslem, and there were fears of religious unrest or of a civil war, as in 1958. The Christians began to leave for their mountain villages.

In the hotel, national qualities were accentuated. The Germans and Swedes drank and grew sullen. The British joked awkwardly. The Americans agitated for something to be done; but the harbour and the

airport were closed and there was rioting round the British and United States embassies. The pivots of security had been struck away so suddenly that it was bewildering to see how frailly they were grounded: the servants bowed and left for the hills; the official was apologetic, hopeless; banks, airlines, travel agencies all shook their heads in regret.

On the second night the United States embassy organized a massive airlift and began herding its nationals into the American University compound, protected by Lebanese soldiers and armoured cars; in this ghetto atmosphere there seemed something final in the farewells to friends, and after more than three thousand had departed, the foreign sector fell silent, so that one could drive along the streets alone …

The war in Beirut happened in people's minds. There was little to show for it in actions. The Shell oil installation was destroyed near the harbour, probably by Palestinian refugees, and the Mobil depot blew up with a disgruntled roar. There were sporadic attacks on the embassies, where cars were burnt and people wounded, and Moslem riots after Friday prayer. But the army's control of the city was efficient and determined. The foreign and Jewish quarters were picketed by military police, who sat entrenched behind the railings of villa gardens and patrolled the streets at night, when the black-out was so effective that they bumped into lamp-posts …

There was an eloquent contrast between the crowded, effervescent Moslem quarter and the quietness of the Christian one. In the large hotels the deck-chairs were still ranged in the sun about the swimming-pools, but nobody was to be seen there. The five-hundred-room Phoenicia was occupied by twenty people, mostly from Damascus embassies, and its great escalator moved up and down in darkness.

The Moslems reacted as the Arabs like to, with fervent decision. They were jubilant and bellicose. But the Christians, who equally distrust Nasser and dislike Israel, were muted and circumspect. Their fear of becoming a tiny minority in a united Moslem world, of Egypt eventually dominating Lebanon, is kept sharp by the disaffection of the Moslems who prevail in the cities: Tripolis, Sidon, Tyre, half Beirut. Their commerce and their tourist trade had foundered, and this they bewailed with a Phoenician common sense.

Those first three days might have been years. Bewilderment changed to loneliness, then to emptiness of feeling. The long walk among mountains, and the peasant quietness, seemed irrecoverable. It was decadent to find significance in anything but the tragic present. History was all around us now. There was no meaning left in cities ruined by more ancient wars, or in the intimations of what men had once believed. And my stay might have to end prematurely, the war-god obstructing the quest.

1975–90 CIVIL WAR AND BEYOND

The 1958 Crisis soon blew away, at least on the surface; the 1967 War happened elsewhere, though its long-term consequences had deadly, lasting implications for Lebanon. During those decades and well into the 1970s, the tourist brochures did not need to exaggerate the relative charms of a relaxed, foreigner-friendly, multilingual country where you really could ski in the morning and swim in the Mediterranean in the afternoon, exhaust yourself before running out of Roman temples and Crusader castles to visit and party the night away in nightclubs as glamorous or seedy as you like. Until quite recently, Lebanon's reputation was as the 'Switzerland of the Middle East' – incongruously, with Beirut as its 'Paris'. This was now superseded by hard-won and unenviable fame as a dangerous, unstable stage where the various causes and griefs of the cause- and grief-laden Middle East are acted out. A good place to avoid; a sort of Emergency Room vestibule to a ramshackle regional hospital for lost causes, desperate fanatics, ruthless mercenaries, unscrupulous politicians, superpower surrogates and madmen.

Most of the books which purport to give an idea of how this country got from A to B in such a short time are exercises in blame. The best examples are those written by journalists to record their stint in Beirut at various times during the unfolding of what has come to be called the Civil War, what the Lebanese call *al-hawadess*, the 'Events'. One can amuse oneself by picking out the favourite bias of each author: this Englishman hates the Frenchified Maronites (many English-speaking reporters, like Lawrence, saw Beirut as 'bastard French in feeling as in language'); an American reporter viscerally detests the Israelis and their local proxies; a French writer attributes all evil deeds to the invisible hand of the CIA. Most residents of Lebanon were in fact convinced that it was all part of a vast conspiracy, a Grand Design cooked up by master-chef Kissinger. But neither assigning blame, nor identifying bias, nor discovering conspiracies – and God knows how much of all that is justified – can explain why men would destroy a unique and beautiful thing. Rather than try to explain the inexplicable, or give our own potted history of the 'events' since 1975, which would inevitably include our own bias, our own assignation of blame, we will let various writers who lived through one or more of the stages of the thirty-plus-year drama speak for themselves.

There are many war memoirs, diaries and stories to choose from. Some of these are written by journalists following a brief tour or a posting, and present the outsider's point of view, that of an observer whose observations are necessarily influenced by his sources of information and the people he knows, some of whom may deliberately seek his company to further an agenda. Some are by foreigners held hostage during the horrific chaos of the late 1980s, whose accounts make up in poignancy what they must lack in perspective. And some are the testimony of local inhabitants, Beirutis, hyphenated Lebanese, Palestinian and other exiles, a cross-section of Lebanon as it was. Their stories are as diverse as their backgrounds and their individual experiences.

Thomas Friedman: *From Beirut to Jerusalem*

Thomas Friedman is an exception among exceptions: not just a Western journalist, as he describes himself in From Beirut to Jerusalem, *a Jewish American thrown into the deep end of Beirut at war. Friedman learned Arabic and Hebrew in the course of his postings (Jerusalem followed Beirut). This gave him the communication tools to make his book an inside story rather than a catalogue of battles, speeches, massacres, betrayals and second-hand misinformation like so many of the books written by foreign observers. It is thoughtful, informative, inclusive and, at times, touching: clearly the story of a good person quite unable to comprehend the horrors he witnessed.*

Shortly before I left Beirut in June 1984, I decided that I wanted to see what remained of the Beirut National Museum, which was located right on the Green Line. The aged director, Emir Maurice Chehab, was only too happy to give me a tour I shall never forget.

Soon after the Lebanese civil war began, and the museum was engulfed in cross fire, the most precious pieces were spirited away and hidden, but the big statues, bas-reliefs, and stelae in the main halls were impossible to move. So Chehab had wooden frames built around each piece and then filled those frames with poured concrete, leaving each priceless object encased in a foot of protective cement that would repel any bullet or shell. When the war ended they could be chiselled out. This made for a rather unusual display, because when you entered the Gallery of Ramses on the ground floor, what you saw were huge square pillars of cement reaching up from the floor to various heights. But Chehab, who had been the director of the museum for ages and knew every piece by heart, gave me a tour anyway. He would point to a 15-foot-high, 5-foot-wide block of cement and say, 'Now, here we have a spectacular Egyptian statue found at Byblos.' Then he would walk a few paces and point to another identical block of cement and say in a voice brimming with enthusiasm, 'And here is one of the best preserved stelae of early Phoenician writing.' For emphasis he would pat the pillar of cement. After about an hour of this I started to believe I could actually see the objects he was describing.

Whenever I think of Lebanon today, I am reminded of that tour. I still feel that there is a core of the original Levantine spirit left in the place, if only it could be chiselled out from under the layers of scar tissue built up over so many years of civil war.

In September 1988, Amin Gemayel's term as President expired, but the Muslim and Christian parliamentarians were unable to agree on a successor. A Maronite Lebanese army general, Michel Aoun, was appointed by Gemayel as a caretaker chief of state until elections could be held. The Muslims, however, refused to recognize Aoun's authority and have appointed the Prime Minister, Selim al-Hoss, as their acting chief executive. As of this writing, there is a Lebanese government in West Beirut and a Lebanese government in East Beirut. Despite this split, those radical Christian or Muslim groups which are calling for formal partition have found little support. Each side has insisted on keeping up the facade of Lebanese statehood and legality and maintaining the option of reunification. Even today, the ideal political future for most Lebanese still seems to be a new, reformed version of the old unified Lebanon.

Even the vast majority of Shiites in Lebanon just want to be Maronites – not religiously, but socially, politically, educationally, and materially. Now that they have inherited Lebanon's ruins, most Shiites seem to long for some of its old content. Now that they have earned an equitable slice of the pie, they want there to be a pan again.

Nadine Camel-Toueg, the young Christian journalist from West Beirut, told me in 1987 that for years her apartment building had had a Christian doorman named George, but during the Shouf fighting George had fled to East Beirut and was replaced by Hassan, a devout Shiite from a village in south Lebanon. One morning while Nadine was sitting in her living room, Hassan the Shiite concierge came up and knocked on her door.

'He was standing there holding a piece of paper,' recalled Nadine. 'He said to me, "Could you please fill out this application for me." I said, "Yeah, sure." So I read it and it was an application for a very posh school – the College Protestant. He tells me his daughter is living in the Ivory Coast and there are no good French schools there, so with the money she is making she wants to put her kids in a good French school in Beirut. Then he tells me, "You know, if we were living in south Lebanon there is great French school there – even better than all these in Beirut – they don't even allow the kids to speak Arabic during recreation." The guy is a Shiite, he has "There is no God but Allah" written in Arabic all over his door, but he wants to send his kids to a French school where they don't allow them to speak Arabic. That tells you something.' ...

Shortly before finishing this book, I had a reunion in London with my closest Lebanese friend, a quintessential Lebanese optimist, Nawaf Salam. Salam, a Sunni Muslim academic and a member of the elite Salam clan which once ruled West Beirut before the rise of the Shiites, explained to me the facts of life back in West Beirut, which he staunchly refused to leave, let alone give up on.

'All the myths are gone now,' said Salam, 'but maybe that is the beginning of wisdom. That is what keeps people like me going. We now know that the democracy we had was not a democracy at all but a sectarian balance of power. Liberty was not real liberty, but a kind of organized anarchy, and the diversity of press was largely a cacophony of voices subsidized by the Arab world. But even with everything having fallen apart a certain open society still exists. A united Lebanon is still the first choice of the Maronites, not a separate state, and a united Lebanon is still the first choice of the Shiites, not an Islamic republic. With no water, no electricity, and no police, we still enjoy a certain quality of life that you cannot find in any other country in the Arab world.

'There are still more books published today in Beirut than anywhere else in the Arab world. There is still more of a free press today in Beirut than anywhere else in the Arab world. Even today I will take the American University of Beirut over Amman University. I will take *An-Nahar* newspaper over [*the Syrian daily*] *Al-Baath*. Even with everything destroyed, the idea of Beirut is still there. The challenge now is to rebuild it on real foundations, not phony ones.' It is said that some men are born to times they cannot change.

As I listened to Salam across the dinner table, I wondered if that would be his fate: a good man born in a bad neighborhood, an optimistic soul born to a bad time he simply could not change.

But the more I listened to his enthusiasm and optimism, the more I thought I had better hold off on writing Lebanon's obituary.

ﺀ

Lina Mikdadi: *Surviving the Siege of Beirut* (1982)
Lina Mikdadi describes the summer of 1982, when Ariel Sharon got a green light to 'go all the way'; the summer that saw Israeli tanks at Broummana high up on Mount Lebanon, the comic-opera negotiation with the PLO for its withdrawal, and the final catastrophe as rogue militiamen took advantage of the Israeli presence to carry out murderous ethnic cleansing at Sabra and Shatila.

August 1st, and I wake up at 3.15 in the morning. I had a nightmare: rats, snakes and cockroaches crawling over me. I don't want to go back to sleep – I can still see the rats. Should I take a valium just because of a nightmare? I try to go to sleep while thinking of Leyla and Rasha. I miss them …

At 3.16 it's pitch black outside and Armand is very still. Has the little lemon tree sensed something? It's hot and sticky and I need to go to the bathroom. I don't feel like getting out of bed; it's so eerie outside …

At 3.17, one explosion follows another; the gunboats and field artillery have simultaneously gone into action. God, what's happening? It's suddenly light not dark, but we're a long way from dawn. The flare-bombs have gone into action too. Today, Sunday August 1st, is my cousin Ghada's birthday. It is Menahem Begin's birthday too. Along with the birthday cake in the shape of a tank, he has clearly decided to give himself an extra present. Happy Birthday, Mr Begin, from all the children of Lebanon. I hope you've decided to have a short ceremony.

By 6.07, it looks as if Begin does not want a quick party. The bombers have arrived to take part in the festivities. Sixty F-15s and F-16s give cover to air raids by the Skyhawks; they come and go in waves. I look out from the balcony: the refugees in the public garden of Sanayeh have nowhere to go for shelter. Some of the children even stand in queues to fill the family gallons [water-containers] *at* burst water pipes. A bomb a second; at $1,000 a bomb, that's quite an expensive birthday present for the sixty-nine-year-old Mr Begin.

⚘

Mahmoud Darwish: *Memory for Forgetfulness: Beirut, August, 1982*

Mahmoud Darwish, who died in 2008, was one of the most respected Palestinian-Lebanese writers and poets; he wrote about the same summer of 1982, a summer so violent that it created a cleavage within the Lebanese, or at least Beirutis. You were either there with us, or you were somewhere else, even (or especially) in mostly Christian East Beirut, where life went on with some semblance of normality, if less than complete safety. His 'we did not understand Lebanon' is the voice of the Palestinians who took refuge in Lebanon, some after 1948, others in 1967 or during the 'Black September' of 1970 when PLO fighters and families were violently expelled from Jordan.

The hysteria of the jets is rising. The sky has gone crazy. Utterly wild. This dawn is a warning that this will be the last day of creation. Where are they going to strike next? Where are they not going to strike? Is the area around the airport big enough to absorb all these shells, capable of murdering the sea itself? I turn on the radio and am forced to listen to happy commercials: 'Merit cigarettes – more aroma, less nicotine!' 'Citizen watches – for the correct time!' 'Come to Marlboro, come to where the pleasure is!' 'Health mineral water – health from a high mountain!' But where is the water? Increasing coyness from the women announcers on Radio Monte Carlo, who sound as if they've just emerged from taking a bath or from an exciting bedroom: 'Intensive bombardment of Beirut.' *Intensive bombardment of Beirut!* Is this aired as an ordinary news item about an ordinary day in an ordinary war in an ordinary newscast? I move the dial to the BBC. Deadly lukewarm voices of announcers smoking pipes …

We did not understand Lebanon. We never understood Lebanon. We will not understand Lebanon. We will never understand Lebanon.

We saw in Lebanon only our own image in the polished stone – an imagination that re-creates the world in its shape, not because it is deluded, but because it needs a foothold for the vision. Something like making a video: we write the script and the dialogue; we design the scenario; we pick the actors, the cameraman, the director, and the producer; and we distribute the roles without realizing we are the ones being cast in them. When we see our faces and our blood on the screen, we applaud the image, forgetting it's of our own making. And by the time production goes into postproduction, we are only too ready to believe it is the Other who is pointing at us …

Is it simply because Lebanon is like that – difficult to study and understand? Or is it because we had no tools for knowing Lebanon other than this manner of adapting?

I'm not so much getting entangled in answering as I'm forcing myself into a quandary. No one understands Lebanon. Not its supposed owners or its makers; not its destroyers or its builders; not its allies or its friends; and not those coming into it, or those leaving it. Is it because disjointed reality cannot be grasped, or because disjointed consciousness is unable to grasp?

And I don't want a correct answer as much as I want a correct question …

The sky of Beirut is a huge dome made of dark sheet metal. All-encompassing noon spreads its leisure in the bones. The horizon is like a slate of clear gray, nothing coloring it save the playful jets. A Hiroshima sky. I can, if I want, take chalk in hand and write whatever I wish on the slate. A whim takes hold of me. What would I write if I were to go up on the roof of a tall building? 'They shall not pass'? It's already been said. 'May we face death, but long live the homeland'? That's been said before. 'Hiroshima'? That too has been said. The letters have all slipped out of my memory and fingers. I've forgotten the alphabet. All I remember are these six letters: B–E–I–R–U–T …

The hours of the afternoon. Ashes made of steam and steam made of ashes. Metal is time's master, and nothing cuts one metal except another that carves a different history. The shelling leaves nothing alone, and there appears to be no end to this day. August is the cruellest month. August is the longest of months. And today is the cruellest day in August, and the longest. Is there no end to this day? I don't know what is happening on the outskirts of the city because the roar of metal has put a barrier between us and the deafening silence of our Arab brothers. A barrier between us and the silence of kings, presidents and ministers of defense, who are busy not reading what they read. Nothing is left for us except the weapon of madness. To be, or not to be. Not to be, or to be. Nothing is left except madness.

> Block your blockade with madness
> Madness
> With madness
> And with madness
> They have gone, the ones you love. Gone
> You will either have to be
> Or you will not be.

⁂

Jacobo Timerman: *The Longest War* (1982)

Jacobo Timerman was not a lucky man. From his Prisoner without name, cell without number *you can tell that he loved his native Argentina, even struggling to do so when it was hijacked by a ruthless military junta that imprisoned him for his liberal ideas. On release, he emigrated to Israel, just in time for the invasion of Lebanon. This he covered as a journalist, and in the process lost his idealism for Israel, or at least for its government at the time. Timerman makes us feel the dizzying heat of that summer of 1982; his story proves, if proof is required, that there were those on the Israeli side who did not agree with what was being done.*

General Ariel Sharon launched his offensive and began his war at eleven o'clock in the morning of Sunday, June 6, 1982 …

In the last week of the second month of the war, Beirut, an open city, has been bombarded by our army, navy, and air force with all the means at their command. We're told that terrorist emplacements and fortifications were attacked, that we had no casualties, and that all our planes returned to base.

The best way to withstand the heat is to talk about the war without getting to the bottom of the subject. Besides, who in this heat has the strength to meditate on the daily communiqués that are so easy to ignore? Who can devote himself to reconstructing the scenes, the details the government is trying to hide? The heat and dust of Beirut, the crumbling buildings, the lack of water, the wounded without hospitals, the dead without burial, and the desperate parents shattered by the guilt of being unable to protect their children, to hide them someplace, not to see them mutilated.

Six days of bombardment. One bombardment lasts twelve hours …

On my return to Tel Aviv I am informed that the army's chief rabbi, General Gad Navon, is distributing a map on which Lebanon is marked as the territory that was occupied in antiquity by the Israelite tribe of Asher. The city of Beirut has been Hebraized, appearing as 'Be'erot' …

Yesterday ten Israeli soldiers who fell in the last attack against Beirut were buried with full military honors. The other nine will be buried today, Friday, August 6. In the same battle, 350 Palestinians and Lebanese, who will not have a burial for a while, also died; the rats will take care of a few. The 65 Israeli wounded are already being treated in the best field hospitals in the world – there are no hospitals for the 670 Palestinian and Lebanese wounded. It's possible that not all of them will perish from their wounds, and that some will survive the thirst.

Psalm 137 says I should never forget Jerusalem. I have never forgotten her. With that same fervor and tenderness, I will never forget Beirut.

⁂

Brian Keenan: *An Evil Cradling*

The late 1980s were an especially terrible time in Lebanon, when civilians were executed for having the wrong religion on their identity card and foreign residents or visitors were taken hostage by shadowy groups professing more or less incoherent revolutionary ideas. Some westerners, like the high-profile Terry Waite, were held for several years in conditions of severe humiliation and brutality, and then released when the political winds changed, or when a ransom was paid. Others were executed after a short spell in captivity, more through bad luck than for any logical reason that outsiders could fathom. Most of the survivors went on to write about their experience. Some of their books are cathartic, most are understandably self-centred; few tell very much about Lebanon. Indeed only a few of the hostages had been there long enough to have much to say in that respect. Brian Keenan had only been teaching at the American University for four months when he was abducted, but he is not an average person. The product of Belfast's gritty working-class streets, he knew the meaning of fanaticism and violence. Beyond that, he is an unusually sensitive and humane person, and the best writer of the group (as evidenced by his poem, 'Remembering Beirut'). He comes closest to an empathy with, or at least a recognition of the humanity of, his captors, which most people would find impossible. If his book does illuminate some of the nightmarish facets of Lebanon at that time, its chilling message transcends any specific place and time.

We often noticed that the food we handed back, such as hard-boiled eggs, was thrown into the guards' rubbish. Our unclean hands had touched it and thus it was forbidden to the zealots that held us. Each time I saw this I was angry. To be considered unclean and untouchable was a humiliation I would not stand. This absolute judgement was without logic, reason, understanding or humanity, and devalued me beyond all comprehension. To concede this was an admission of defeat. I hated the waste. I remembered what they had said to me in my first imprisonment when I refused to eat and they simply shrugged their shoulders saying, 'There are many people hungry in Lebanon; if you do not eat, we do not care.'

As we sat in our cell passing those long hours, John [*McCarthy*] and I often discussed the Lebanon we had got to know before we were taken captive. During my four months teaching at the university, I had been fortunate enough to travel around the country, usually going out with a colleague for dinner and driving up into the hills, or perhaps to Sidon. I had seen much of how the land had been devastated and was aware of the grinding poverty with which the people from the southern suburbs had to contend. Lebanon is a country of vast extremes, of great wealth set side by side with the most abject poverty. Its different religious groupings, each of them insisting on the absolute correctness of its own system of belief and way of life, had made impossible the kind of compromise and acceptance of each other's traditions that could have more equitably distributed the country's wealth. Lebanon is crippled by a kind of tribalism, its peoples afraid of one another though they live so close together in this tiny land mass …

I told John the story of the Turkish villa in which I lived before being taken. It was set high off the ground and surrounded by its own gardens. Beside the entrance steps was a small Christian grotto. The Virgin stood angelic in her blue and white. At Easter-time I watched old women walk past and push lighted candles through the gate and rails that set the villa off from the street. They left them there, crossed themselves and prayed. I used to stand and look out of the villa at this. I wanted to open the gate to let them walk through the garden and pray beside the object of their veneration, but I could not. I was living near the Green Line that divides Christian East from Muslim West Beirut. My self-interest prevented me from opening the gate for them. I felt deeply ashamed. Behind me lived poor Armenians and near them even more impoverished Shias who had been dispossessed of their homes in the south of Lebanon. Overnight they had become urban citizens. Their whole way of life and their traditions had been stolen from them, obliterated overnight by the gratuitous and monstrous slaughter of the Israeli invasion of 1982. The city was a refuge but it was also a place alien to them. They were literally strangers in their own land ...

It is always the case when a people feel themselves so totally dispossessed, so unjustly condemned to a condition of absolute poverty that the anguish of it forces them to seek an escape. The need to escape becomes stronger as each community acknowledges its dispossession. Such acknowledgement always carries with it, hidden beneath the surface, a kind of shame and guilt, an admission of loss of identity, of full humanity, and that shame and guilt grows into anger. When the anger can find no outlet, when there is no recourse within the social structure for redress of grievances, the anger turns inward and festers. They cannot find value in themselves; they reject and loathe themselves. A man can then no longer surrender to such a monstrous condition of life. He seeks power, power that will restore his dignity and his manhood; that will let him stand with other men and know himself to be their equal and restore him to the community of humanity. But so filled with anger is he that he must act to reclaim meaning and purpose. With one great leap he tries to exorcize his fury.

The man unresolved in himself chooses, as men have done throughout history, to take up arms against his sea of troubles. He carries his Kalashnikov on his arm, his handgun stuck in the waistband of his trousers, a belt of bullets slung around his shoulders. I had seen so many young men in Beirut thus attired, their weapons hanging from them and glistening in the sun. The guns were symbols of potency. The men were dressed as caricatures of Rambo. Many of them wore a headband tied and knotted above the ear, just as the character in the movie had done. It is a curious paradox that this Rambo figure, this all-American hero, was the stereotype which these young Arab revolutionaries had adopted. They had taken on the cult figure of the Great Satan they so despised and who they claimed was responsible for all the evil in the world. Emulating Rambo they would reconquer the world and simultaneously rid themselves of that inadequacy which they could never admit ...

One afternoon when the other guards had left Said alone with us, John was dozing, tired from the constant early morning prayers that ripped into our sleep. I lay half awake, trying to enjoy what little sunlight filtered through the guards' side of our room. The sheet that separated us from them was hung just above head height and with the high ceilings in this old Arabic building we could catch some light. Said was moving about restlessly. The radio was on; Said always needed noise, he needed to distract his mind, and this was common to many of our captors. He began talking to himself, speaking words in English, which he had obviously learned from TV from those violent films. For hours they all watched them in awe-struck wonder. Said spoke: 'You bastard, I kill you ... you bastard I kill you, bastard, bastard, bastard,' he repeated, trying to imitate the aggressive manner in which he had heard the expression used. Then he was moving about the room again, distracted and restless. As if he was looking for something, anything to occupy him.

My own mind was equally restless, seeking out something on which to concentrate and evade the crushing boredom of the coming hours. The room was flushed with the morning's half-light. Birdsong sparked softly outside. Said and I were caught up in our mutual rapture, drifting heedlessly around one another like fish in a tank. Suddenly the dreaming silence was shattered. Said was weeping great shuddering sobs. This was a different kind of weeping from the automatic religious melancholia of his prayers. He walked around the room crying, the whole room seemed to fill up with his anguish. I felt, as I have never felt before, great pity for the man and felt if I could I would reach out and touch him. I knew instinctively some of the pain and loss and longing that he suddenly found himself overwhelmed by.

The weeping continued. Said became fleshy and human for me. Here was a man truly stressed. His tears now wrenched a great well-spring of compassion from me. I wanted to nurse and console him. I felt no anger and that defensive laughter which had before cocooned me was no longer in me. I lay on my mattress and looked over the top of the sheet. Said's shadow, caught in the sunlight, was immense. It flowed up the wall and across the ceiling. He was now chanting, fleeing from his sadness into recitation. His hands were clasped on the top of his head in the gesture of prayer. His body swayed and turned in a slow chanting circle. The room was filled with his eerie shadow and the slow rhythmic utterances choked with sobs. At times his voice broke and he cried out in desperation for Allah. I felt my own tears. I was transformed with a deep and helpless love for him. I had become what he was calling out for.

I woke John. 'Look at his, look at this,' I urged quietly. We both stared at the great moving shadow, fascinated and compelled. After a few minutes, John, exasperated, sighed in disgust and turned away. I remained watching. There was something unbearably beautiful about it. At once terrified and intrigued, my loathing for this man began to fall from me. I no longer thought of him as nothing, and felt guilty for having dismissed him so completely. Said's violence against us was a symptom of his need for us. Here was a man whose mind was forever locked in that desert wilderness that I had known during my worst moments in isolation.

*   *   *

Beirut Remembered

Dawn is cruel in Lebanon.
Rocket holes have gutted this place
As would a blunt and rusted blade
In the flesh of a fish.
An unkempt forest of rushes sprouts
Amid minefields
Fed on sewage, watered by years
Of unstaunched pipes.
The ghosts of the night have no place
In Lebanon.

Here they are masters of the light
Made substantial by the sun.

Today,
L'Orient le Jour has a headline
'Decouverte Macabre'.
A record of bodies discovered the previous day
Spills out,
Like the innards of a disembowelled animal.

One dawn, perhaps
Such secrets may not be
The burdensome fruit
Of Lebanese earth.

ﻙ

P. J. O'Rourke: *Holidays in Hell* (1989)

American journalist-satirist P. J. O'Rourke wrote a collection of travel writing that will definitely not inspire anyone to get out of his or her armchair (Holidays in Hell); *his next book was called* Give War a Chance. *He describes serious events and dangerous times with flippant, sometimes laboured irreverence. The Lebanese also used humour to help themselves survive years on end of indescribably depressing events. O'Rourke picks up some of the jokes, including several of the Syrian-Checkpoint-Joke genre – like the one where the soldier insists on opening the rear hatch of a Volkswagen Beetle, exclaiming: 'Ah, you have just stolen a motor!' And there is serious matter beneath the sarcasm: his reflection on why the Lebanese of all people, with their huge baggage of history, could lock themselves into yet another infernal spiral of violence-begetting-violence, is telling.*

There are a number of Beirut hotels still operating. The best is the Commodore in West Beirut's Hamra district. This is the head-quarters for the international press corps. There are plenty of rooms available during lulls in the fighting. If combat is intense, telex Beirut 20595 for reservations. The Commodore's basement is an excellent bomb shelter. The staff is cheerful, efficient and will try to get you back if you're kidnapped.

There's a parrot in the bar at the Commodore that does an imitation of an in-coming howitzer shell and also whistles the 'Marseillaise'. Only once in ten years of civil war has this bar been shot up by any of the pro-temperance Shiite militias. Even then the management was forewarned so only some Pepsi bottles and maybe a stray BBC stringer were damaged. Get a room away from the pool. It's harder to hit that side of the hotel with artillery. Rates are about fifty dollars per night. They'll convert your bar bill to laundry charges if you're on an expense account.

Beirut, at a glance, lacks charm. The garbage has not been picked up since 1975. The ocean is thick with raw sewage, and trash dots the surf. Do not drink the water. Leeches have been known to pop out of the tap. Electricity is intermittent.

It is a noisy town. Most shops have portable gasoline generators set out on the sidewalk. The racket from these combines with incessant horn-honking, scattered gunfire, loud Arab music from pushcart cassette vendors, much yelling among the natives and occasional car bombs. Israeli jets also come in from the sea most afternoons, breaking the sound barrier on their way to targets in the Bekaa Valley. A dense brown haze from dump fires and car exhaust covers the city. Air pollution probably approaches a million parts per million. This, however, dulls the sense of smell.

There are taxis always available outside the Commodore. I asked one of the drivers, Najib, to show me the sights. I wanted to see the National Museum, the Great Mosque, the Place des Martyrs, the Bois des Pins, the Corniche and Hotel Row. Perhaps Najib misunderstood or maybe he had his own ideas about sight-seeing. He took me to the Green Line. The Green Line's four crossings were occupied by the Lebanese Army – the Muslim Sixth Brigade on one side, the Christian Fifth Brigade on the other. Though under unified command, their guns still pointed at each other. This probably augurs ill for political stability in the region.

The wise traveller will pack shirts or blouses with ample breast pockets. Reaching inside a jacket for your passport looks too much like going for the draw and puts armed men out of continence …

We went back and forth across the Green Line six times, then drove into Beirut's south suburbs. This area was once filled with apartment buildings housing the Muslim middle class. The buildings were destroyed by Israeli air strikes during the invasion of 1982. Modern construction techniques and modern war planes create a different kind of ruin. Balconies, windows and curtain walls disintegrate completely. Reinforced concrete floors fold like Venetian-blind slats and hang by their steel rebars from the building's utility cores. Or they land in a giant card-house tumble. Shiite squatter families are living in the triangles and trapezoids formed by the fallen slabs. There's a terrible lack of unreality to this part of the city ...

Downtown on the Corniche you can lunch at the St Georges Hotel, once Beirut's best. The hotel building is now a burned shell, but the pool club is still open. You can go waterskiing here, even during the worst fighting.

I asked the bartender at the pool club, 'don't the waterskiers worry about sniper fire?'

'Oh, no, no, no,' he said, 'the snipers are mostly armed with automatic weapons – these are not very accurate.'

Down the quay, pristine among the ruins, chez Temporal serves excellent food. A short but careful walk through a heavily armed Druse neighbourhood brings you to Le Grenier, once a jet-set mob scene, now a quiet hideaway with splendid native dishes. Next door there's first-rate Italian fare at Quo Vadis. Be sure to tip the man who insists, at gunpoint, on guarding your car.

Spaghetteria is a favourite with the foreign press. The Italian specials are good, and there's a spectacular view of military patrols and night-time skirmishing along the beach front. Sit near the window if you feel lucky ...

On up the coast road, twenty-four miles from Beirut, is Byblos. Since the Christians were run out of the Beirut airport, the Phalange has taken to landing planes on the highway here. Expect another traffic jam. Byblos was considered by the ancients to be the oldest city in the world. In fact, it has been an established metropolis for at least six thousand years. Main street, however, looks like the oldest part of Fort Lauderdale.

By the seaport, however, is an Arab fortification atop a Frankish castle constructed with chunks of Roman temples which had been build over a Phoenician town that was established on the foundations of a Neolithic village – quite a pile of historic vandalism.

The war has not touched Byblos except to keep anyone from coming here. We found one consumptive tour guide playing solitaire in a shack by the entrance to the ruins. He took us through the deserted remains spieling, with pauses only to cough, a litany of emperors, catastrophes, and dimensions.

The Lebanese are chock-full of knowledge about their past. Those who *do* learn history apparently get to repeat it of their own free will …

ڪ

Jean Said Makdisi: *Beirut Fragments* (1989–90)

Among the plethora of war diaries, that of Jean Said Makdisi is one of the most thoughtful and human, with its horrible and improbable – but documented – account of the botched public hanging of a murderer in Beirut in the middle of the war. By now we are in 1989-1990, supposedly the final months of the war. We reproduce her 'Alphabet', a telling recapitulation of the exhaustion that follows a long war, the burned-out and fragile lucidity that changes, forever, the way people see the world.

Beirut: An Alphabet

One of the greatest sources of pride in Beirut has been the frequently affirmed claim that the alphabet, which provides language with a controlling order, was invented here in ancient times. Thus, all human advances since are traceable to their bright beginning in this location. Yet it is here that order has been so terribly threatened. In the last years of war, although the state and its institutions came close to collapsing, total social chaos was somehow averted. Perhaps this is due to the momentum of thousands of years of history and civilization, the same source from which the alphabet arose.

Is it possible to hope that from the rubble of the war, which at certain times seemed to have ended civilization, a new form might arise and permit future creativity? There is something of the alpha and omega in this hope, is there not?

Zbale	*garbage surrounds us, everywhere we look, there are piles of rubbish, debris, there is stench and ugliness, we*
Yield	*always we yield to the force of things, we are in danger of surrendering to despair, and to the ease of*
Xenophobia	*there is always someone else to blame for what has happened to us, it's never our fault, oh no, and meanwhile we are*
Waiting	*always waiting, for the others, for the solution, waiting for them to let the water come gurgling into our empty taps, waiting for the walls to crumble*
Weary	*of the never ending*
War	*we listen, overwhelmed with sorrow and anger to the empty*
Words	*the endless empty rhetoric which has only brought more*
Violence	*while the*
Veneer	*of fashion glitters like a worthless, forgotten coin in a mound of rubble as it catches the sun.*
Ugliness	*surrounds us, the ugliness of a broken city, ugly buildings sprouting up everywhere, ugly streets, whole neighborhoods, the beauty of mountains is destroyed by utilitarian ugliness, and*
Time	*weighs heavily on us – our days are long, and we carry History on our backs, an intolerable burden – but History gave us also*
Tyre	*and*
Tripoli	*and*
Sidon	*timeless relics from the past, ancient, beautiful, but*
Scarred	*by war and the suffering of*
Refugees	*We are a land of refugees, a people of refugees, coming from everywhere, going nowhere.*
Refugees	*make beautiful causes, but they are people, their trucks piled high with the pathetic remnants of former lives, mattresses and goats and children and stoves – they have found no*
Quarter	*because this place is like*
Quicksand	*in which everyone sinks. We are in a*

Prison *of violence and forgotten ideals. Still,*

Peace *will come, and*

Oppression *will end, must end, and*

Nemesis *will come, but not with more*

Militias *certainly not with more fighting men, nor with more*

Lies *the lies told by everyone to preserve the war and to prevent the*

Knitting *together of the unravelling whole.*

Justice *In war there is no Justice, and it is not from War that Justice will come.*

Jbeil *ancient Byblos, and*

Jounieh *with its ancient harbors and stunning bay, emerald mountains dipping into the blue sea and reaching into the azure skies, they are in danger of drifting away from us, but someday perhaps there will be*

Joy *and*

Jubilation *when this war ends and the*

Internecine *butchery ends. They say*

Hope *springs eternal and so it does, in spite of the*

Guns *and the*

Fawda *the anarchy which threatens us at every turn, because*

Earth *around us is beautiful: the gray rocks on the sheer cliffs, the shimmering silver leaves of the olive trees, the deep dark green of the ancient cedars, the sweet smell of the pine forests, the oranges dotted like yellow stars in the sparkling groves that lie by the blue seas. Meanwhile, our*

Days *pass, drearily, with explosions shattering the stillness of the nights. Our senses are dulled by the*

Catastrophe *that has been upon us here in*

Beirut *— poor, ugly, stricken Beirut, broken Beirut, unloved city, lost Beirut, like the child in the tale, torn between two mothers, but no Solomon here, no true mother.*

Beirut *pleads to be redeemed, but not by*

Another

Army.

William Dalrymple: *From the Holy Mountain* (1997)

William Dalrymple followed the tracks of the sixth-century Orthodox monk John Moschos, who gathered up the wisdom of all the saintly or merely wise people that he encountered on his journey from Athos to Sinai. Moschos gathered the fruits of his travels into the Spiritual Meadow; *Dalrymple his into* From the Holy Mountain, *an acknowledged masterpiece of thoughtful travel writing. He did not seem to click, spiritually, with the Frenchified clergy or with people he met in Lebanon, so much as with the monks in desert monasteries. He did take the advice of veteran journalist Robert Fisk to interview and record the war stories of one remarkable Beiruti: Lady Yvonne Cochrane. Lady Cochrane, despite her married name, is from one of the principal Levantine mercantile families, the Sursocks (as in Sursock Street, Sursock Quarter and Sursock Museum).*

Everyone I talked to seemed to agree. If I wanted to understand the Maronites there was one place I had to go: Bsharre.

In the cliffs below the town, deep in the Qannubin gorge, the first Maronite hermits had taken shelter when they were driven out of Syria by Byzantine persecution in the sixth century. Fourteen hundred years later, at the end of the nineteenth century, the town produced the Maronites' most famous poet and writer: Khalil Gibran, author of *The Prophet* …

But before I could leave to visit this town which, according to *Lebanon: The Promised Land of Tourism*, 'still rings with the soothing sound of Gibran's peaceful words', I had a morning appointment to keep in Beirut. [*Robert*] Fisk had told me that the opposition to the bulldozing of what little remained of historic Beirut – the so-called Downtown Project – was being coordinated by one Yvonne, Lady Cochrane, who had memorably described the President's ambitious plans for Beirut's redevelopment as 'the dream of a retarded adolescent'. Lady Cochrane was apparently the head of a family of old Beirut grandees who had come by her very unLevantine name when she married a former Irish Honorary Consul in Beirut, now long since dead.

I suppose I had guessed that Lady Cochrane was not going to be living in poverty in some poky flat when, on the telephone, she gave her address as Palais Sursock in Rue Sursock. But even so I had not expected the vision that confronted me when Nouri's taxi dropped me in front of Lady Cochrane's gates.

In the middle of the drive-in Apocalypse that is post-war Beirut, surrounded by the usual outcrops of half-collapsed sixties blocks – conical termite heaps of compacted, crumpled concrete – there stood an astonishing vision: a perfect Italian Baroque palace, enclosed within its own walled garden. Everything was beautifully kept, with wide terraced lawns framed by a pair of date palms looking down over the smart Christian district of Ashrafiyeh to the blue wash of the Mediterranean far below. A double marble staircase led up to the front door; only the broken balustrade which appeared to have received a glancing hit from a mortar or a rocket-propelled grenade indicated that the war had touched this small oasis at all.

I was let in by a servant and conducted to the library. On the wall hung a fine portrait of a seventeenth-century Greek merchant flanked by a series of superb oils of Ottoman townscapes: domes and caiques and wooden palaces on the Bosphorus. Shelves groaned with old leather-bound books; on one side a seventeenth-century escritoire was covered with the latest magazines from London and Paris.

After maybe ten minutes there came the sound of brisk footsteps and a petite but stylish woman walked in, hand extended. She was strikingly beautiful. In the half-light of the library I took her for about forty; only in the course of her conversation did it become clear that she must have been at least seventy, and possibly a good deal older than that.

'Do forgive me,' she said in an old-fashioned upper-class accent, the 'r's slurred almost into 'w's. 'I've been with the lawyer. We're having the most trying time with one of our neighbours. He's recently started behaving like a total gangster. All the institutions in Lebanon seem to have collapsed. Last year this man used his position to help himself to the funds of a hospital donated by my family for the benefit of the poor. Now he is trying to claim a strip of my garden. You see, unfortunately the boundary wall was destroyed in the Syrian bombardment, and that was the start of the whole problem.'

'You were bombarded here?'

'Several times.'

'Who by? I thought this part of Beirut escaped the worst of the war.'

'The first time, in '75, it was by the Palestinians. Then there was a second, more serious bombardment by the Syrians in '76. I was the other side of Beirut when it began again: couldn't get across the Green Line. Eventually I found someone who was prepared to bribe the Syrians, brave the shells and take me across. I arrived to find that the house had been appallingly battered. My son was here giving out water from the well in our garden to queues of people from the street. The Syrians had cut the water supply.'

'But the house was still standing?'

'Just about. This room was blown out by a phosphorus bomb. Came back to find the place looking like a surrealist picture. That entire wall had disappeared, but the bookcase was still standing, upright against the sky.'

Lady Cochrane arched her eyebrows: 'Next door the chandelier was blown apart in the blast, the mirrorwork ceiling was destroyed and my late husband's remarkable collection of fifteenth-century Chinese bowls was smashed.'

She stood up and led the way to the door into the hall. 'I suppose we were very lucky that none of the shells cut the main load-bearing pillars, otherwise the whole thing would have collapsed. But by pure good fortune most of them went straight through: down the passage, into the dining room and out the other side into the garden. Ruined my borders. Holes everywhere.'

'And you carried on living here, despite everything?'

'Oh yes. We lived in the shell for seven years. You can get used to anything. In time.'

'And you didn't rebuild?'

'There didn't seem much point while the shelling was continuing. It was 1985 before we felt it was worth trying to begin restoring the house.'

Lady Cochrane led the way into the main hall, an astonishing piece of mid-nineteenth-century Lebanese architecture enclosed by a quadrant of Saracenic arches. At the far end she pointed to an empty space on the wall; a shadow and a copper picture-hanger indicated where a large canvas had once hung.

'We had to sell the Guercino to the Met,' she said. 'It was painted for one of my ancestors, but the Syrians were shelling and we were left with no money at all. Couldn't even pay the servants. I panicked and sold it for a fraction of its worth.'

'And this?' I asked, pointing to a Venetian canalscape. 'Canaletto?'

'No,' she said. 'It's Guardi. But it's nice, isn't it?'

Outside the door of the sitting room my hostess paused by a small Baroque table with finely carved ball-and-claw feet. On it were displayed a few lumps of twisted metal.

'And these,' I said. 'Giacometti?'

'No, no,' said Lady Cochrane. 'Those are shells. All of that lot landed inside the house. Those ones on the left are mortars: used to come whizzing through the house six at a time. Made a terrible racket. We keep them just to remind us what we went through.'

We sat at a table and Lady Cochrane called for coffee. She then talked about her views on the redevelopment of Beirut: how the town had once been a green Ottoman garden city and should now be trying to return to that ideal rather than aiming at a sort of Middle Eastern version of Hong Kong, all high-rise blocks and plate glass. The brutalist architecture, she believed, was partly responsible for the brutalisation of Lebanon.

'In the past rich and poor had their own green space,' she said. 'A workman had something to look forward to: a peaceful evening sitting with his family round a small fountain surrounded by sweet-smelling herbs. Now he comes back to a concrete box in a slum. His children are screaming, the television is blaring. It's no wonder the Lebanese turned somewhat irritable and aggressive during the 1970s.'

A servant padded in with a tray of coffee. Lady Cochrane poured me a cup. In the background a telephone rang and a minute later the servant reappeared and whispered into his mistress's ear. She smiled a broad smile.

'Good, good,' she said. 'That was my lawyer. He's rung to say my neighbour has just received the order to stop building in my garden.

Ah, but life is so trying these days! The Lebanese who are even remotely civilised are now reduced to a tiny minority. Before the civil war there was an artistic life: painters, musicians, actors. Now there is a terrible exodus of brains and honest people – the best Lebanese, Christian and Muslim, have all left, or are in the process of leaving. Among the Maronites 300,000 – a third of the total community – fled the Middle East in the course of the war. We're left with the bottom of the barrel.'

'Are you a Maronite?'

'I'm Greek Orthodox,' said Lady Cochrane. 'My family were Byzantines from Constantinople: the name Sursock is a corruption of Kyrie Isaac, Lord Isaac. They left at the fall of the city in 1453 and settled near J'bail.'

I asked how much responsibility she thought the Maronites had to bear for what had happened to Lebanon.

'The Maronites presided over both the birth and the death of Lebanon,' said Lady Cochrane. 'Without them, Lebanon would never have existed. With them behaving as they have a tendency to do, it can't go on. Of course, the war brought out the worst in everyone. The Muslims all turned into terrorists and the Christians into mafiosi: kidnapping and robbing people, protection rackets and so on. At the beginning they were so brave and honourable: we willingly gave them money, and even our own sons. But by the end we refused: it was just people like Geagea. Gangsters.'

'I'm off to Geagea territory – Bsharre – this afternoon.'

'Well, you be careful,' said Lady Cochrane briskly.

꙰

T. J. Gorton: *Lebanese Journal 1967–2005*

Extracts from the personal diary of one of the writer/editors of this book cover sporadic vignettes of the period from 1967 to 2005.

This diary begins in August, 1967, when I landed in Beirut to begin my studies at the American University of Beirut. The last entry is dated September, 2005, a time of hope punctuated by deadly car-bombs. A few snapshots in between …

March 25th, 1975. We sit in the library of the old house, windows shuttered against the spring sunshine, sipping thick Turkish coffee after a lunch of garlicky chicken in slimy green *mulukhia* leaves. On the table, sensational headlines cover the French-language *l'Orient-le Jour* and *an-Nahar* in Arabic. King Faysal of Saudi Arabia has been assassinated by his nephew, ending the nervous equilibrium which had been holding the Arab world more or less quiet since the 1973 Arab–Israeli War. Beirut is buzzing with talk of the murder and its effect on OPEC policy, Middle East conflict, and the international financial system; curiously enough, nobody relates it directly to Lebanon.

April 13th, 1975. More sensational headlines, this time reported very differently in Lebanon's politically diverse newspapers. A bus full of Palestinians on their way to a demonstration has strayed, or was deliberately driven, into a staunchly anti-Palestinian working-class Christian suburb, and is riddled with bullets. This could be Lebanon's Sarajevo Bridge: more portentous in the timing than the event itself. Tensions boil over between the Lebanese (mainly but not exclusively the Christians), anxious to preserve the old order – the supersized Republic crafted by France – and the armed and angry Palestinians festering in their camps.

June 6th, 1975. Our daughter is safely born in West Beirut. So I am told, as thankfully the telephones are working; but no question of crossing the city today. Now there is almost no breathing space between the rounds, as the press calls them: as though Lebanon was a gladiator, or a boxer on the ropes, and the world a bloodthirsty crowd shouting for the kill.

August 6th, 1975. Another lull. We have our fourth anniversary dinner on the bayside terrace of the Saint-Georges Hotel. Watching the lights of the city dance in the dark waters of the harbor, we talk of relief that the trouble has passed.

September 23rd, 1975. The end of one round has begun to blur into the beginning of the next. The press has already found a name for it: the Lebanese Civil War. As though there was a blank spot in the future history books, just waiting for this chapter. Each day worse than the one before, punctuated by awful columns of smoke and the intermittent rumble of heavy munitions exploding in residential neighbourhoods. From the impossibly idyllic hills, the dull thud and echo of distant explosions suggest invisible, abstract events, something to read about in tomorrow's newspapers or hear on the BBC.

January 3rd, 1976. Things are not looking good. With binoculars we have been watching troop movements on the coast road north of Beirut, not sure whose they are.

March 22nd, 1976. A terrifying drive to the airport, past the harbour with its sunken freighters poking their already rusting funnels at drunken angles to the sea.

April 7th, 1981. [*We have moved back to Beirut in 1980*] Palm Sunday, noon. I am driving from Beirut up to the mountain, where we have yet again taken refuge as violence again takes over in Beirut and the airport closes. We thought the Lebanese troubles were at last over, not very promising for someone planning to set up shop as a Middle East Expert.

It is a beautiful Mediterranean spring day, and as we drive through the middle-class Christian neighbourhood known as Gemmayzé – or more prosaically, '*Electricité du Liban*' – there are everywhere little girls in white dresses clutching large decorated candles as they are hustled along to church. The traffic is slow. There are Syrian positions on the hills ringing Beirut, where an uneasy truce has reigned for nearly a year, desultory fighting going on at Zahlé and elsewhere in the mountains as the Syrians' allies probe the remaining areas of resistance. It had been a hellish autumn, another gloomy Christmas.

Suddenly an artillery shell falls out of the clear blue sky and explodes on a car ahead of us: flames, screams, chaos. In the panic, some people abandon their cars and run away, leaving an inextricable gridlock. I notice a side street just opposite us, turn the car into it, and we shelter against the side of a building as heavy machine-gun fire peppers the main street. The firing subsides a little; I drive out onto the coastal boulevard linking the port to the suburb of Dora, accelerator pedal to the floor. Five hundred yards of zig-zagging to avoid the bullets raking the road, only one other car trying to do the same, swerving like me back and forth. My eyes meet for an instant those of the other driver. Finally the bend at the ruined mattress factory called Sleep Comfort and relative safety ...

April 21st, 1981. We have had to leave the house on its mountain, warned by the local militia that they cannot hold the area any longer. We rent a fisherman's cottage at Aamchit just north of Byblos. The kids think it is wonderful: springtime on the Med, no school, all cosily living in one room. At nightfall the shelling of Beirut resumes, dull thudding just audible from Aamchit.

April 13th, 1983. The eighth anniversary of the beginning of the war. The Israeli invasion, the horrible siege of Beirut last summer, and the Sabra and Shatila massacres of September have given way to active involvement by the West. There are American Marines at the airport; Italian *bersaglieri* with dyed-black chicken feathers on their helmets drive around in jeeps, French soldiers lounge around and chat up the local girls. The talk in Beirut is of possible international interest in organizing a peace conference to find a new formula for Lebanon.

February 8th, 1984. A previously mothballed World War II battleship, the USS *New Jersey*, which has been patrolling Lebanese waters since the marine barracks bombing last October, fires 288 shells in the general direction of 'Syrian and Druze artillery' that has been pounding Lebanese Army positions. The *New Jersey*'s shells are described by one reporter as 'Volkswagen-sized', an epithet that caught the imagination of the international press.[29] The comparison seems somehow to explain why this relic of military history was firing what might as well have been randomly into the Lebanese mountains, destroying some livestock, a few houses, and a lot of pine trees. Every position and stronghold of the 'Christian-rightist' forces the *New*

---

29 One only has to do an internet search of 'Volkswagen-sized' and 'Lebanon' to see how this strange description has flourished.

Jersey was supposed to be helping comes under attack and falls, notably in Beirut and the Shouf mountains, formerly a real mosaic of Christian and Druze villages, an area of blood-soaked history and indescribable natural beauty. Worth fighting over, perhaps – if only the fighting did not destroy the prize. The Lebanese Civil War is over, the Syrian Occupation of Lebanon begins.

April 20th, 2001 [*We are back on a visit with our two younger children*] Colonel Riyadh's coffee is good, laced with cardamom, topped as it should be by creamy foam. It was hard to get to him. The Lieutenant in the villa at the bottom of the hill sent us to see a Major in the regional Syrian Military Intelligence headquarters in nearby Bois de Boulogne (not a misprint) just beyond Dhour. Colonel is out to lunch, *wallahi* ('by God'), we go down to Bikfaya for a sandwich as there are no shops in Boulogne and Dhour is too sad, not so much the occasional burned-out house as the hangdog look of the people. We return and are received with, '*Tfaddlu, ya hala,*' etc., etc. ('Welcome, please come in, you are so welcome,' etc. – well, it works in Arabic), all with the heavy Syrian accent which the Lebanese love to mock, quietly, in private.

The Colonel is from Der'a, near the Jordanian border. He used to speak French but his private schooling in a French convent school (where the pupils were punished for speaking Arabic) ended when he was nine: he was sent to a public high school where they were forbidden to speak anything but Arabic. *Unspoken*: ended, because of the Ba'athist revolution which confiscated bourgeois assets and closed foreign schools. More coffee and more chitchat around the kerosene stove: the cold winters in Dhour, where did we live in America, how is life there, yes, *better stay there with your family*; everything except anything about the Syrian army in Lebanon. He telephones the cautious Lieutenant at the barracks down the hill, explains that the owner of the house was coming with her family to see it, says you send a soldier up with them and let them stay as long as they want.

The children, then fifteen and seventeen, loved it. After their childhood inside the Washington DC Beltway, the whole experience is like some weird theme park set in an idyllic natural environment, with tanks and foreign-looking soldiers and guns and a heavy atmosphere of Things One Does Not Mention. Then to the visit,

College Hall, American University of Beirut

bumping up the hill road rutted by tanks, a young recruit named Arfan trotting next to the car, bayonet fixed on his Kalashnikov.

The living room is a barracks, the picture windows with the view down to the sea gone and the holes boarded up, the garden wall has lost half its stones, the now gateless arch over the entrance road has a portrait of Hafez Assad painted on it. Many of the walls bear graffiti: mostly the names of bored soldiers, a few slogans, none more original than 'Assad forever'. The general filth is perhaps to be expected in the absence of running water, though the conscripts had sloshed a few buckets of water around inside following the Colonel's call, creating mud and reviving rather than removing the smells.

The former studio and library on top of the house still has the best view of all, up to Sannine and down to Bikfaya and the Mediterranean. It is not now a nice place to visit, walls blackened by fire and with a gaping hole facing the cannons of Dhour. Dirty scraps of typescript scattered everywhere turn out to be pages torn from the carbon copy of our PhD theses from all those years ago, bearing graphic witness that, if the soldiers did not know what to make of Andalusian poetry or Bronze Age Egyptology, they knew just what to do with flimsy paper. We do not linger.

From *Lebanon, Lebanon,* ed. Anna Wilson
[Israel–Hizbullah conflict, July–August 2006]

Finally, three passages from Lebanon, Lebanon, *an anthology of poetry, prose and graphic art inspired by the events of the summer of 2006, all profits from which go to children's charities in Lebanon. Hassan Daoud and Robert Fisk contribute their own diaries of that summer; and Alexandre Najjar enables us to end this section with a frail glimmer of hope.*

Hassan Daoud: *They Destroy and We Build*
The switch from peace to a state of war is the fastest transition of all. The few minutes leading up to 9.30 am on Tuesday were a world away from the minutes that followed it. There had been no warning …

none of the usual signs that war was about to break out. On Tuesday, most Lebanese were contentedly reflecting on the steady rise in the number of tourists flocking to the country. Two days previously, the minister of tourism had announced, 'This year, the figure will reach 1.3 million.' The streets were filled with cars displaying banners bearing the names of all the countries whose inhabitants were coming to Lebanon to spend their holidays. There was no warning. The annual influx of expatriate Lebanese to their homeland for the months of July and August had begun in earnest. Before arriving, many of these homeward-bound expats had asked their relatives and friends to reserve tickets for the Fairuz concerts due to begin on 14 July. Seats had sold out more than a month ago. Now, focusing on the trivial to avoid the more fateful developments unfolding around us, we wonder what all these would-be concert-goers are going to do with their worthless tickets.

In the space of a single day, everything changed. The crowds on Verdun Street have vanished into thin air and the chaotic uproar that emanated from its coffee shops during the World Cup has faded into silence. Indolence and fear are writ clear on the faces of the Amore Café's few remaining patrons. The inhabitants of Lebanon's south, who until Tuesday must have thought that the days of artillery bombardment and internal migration were over, have reclaimed their familiar postures on our television screens: trudging along country roads and stumbling across bombed-out bridges with their scant possessions stuffed into small suitcases and nylon holdalls. The most frequently heard remark on Hizbollah's abduction of two Israeli soldiers (the pretext for the bombardment that followed) is 'bad timing'. This diplomatic phrase allows the speaker to avoid an open declaration of disgust at the kidnap operation, in case any Hizbullah supporters happen to be within earshot …

On Wednesday evening a pro-Hizbullah talking head appeared on TV and stated that everything that the Israelis destroyed could be easily repaired. According to him, houses could be rebuilt and bridges restored by the army engineers. Even as he spoke, Israeli warplanes were loading up to go and destroy more bridges; and the next day and the next, they did exactly that. It was distinctly similar to what one of our top officials said about Israel when he came to office: 'They destroy and we build.' He sounded bizarrely confident – as if the country Israel was destroying and the country we were rebuilding were two different places …

ৠ

Robert Fisk: *One Week in the Life and Death of Beirut*

Sunday 16 July It is the first time I have actually seen a missile in this war. They fly too fast – or you are too busy trying to run away to look for them – but this morning, Abed and I actually see one pierce the smoke above us. 'Habibi [my friend]!' he cries, and I start screaming 'Turn the car round, turn it round,' and we drive away for our lives from the southern suburbs. As we turn the corner there is a shattering explosion and a mountain of grey smoke blossoming from the road we have just left. What happened to the men and women we saw running for their lives from that Israeli rocket? We do not know. In air raids, all you see is the few square yards around you. You get out and you survive and that is enough.

I go home to my apartment on the Corniche and find that the electricity is cut. Soon, no doubt, the water will be cut. But I sit on my balcony and reflect that I am not crammed into a filthy hotel in Kandahar or Basra but living in my own home and waking each morning in my own bed. Power cuts and fear and the lack of petrol now that Israel is bombing gas stations mean that the canyon of traffic which honks and roars outside my home until two in the morning has gone. When I wake in the night, I hear the birds and the wash of the Mediterranean and the gentle brushing of the palm leaves.

I went to buy groceries this evening. There is no more milk but plenty of water and bread and cheese and fish. When Abed pulls up to let me out of the car, the man in the 4 x 4 behind us puts his hand permanently on the horn, and when I get out of Abed's car, he mouths the words '*kiss ukhtak*' at me. 'Fuck your sister.' It is the first time I have been cursed in this war. The Lebanese do not normally swear at foreigners. They are a polite people. I hold my hand out, palm down and twist it palm upwards in the Lebanese manner, meaning 'what's the problem?' But he drives away. Anyway, I don't have a sister ...

Wednesday 19 July Now that the Israelis are destroying whole apartment blocks in the Shi'i southern suburbs – there is a permanent umbrella of smoke over the seafront, stretching far out into the Mediterranean – tens of thousands of Shi'i Muslims have come to seek sanctuary in the undamaged part of Beirut, in the parks and schools and beside the sea. They walk back and forth outside my home, the women in chadors, their bearded husbands and brothers silently looking at the sea, their children playing happily around the palm trees. They speak to me with anger about Israel but choose not to discuss the depth of cynicism of the Shi'i Hizbullah who provoked Israel's brutality by capturing two of its soldiers. As well as the Hizbullah, the Israelis are now targeting food factories and trucks and buses – not to mention 46 bridges – and the bin men are now reluctant to pick up the rubbish skips each night for fear their innocent rubbish truck is mistaken for a rocket launcher. So no rubbish collection this morning ...

The minister of finance holds a press conference to talk of the billions of dollars of damage being done to Lebanon by Israel's air raids. 'We have pledges of aid from Saudi Arabia, Kuwait and Qatar,' he proudly announces. 'And from Syria and Iran?' the man from Irish radio asks, naming Hizbullah's two principal supporters in the Muslim world. 'Nothing,' the minister replies dismissively.

Alexandre Najjar: *Hope*

The war that ravaged Lebanon from 1975 to 1990 did not spare a thing: the economy, national unity, the joy of living ... I remember the horrific nights lit by fire, the deafening din of shelling, the whistling of the militiamen's bullets; I recall the dead transported in bin liners, the injured piled up in ambulances, the refugees sleeping in car parks, the car bombs, the devastated buildings, the shattered windows and the barricades; I can still smell the odour of blood, of powder, of dirt ... And I ask myself how and why I came out of it unharmed, though I guess one is never quite unharmed after such an ordeal.

During the war, my father, by nature an optimist, developed projects for the future, urged his relatives and friends not to abandon ship, convinced that the 'good Lebanese' ought to stick together and not desert their country. To those who came to him to lament the loss of their belongings, he promised better days; to those who felt despondency take over them, he assured the imminent end to the fighting; to those who wished to take the path of exile, he explained that exile was not a remedy, but poison. Was he himself convinced of what he was preaching, or was he bluffing in order to persuade them to stay? He felt, I think, entrusted with a national, almost divine mission to preach hope; people came to see him discouraged, they left confident, with a skip in their step.

One day, when the bombs were raining down, my mother came to find him with a worried look on her face:

'What's wrong?' he asked her.

'I fear protests in front of our house.'

My father frowned, walked towards the window and drew the curtains.

'Protests? Who would want to protest in front of our home?'

My mother shrugged and answered in a deadpan tone: 'All those to whom you gave false hopes, who remained in Lebanon because of you; all those whom you comforted, and who, at this hour, are hiding underground like rats to escape the shelling!'

My father always looked on the bright side, would see that the glass was half-full. He was so optimistic that he had the utmost difficulty in imagining old age or death. At the age of seventy-three he was offended when I classed him in the category of elderly people: 'I am not old,' he corrected me sternly. And when my uncle passed away suddenly, I recall my father full of hope in the car leading us to the hospital, incapable of imagining his brother dead. When we reached the emergency room and my tearful sister told us it was over, he looked lost for a while with a haggard gaze and pursed lips.

'It's impossible,' he stammered, shaking me like an apple tree. 'We have to save him, it's impossible!'

'There's nothing we can do, Dad. He's gone.'

'It's impossible,' he repeated, 'It's impossible … '

Indeed it was possible. Death had taken away my uncle, he who was goodness itself, he who, in a letter sent to Dad, had written these words: 'You are a father to all of us; you are and you will always remain our last recourse.'

Another day, during the most critical stage of the war, while we were always in shelters, confined to an obscure and malodorous room, listening to the sound of explosions that were shaking the city above our heads, we saw my father (who was a lawyer) arrive with a candle and a pile of folders.

'What are you doing, Dad?'

'I have these files to finish,' he answered, settling himself in a corner of the shelter.

'What files? The country is ruined. There are neither clients, nor tribunals, nor judges, nor justice … What's the point?'

My father nodded and said these magnificent words: 'Tomorrow peace will come and I need to be ready.'

Translated by Yasmine Gaspard

LITERATURE OF CONFLICT AND SOLIDARITY

It should come as no surprise that in a disintegrating society – where as someone said, 'even the law of the jungle does not apply' – it is women's voices that ring most true, that go beyond newsreel descriptions of daily horrors. Almost without exception it is in their stories, journals, novels and poems that one finds the human side of war, not the parties and armies and ministers and destructive technology that men busy themselves obsessively with, hiding behind meaningless distinctions, slogans and logistics.

This harks back to an ancient Arab tradition, before Islam, when wars were small-scale struggles for tribal dominance and, especially, honour. Their relatively small scale did not mean that they were not bloody. So constant were the wars and battles and duels that hardly a mother was outlived by her sons; widows and bereaved sisters were probably a majority of the population. And so they excelled at one genre of poetry: the *ritha'* or *marthiya*, the eulogy for the dead. In this genre, even the compilers of anthologies (all men of course) had to admit their supremacy. Sometime in the sixth century AD, Al-Khansa's brother was one of many killed in a particularly devastating battle:

> I can still see them before me: the mother grieving for her
> dead child,
> The wife, wailing over her dead husband on that day of woe…
>
> Woe is me, and woeful too our mother – Can it really be,
> He spends the morning in that grave, and then the evening too?

In their stories one can at least look for questions, if not answers: How do ordinary people cope with violent chaos when it goes on for years, decades, a generation? What does it do to them, and what is left of their former selves, after the worst is over?

Emily Nasrallah: *The Green Bird*

Some may find Emily Nasrallah's story 'The Green Bird' hard to take. It is a hard story, obviously drawn from personal observation: there are some scenes, some emotions that cannot be merely imagined. But the green bird of the title clearly – though never explicitly – harks back somehow to Tammuz-Adonis and the cult of the Green One that lingered wherever the cult of the murdered, beautiful young hero had flourished. Nasrallah was born in 1931 and raised in the small Lebanese village of al-Kfayr at the foot of Mount Hermon. She is an established novelist and storyteller, writing in clear, no-nonsense Arabic.

For a week now, that man has been sitting on the cement block facing my building. I don't know what winds blew him our way – a strange man. But who would dare ask these days? Who would query someone at the corner of a street in Beirut? Or in a bomb shelter? Or a hideout? Who would dare question anyone, whether man, woman or child? In Beirut these days no one would ask questions like 'Who are you? Where have you come from? Why are you here?' It would be like striking a match to the fuse of a bomb.

He has been sitting in that same place for a week now, immobile, not eating or drinking, nor even moving to answer the call of nature … Or at least that is how it seems to me. I see him every time I walk in or out of my house – there he is.

How can I avoid looking at him? He is sitting there, facing the entrance. Not crouching in a corner, not blending into a wall, not squatting behind the trunk of what used to be a tree. Just sitting. Simply sitting on that concrete block – half a metal barrel, actually, filled with cement, used as a shield by a fighter at some point during the war. (Don't ask who poured the cement into the barrel, or when or for what purpose, for that is another long story – a nine-year-old story and growing older, its action taking place in this neighbourhood and that and the other …) In any case, that is what he is sitting on, a makeshift stool he has turned into his makeshift headquarters, from which he darts his nervous glances. This man seems to be living on the cement barrel. And I cannot avoid looking at him as I come and go. He's sitting in that strategic spot and watching me. Every time I open my door I see him watching me: every time I step out of the building, he's watching, or so I think, for I have not had the courage to make a move towards him, maybe get closer to him, introduce myself to him, get to know him … I wouldn't dare.

'Get to know him? Whatever for?' I ask myself as I slam the car door and take off as far away as possible from his piercing gaze …

Why? A huge 'why?' An enormous question mark. It escapes me and hangs in the air and becomes part of the echoes around me. It obsesses me.

I could save myself this worry and gnawing curiosity and ask an alert neighbour – the one who lives at the intersection of other people's lives, recording every movement of their traffic. Or I could ask the building janitor.

Yes! Great idea! And so simple – why hadn't I thought of it before?

Naturally, he answers my 'why' with a smile that says he 'has it all under control'.

'Who? That man? He's one of the refugees, the displaced.'

He waits for me to ask him the very obvious next question, 'Where from? What part of the country has he run away from?'

He opens his book of war days, in which he's written newspaper headlines and news reports and radio broadcasts and analyses and rumours and stories that float in the air. 'What does it matter?' he says finally. 'He's a refugee and a stranger to this neighbourhood.'

'Have you spoken to him?'

'Yeah, the first day. He's from one of the really hard-hit areas. His people have taken refuge in the building facing ours – you know that, of course. There are twenty families. They've taken over all the empty apartments whose owners are in Europe.' Sarcasm tinges his words.

He stops there to see whether I am satisfied with the information he has provided. Then he looks at me, a pregnant, knowing look and the same confident, all-knowing smile of a simple man that says, 'It's under control, I've got it all under control.'

'Blessed are the simple people', I think to myself: 'Blessed are their simple, uncomplicated hearts … It is not easy in these times to be so simple-minded. Oh, how very difficult it is!'

'So, madam … ' he continues when he realises that I am not going to ask any more questions. He continues because the story has been knocking on the walls of his conscience. It pushes him to tell it. 'The man has a story, madam. No, a tragedy is what it is.'

I object to hearing this. Immediately I stop him. 'He must have relatives or a family.'

'Yeah, sure he does. They took the second floor in the building. But he refused to go up there, to stay there. The family is made up of … '

I interrupt him again: 'It may be the shock of having to move. He'll soon get used to it and start leading a normal life …' I move, I shuffle. I want to run away. I have no desire to hear what happened to the family, how many they are, how they live. I certainly don't want to hear the details of the tragedy that has befallen them. It has befallen the entire country. It has engulfed us all … What good will the details do me? No, I certainly do not want to hear this story. 'Do you hear me, man? What good are details once the whole is lost?'

'Ah, but some details are important. Some details carry within them the essence of the whole.' My simple building janitor waxes philosophical, the words gushing out of him. He no longer awaits my questions or comments.

The door is half open and I try to leave, but he stands in front of it and points to the man sitting on his barrel, his voice an odd mixture of pity and mockery. 'This man has lost his mind,' he says. 'And who would blame him, really. Man is not made of stone, you know. Some tragedies are just too big. More powerful than he is. They destroy him.'

Again I try to get away from the circle his words have drawn around me. But the door is half closed in front of me and the janitor has saddled his story and is preparing to take off on it.

'He keeps saying, "He'll be back." Do you know the story of the Green Bird? It's an old story. One of our forgotten legends told in the villages. "I am the Green Bird. I walk with a swagger." This is how it begins. You know it, the mother revives her son from the dead, rejuvenates his dried bones … '

'He quotes again, "My dear Mother/picks up my bones/places them in the marble urn … " Do you remember? The other woman, the stepmother, had conspired against the beautiful young boy and killed him, and made his body a feast for her friends. But his dead mother's soul revived him. It gathered his bones into a marble urn and nurtured them with drops of water until they came alive again! But her young son could not return as human flesh. He turned into a green bird and started haunting the other woman in dreams and wakefulness, hovering over her, plucking at her, reminding her of her crime and that Judgment Day was near.

'This man here, he awaits the return of the green bird. He says he's afraid to close his eyes lest the green bird returns and he does not see it. He stays up all night, his eyes roaming all over the place. He's afraid to close his eyes and not see the green bird when he comes.'

'Who is this green bird he talks about, anyway?' I hear myself asking the janitor, almost against my will. The story has conspired against me, and it hooks me, and I cannot free myself. 'What is the green bird to this man?' I ask again.

My storyteller smiles, an almost mocking, nearly sad, slightly humorous kind of smile, and I think, 'What is there to smile about? Didn't he say the story was tragic? Yes, but isn't there a saying that goes, the most tragic events are those that induce laughter?'

'It's his son, madam. His eldest son, his only son among five girls. He brought him up, educated him and put him through university and pinned all his hopes upon him. He sold everything he owned to put him through medical school. Yeah, he's a poor man, but he managed to put his bright son through university to become a doctor. Being bright, at least, is not the privilege of the upper classes alone, you know. God gave him a bright young boy, and through His divine guidance, the man educated the boy.

'He would have graduated from medical school at the end of the year. Then he would have been able to carry some of his father's burden. Maybe even put his sisters through school… Who knows, one of them may even have been able to go to university herself.

'Who knows what the future would have held for the young man before the …'

'Before what?' I scream the question at him but he continues, calm, unperturbed. 'Yes, madam … Before that shell found him and … he exploded.'

The janitor shifts from philosophy to literature and waxes poetic. He draws the clearest of pictures for me and slaps me with it, using that one expression 'he exploded', with all its literal connotations. I have certainly never heard it before – war slang, no doubt. And as he continues speaking, frame by frame the scene he describes plays out behind my eyes, and I am transported to a different time and place. The scene unfolds before me, running alternately in fast and slow motion, very slow motion.

'The shell surprised him as he was coming out of the bomb shelter. He had wanted to take advantage of the calm. He thought it was a truce or a ceasefire. He told his mother: "I'll just go out for a minute and move the car to where it'll be safer." That's when it surprised him. First one shell then the other … They slammed him against the wall … That's how they found him. His mother, his father, his sisters … that's how they found him. Splattered across a wall in a hail of shrapnel and rockets and shells. It was raining bullets as the father gathered his son's remains into his bosom.

'One entire night the man sat in that pool of blood, his son's remains in his arms. One whole night. Then in the morning they had to pry what was left of the body from his arms in order to prepare it for burial. They had to pry it by force from his arms!

'He spent the entire night talking to his son, soothing him. "You are cold. The night is cold and dark. Listen to the thunder and the rain. My child is so cold. Leave him, leave him in my arms. I am keeping him warm." The neighbours had to all work together to pry it away from him. Like prying open a clam shell to remove the precious pearl in order to bury it in the earth.

'Here he is now. He's lost his home and shelter and left the last of his rational mind in that pool of blood. If you go near him he'll ask you, like he asks everyone else, "Have you seen him?" And you would say, "Who?" And he'll tell you, "The green bird, of course, who else? He's coming, don't you know. Come sit next to me. He'll be here any minute now."'

Translated by Thuraya Khalil-Khoury

Nadia Tueni: *Lebanon: Poems of Love and War*

Nadia Tueni was born in 1935 to a princely Druze family in Baakline up in the Shouf Mountains, the heartland of Druze country near the palace of Beit ad-Din. A famous beauty, she died in 1983; her son Gebran Tueni, who had taken over from his father Ghassan as publisher of the best Lebanese newspaper, an-Nahar, *was killed in one of the series of car-bombings that silenced some of the most reasonable voices in Lebanon, including former Prime Minister Hariri, in 2005-6. Her* Lebanon: Poems of Love and War *is a posthumous collection of her poems written during the first, violent phase of the Civil War.*

In the Lebanese Mountains

Remember – the noise of moonlight
when the summer night collides with a peak
and traps the wind
in the rocky caves of the mountains of Lebanon.

Remember – a town on a sheer cliff
set like a tear on the rim of an eyelid;
one discovers there a pomegranate tree
and rivers more sonorous
than a piano.

Remember – the grapevine under the fig tree,
the cracked oak that September waters,
fountains and muleteers,
the sun dissolving in the river currents.

Remember – basil and apple tree,
mulberry syrup and almond groves.

Each girl was a swallow then
whose eyes moved like a gondola
swung from a hazel branch.

Remember – the hermit and goatherd,
paths that rise to the edge of a cloud,

the chant of Islam, crusaders' castles,
and wild bells ringing through July.

Remember – each one, everyone,
storyteller, prophet and baker,
the words of the feast and the words of the storm,
the sea shining like a medal in the landscape.

Remember – the child's recollection
of a secret kingdom just our age.
We did not know how to read the omens
in those dead birds in the bottoms of their cages,
in the mountains of Lebanon.

Hoda Barakat: *The Stone of Laughter*

Hoda Barakat was born in Lebanon in 1952, in the Maronite stronghold of Bsharre (Khalil Gibran's hometown). She shocked that society by marrying a Muslim at the height of the Civil War; she now lives in Paris. Her first novel (Hajar ad-dahk, *'Stone of Laughter') was published in 1990, and is written in the voice of a homosexual man, all very daring for a woman writing in Arabic.*

Khalil went out of the building and began to walk towards his room … there were few people in the road, the lucky ones were sweeping up the glass … most people were outside looking at the houses from the streets … most of them were silent, dumbstruck, looking closely but without surprise and some had raised their hands to shield their eyes from the sun … a woman with wild hair and bare feet was weeping out loud as she pointed to her home on an upper floor, no one paid her any attention … only a boy standing near her was looking at the place she was pointing to.

Khalil went slowly on his way … the only noise to break the silence of the street where he walked was an occasional ambulance siren … some of those who watched the ambulance pass had their mouths open in what looked like a grin as if they were saying over and over again, 'we're not in it … we're not in it … we're not in it … '

The bombing had only stopped … a few hours ago, so Khalil was deeply astonished to see pictures of the new young men on the walls of all the buildings … how did they find the time to prepare the posters and pictures and spread them all over the walls … the pictures were, perhaps, stuck onto ready-made notices, prepared in advance in the offices of the parties and organizations … printed and run off in underground presses, in secure places …

The fresh heads coming out of the walls still looked exactly like the ones that had just been buried, or were on their way to being so … death had not yet done its work… the original faces were still alive, the pictures all but spoke, for enough time had not yet passed to raise them to the divine world of martyrdom …

When the rich used to get too unsettled by the many check-points in the streets at night, they used to hire out an ambulance from one of the hospitals to take them to nightclubs, which continued to operate in the same way, inviting rising singers with a talent for provoking laughter and ridicule from the audience. These talents were the favorite with the late-night clientele because they were as far as they could be from being serious, they did not make them feel sad or call upon them to sigh, or think deeply. They cleared the way, with their enormous humility, for every man or woman to hope that they had a presence equal to the singer's presence and to become, consequently, the hero of the evening, the funniest, the noisiest, and the most devastating on the dance floor.

This is the 'love of life' that the western and Arab newspapers talk about … Khalil thought, as he started off again … people in our country love life in a way that surprises the scholars who, whenever they speak of us, express their surprise at this formidable ability of ours to love life … so much that some of those countries have managed to get hold of videotapes, from their correspondents, of those evenings where the dance floor is raised and everyone dances on the tables to the melody of songs that have nothing to do with, not one of them, with the tunes that the singer is desperately trying to bring to their ears …

Viewers around the world may be much more surprised to see us spending our evenings this way than by the sight of people patching over the holes in the houses and their walls, or the spectacle of people swimming over a surface of several dozen yards of blazing Green Line, or the sight of the tomato growing on the old sand barriers which one of the boys, whose wide black eyes pulse with love for life, plucks.

Khalil began to remember incredible scenes from one of those parties that was shown on television during a series of shows put on with the aim of raising the people's morale. He began to remember it and, as if reproaching himself, remembered that it was boring, that it made you want to choke, that it was unbearable, and that it made you feel artificial, it had nothing to do with people. These are people, the people, thousands upon thousands of miles of nerves and coronary arteries. People who look like you whether you like it or not, people to whom you flee whenever you are struck by a touch of madness and megalomania, people whom you implore to take you into the tender embrace of their multitude. People with more feeling than you, you Khalil who are so sensitive, because they are real people. Human beings who weep, who fear the bombing, who dream of infatuation, but who dance …

Time is not a steed that eats to keep going.

Time is a sugared doughnut. Little pieces strewn about empty, even, of their soft fragility.

In a city like ours, your life is like a butcher's block. And your time, you stand at the sink rolling your sleeves up over your arms and begin to mince it up into little pieces and eat. Tiny bits which get more minute whenever they are gathered together … the more you mince them, the tinier the bits become, until they vanish. Nothing holds your time together and gives it its essence or content except the bombing. The bombing rearranges the city's schedule like the calendar of the fast does in Ramadan. Before the bombing – during the bombing – during the long bombing after the bombing – before the bombing. All sorts of bombing.

Everything is minced into tiny pieces, a puff of dust, except during the bombing. On the radio you hear nothing but fragments of words and songs ... of long songs, such as Umm Kalsoum sings, you hear – when the bombing has stopped – nothing but very short snatches, because everyone is in a hurry. When the bombing becomes intense, you can hear these songs from start to finish since the presenters of the live shows are busy with themselves, with their safety, with listening to the news here and there so they give the singers who like to sing long free rein ... the people who prepare the short programs cannot, for the most part, get to the broadcast transmission centers and the live shows, such as those that cover artistic or social activities or that aspire to broadcast witty interviews with artists, become impossible to put into effect ... then, the bits of time grow large and round and you hear the sort of thing to which listening time should be devoted.

The auspicious bombing returns primal time to you and restores the city's first coherence. Death is the only spur to the city, for it is death that gathers the city's many little splinters and holds them to itself like iron filings.

Death is the only man in the city. When the city is plunged deep in her seductions and games he twists her arm and, in one swoop, holds it fast towards him and she leans on him and calms down and she begins to breathe regularly.

He gives the city her real flavor which she forgets, when the bombing starts. It is death who is the father of the city, who always reminds her that she must refrain from standing by the window ... who chides her, holding her back from the dreams that tempt her to play outside the fence, to talk to strangers, that tempt her to the desire to be like the distant world that sends the city its disgusting pictures in magazines, in immoral books, and on television.

When the bombing becomes intense, death sits at his desk. He cleans his spectacles thoroughly before picking up the long ruler and the pen to draw up a plan for the city as befits a great architect. Only those who have some connection go out into its streets: the fighters and the death squads. As for those who have no job, they loiter in his vaults, in his natural places. Things are not confused, the lion does not lie with the lamb, this is one of Nature's catastrophes, one of its bitter peculiarities. There is no place for confusion, no place for you to wonder whether the shoeseller is a blood merchant, or sells plundered electrical goods. Even the petty thieves restrain themselves and take their family life seriously …

Khalil noticed that there were no pictures of the martyrs who had been killed on the walls of the street. Only shreds remained. Shreds of lines and shreds of old pictures which the rain and children's hands had torn down. So then, the walls of the streets of our city will clean themselves, one day …

⚜

Nada Awar Jarrar: *Dreams of Water: my family, my life, my Lebanon*
Born in Beirut of a Lebanese (Druze) father and an Australian mother, Nada Awar Jarrar spent long periods outside the country during the Civil War. Written in English, her first novel (Somewhere, Home) won prizes for its depiction of the pangs and confusion of exile. Dreams of Water tells the story of a family whose son was kidnapped and presumed killed during the war, the pain of uncertainty and lack of closure. She somehow manages to write on such a subject without bias, without politics, almost without clues as to the religious affiliation of the family, which is next to impossible in the Lebanese context.

These are the hours of her undoing, long and sleepless, solitary. She shades her eyes and reaches for the bedside lamp. When she lifts herself off the bed, her body shadowing the dim light, she lets out a sigh and shakes her head.

Her dreams, gathering all her fears together in one great deluge until there seems to be no means of overcoming them, were once again of water, the images behind her eyes thick and overwhelming, her pulse quickening and then suddenly stopping in the base of her throat.

She tiptoes into the living room in bare feet, switches on the overhead light and stands still for a moment.

'Aneesa,' Waddad calls out from her bedroom. 'Are you all right?'

'I'm fine, mama. Go back to sleep now.' Her mother coughs into the night.

'Don't stay up too late then, dear.'

Aneesa steps out on to the balcony. Beirut in early autumn: the nights are getting cooler though the air remains humid. She wraps her arms around her body and looks down on to the street where there is absolute quiet.

She feels a sudden longing for permanence and certainty, for the hardiness she has seen in large oak trees in the West, unwavering and placid too. For a moment, as a breeze comes in from the sea, she wishes she could fly back with it to anywhere but here.

Months after her return, she is still unused to the feeling of always being in familiar places, indoors and out, as if enveloped in something almost transparent that moves with her, a constant companion. These streets, she thinks when she wanders through them, are a part of me, how familiar are the smells that emanate from them, fragrant and sour, the sun that shines or does not on their pavements, and when the rain falls I, umbrella in hand, mince my way through the water, through the cold.

The first letter arrived not long after Bassam's car was found abandoned and empty in a car park not far from the airport. My mother saw the white envelope addressed to her on the doorstep when she opened the front door to put out the rubbish. She brought the envelope inside, and sat down heavily on her favourite kitchen chair before handing it to me. Open it, she said.

I tore open the envelope with trembling hands, pulled the letter out and began to read.

My darling mother – I cannot imagine how difficult it has been for you and Aneesa these past few weeks and I am sorry for it. [I looked up at my mother and she nodded for me to continue.] I have already begun negotiating with my captors for my release. It's a long process, mama, so it might be a while before I see you and my darling sister again. I do not know which part of the country we're in but please don't worry about me. I am well and getting plenty of food. I have even made friends with one of the guards here and he has agreed to take this letter for me. I cannot say much more and don't know when I'll be able to write again. I love you both very much.

I reached out and placed a hand on my mother's shoulder. Bassam is alive, *mama*, I said.

She took the letter from me and put it back into the envelope. Then she stood up and began to pace across the kitchen floor.

He may have been alive when he wrote this but how do we know what's happened to him since? my mother asked. The only way we'll know that he's still alive is if we see him again. And with that, she turned abruptly to the sink and began to wash the breakfast dishes.

When we were children, I used to place my hand on my brother's forehead as he slept and try to will him to dream of a stronger, hero-like self, of the man he would be, until he woke up and pushed my hand away. Aneesa, what are you doing here in the middle of the night? Let me sleep now.

That moment in my mother's kitchen, suddenly realizing that Bassam's living and dying, both, were endless, our fears and hopes entangled between them, I shuddered.

Another letter, I murmured to my mother's back.

Another letter?

They drive south along the coast and then turn up into the hills east of Beirut. When they are halfway there, Aneesa stops the car and steps out to look at the view. The sun is shining, the sea is bright and blue, and the air is so much cleaner up here that she feels she is breathing freely for the first time since her return. She gets back into the car and realizes how much she has missed the mountains.

When they arrive at their destination, Waddad and Aneesa stand at the terrace's edge and look down to the valley, into the distance. There are pine trees and gorse bushes and a soft haze in the air. Behind them are mountains of grey rock and fine, violet-coloured earth.

'Shall we go into the shrine now, *mama*?'

'We'll have to put these on.'

Waddad opens her handbag and takes out two long white veils. Aneesa shakes out a *mandeel* [*scarf*], jerking it up suddenly so that it will not touch the floor. The delicate spun cotton flutters outwards. She places it on her head, throws its folds over one shoulder and takes a deep breath.

'It smells so sweet.' Aneesa smiles at her mother.

Waddad reaches for her daughter's hand and the two women make their way to the shrine. They take off their shoes, placing them neatly outside the door before stepping into the large, square-shaped room.

Several people stand leaning against the iron balustrade around the shrine. Aneesa watches a woman who is kneeling, both her hands wrapped around the railing and her eyes squeezed tightly shut.

'Let's sit over there.' Waddad motions towards quilted cushions placed over the large Persian carpet that covers the floor.

They move to one corner of the room and sit down, their legs tucked beneath them. Waddad places her hands on her thighs, stares straight ahead and begins to mutter softly under her breath. She has a serious look on her face and the edges of the *mandeel* rest open against her large ears. Aneesa tries to suppress a smile and fails.

Some moments later, a man tiptoes into the room in his socks. He must be taking a break from work, Aneesa thinks, because he is wearing navy trousers and a beige shirt that are dotted with dust and paint. He walks up to the shrine and pushes a folded banknote into the collection box hanging on the railing. He stands still for a moment and taps his roughened hand on the wooden box, while gazing at the shrine. Aneesa wonders what he is praying for and watches as he silently steals back out of the room. The kneeling woman is weeping quietly to herself. Aneesa stretches her legs out and coughs quietly.

She feels her mother's hand on her arm.

'Shush, dear. I'm trying to concentrate,' she whispers.

'What on?'

Waddad presses her lips together and shakes her head.

Moments later, she stands up.

'Come on, Aneesa,' she says, 'let's go.'

When they are back in the car, their heads bare and shoes on their feet, Aneesa and Waddad sit quietly for a moment.

'I was praying for your brother's soul,' Waddad finally says.

'What good does it do?' Aneesa rolls down her window and lets in a cool breeze that touches their faces. She reaches a hand up to her hair, missing the feel of the veil around her head and on her shoulders.

'What other choice do we have?' Waddad asks.

جه

Ghazir

Mishka Moujabbar Mourani: *The Fragrant Garden*

Mishka Moujabbar Mourani is a typical West Beiruti, born in Egypt of Greek and Lebanese parents. Her story 'The Fragrant Garden' is a mezzotint portrait of the post-Civil-War atmosphere in a part of Beirut that time seemingly forgot, a triangle of old houses and secluded gardens bounded by the teeming Port, a flyover, and a major road, now hemmed in by construction sites throwing up high-rise beehives and shopping centres.

The neighbourhood of Gemmayzeh, just beyond Beirut city centre, was too close to the demarcation line during the war. As a result, for twenty years the area had been left pretty much to its own devices. While the war raged on, its ancient alleyways and traditional houses were abandoned or occupied by cowering people who had nowhere else to go.

For various reasons, the reconstruction that followed the war did not quite reach this quaint quarter either. Some of the old houses were renovated and transformed into expensive villas by an enterprising woman who was keen on both charging rent and preserving what little heritage remained in Gemmayzeh. Apart from that, the area remained untouched.

One evening we were invited to the home of some friends who lived in the area overlooking Gemmayzeh. When we arrived we found them sitting in the garden with their guests. It was a lovely October evening, and the air was heavy with the scent of jasmine.

As is often the case when Beirutis get together, the conversation somehow managed to turn to the war years, even though the war ended some fifteen years ago.

'The other day my daughter asked me if the war had left any scars,' said a lawyer who had shuffled back and forth between Tripoli and Paris. 'It seems her teacher had been discussing post-traumatic stress disorders and the problems faced by the lost generation.'

'What did you tell your daughter?' asked an attractive artist in her forties.

'I was taken aback by the question, actually. I didn't think that I was scarred. But then my daughter asked me a curious question. "What about *Teta* [grandmother]? Did the war affect her?" Suddenly, I started to weep because when my mother had died during the war I was unable to attend her funeral.'

'I feel like I wasted my youth,' said the artist. 'I still can't account for those fifteen years of war, or even the years that followed. Many of my friends never married, and in our culture women marry young.' Then she turned to me. 'Where were you during the war?'

'I stayed in Beirut.'

'Here in Gemmayzeh?'

'No, I lived in West Beirut. I moved after I got married, but by then the war had ended.'

'I went to Paris soon after the war started,' said our hostess. 'I couldn't risk staying. My son had just been born and my husband was able to relocate his work. I know it must have been a horrible time to be in Lebanon.'

I thought for a moment. 'There was much that was terrible, yes, and yet, in an odd way, it was a unique experience. I have never lived as intensely as I did during the war.'

'Intensely?'

'Perceptions were heightened, experiences were more vivid. I can't explain it. I felt I was really alive. I wrote poems mostly, that were compact and intense reactions to what was happening. I looked forward to going to school, to spending time with the kids I taught. There was heightened meaning to our everyday lives. In fact, I haven't felt that way since the war ended.'

'I remember the summer of 1989,' my husband said. 'I was one of the few people remaining in Beirut. My wife's family had gone to the US and left me the key to their apartment, on the sixth floor of a building in Zarif. I had offered to feed the cat and water the plants while they were away. My sister and her family had gone to the mountains in the north, and she too had a cat; so she left me the key to her place on the seventh floor of a building about a ten-minute walk from the Zarif apartment. I lived on the eleventh floor of a building in Kraytem, about a half-hour away from both houses. By then the war had been raging for fourteen years, and, although I'm a Maronite, living in West Beirut was the only choice available to me.'

My husband was keen to share his war experience. 'The shelling that summer ravaged the city. Fuel was scarce, and basic amenities were unavailable, but I soon developed a ritual. Because the electricity was cut most of the time, I had to walk down the eleven flights of stairs before heading to the Sporting Club where I would swim for an hour. The beach was the only place I could have a shower, albeit with brackish water, since there was no running water in any of the flats. Occasionally I played chess with some of the regulars there, but mostly I donned my mask and flippers to go skin-diving, relishing the cool serenity of the Mediterranean,' he explained to the interested guests.

'Every afternoon I walked to my sister's house as there was very little fuel and taxis were a luxury. Once there, I climbed the seven flights of stairs to her apartment, fed the cat, walked down again and headed to Zarif to do the same thing. It was a thirty-minute walk back to my building and, once again, I had to climb up eleven flights of stairs to my apartment. I developed different ways of making the trek up the stairs easier. Sometimes maintaining a steady, slow pace helped preserve energy. Or counting backwards and focusing on how many floors were left rather than how many I had climbed,' my husband continued.

'In the evening, I would often meet my neighbour, a gnarled and gruff Sunni, on the landing between our two apartments; it was the safest place to be during heavy bouts of shelling. Like underground garages, these spaces became the community centres of wartime Beirut. People who barely acknowledged each other before the war began to spending long, intimate evenings together, united by their need for preservation and survival,' he said with a distant look in his eyes.

'My neighbour and I found we had a lot in common. We had long discussions over bottles of whisky in the dim light of a battery-powered lamp. Confidentially he would tell his friends that he really liked his Maronite neighbour. "An excellent young man, were it not for his name!"' The guests in the garden chuckled. My husband's name literally means 'the Maronite'.

'Funny thing about all this is that when the horror of the shelling stopped, and a ceasefire was agreed upon, eventually leading to the end of the war some months later, I was miserable,' my husband admitted. 'Many of the people who stayed behind had the same reaction. Instead of feeling relieved or overjoyed, I was upset, lost. People returned from wherever they had taken refuge. Normal life resumed, but I couldn't take it. My space was suddenly invaded by all the people returning from cities where normal life is taken for granted. They had no idea what every shell hole in the wall or every pothole in the street meant. The pace of life quickened and became banal. People were busy again. It actually made me nauseous.'

Our host shook his head: 'and here we are fifteen years later still coming to terms with this devastating war'.

The delicate jasmine blossoms shivered in the breeze, wrapping us in their fragrant perfume. The white flowers fell gently in our laps as we sat silently in the fragrant garden, an anachronism in this city of unruly concrete.

The coast near Batroun

Afterword:
Further Reading, Practical and Otherwise

Travelling to Lebanon

The beautiful side of Lebanon is still very much there, and all the years of turmoil have not spoiled the Lebanese' prodigious talent for welcoming visitors. In fact, one legacy of the 'Events' is that there are fewer tourists than before, which has two good sides: the sites are not crowded, and the locals are all the more glad to see the tourists who do come. It would be irresponsible not to point out that there are still dangerous spots in the country and that the neighbourhood is still a rough and unsteady one, however. Thus, from the Lonely Planet website, 2007:

> The security situation in Lebanon remains very uncertain. Violent clashes have taken place on the streets of Beirut and further unrest is predicted. Travellers should exercise extreme caution, avoid any demonstrations and monitor the news for any developments. Beirut airport has reopened but damage from the conflict remains significant throughout the city. The presence of unexploded ordnance is a real threat, particularly in the south.

They are obviously taking no chances and they are right. The hairy days described (with some hyperbole) by P. J. O'Rourke are behind us, one hopes, permanently. The fact remains that reliable practical information for planning and making a visit is much less abundant than for more obvious destinations. The following is a survey of published guidebook-type resources currently in print (for older books, prices given are those we found for second-hand copies on the internet; no guarantee of availability at those prices).

One new development is the Lebanon Mountain Trail. This well-marked hiking trail runs 440 kilometres down the backbone of

Lebanon. It was partly financed by USAID in what must be one of the more enlightened projects it ever supported. One section of the Trail is devoted to literary nostalgia (the Baskinta Literary Trail) and takes one to the origins or haunts of famous Lebanese novelists and poets such as Khalil Gibran, Mikhail Naimy, Amin Maalouf, Abdallah Ghanem, Suleiman Kettaneh, Rachid Ayoub and Georges Ghanem. The best way to find out about it is from the Trail Association's website, http://www.lebanontrail.org/default.asp.

Guides Visa (Hachette): Au Liban (1997) (available from amazon.fr or chapitre.com) is an excellent guidebook, in French. The historical and cultural background, enlivened with alluring photographs and appropriate literary texts, make it the best for reading early in the process of beginning with deciding whether to go and, once decided, what to include. It is less helpful on the practical details, which is just as well as they would be out of date by now.

Guide Petit Futé: Liban by Dominique Auzias et al (2005). Full of the kind of practical details the more sumptuous *Guide Visa* lacks.

Lonely Planet: Jordan, Syria and Lebanon by Siona Jenkins (2000).

Syria and Lebanon by Terry Carter et al (2004). Typical Lonely Planet: practical but somewhat superficial.

Footprint: Syria and Lebanon Handbook: The Travel Guide by Ivan Mannheim (2001).

Insight Guide: Syria and Lebanon (2000).

Lebanon: A Spy Guide International Business Publications Inc (2005).

In the Levant, Travels in Palestine, Lebanon and Syria by Charles Dudley Warner (2002).

Lebanon: An Insider's Guide by Blair Kuntz (2001).

GEO Projects Ltd: Beirut and Mount Lebanon (2001).

Bradt Travel Guides: Lebanon Guide by Lynda Keen (1999).

Travellers Survival Kit Lebanon 2nd Revised Edition (1999).

A Hedonist's Guide to Beirut by Ramsay Short (2005).

Bibliography

Note. We have not included works of political analysis and/or polemic writing about the 1975–90 crisis. This is of easy access on the Net and elsewhere, and beyond the scope of this book.

Adler, Marcus Nathan, *The Itinerary of Benjamin of Tudela: Critical Text, Translation and Commentary*, New York, Phillip Feldheim, Inc., 1907

Awar Jarrar, Nada, *Dreams of Water: my family, my life, my Lebanon*, London, HarperCollins, 2007

Barakat, Hoda, *The Stone of Laughter*, translated from the Arabic *Hajar ad-Dahk* by Sophie Bennett, Northampton, Massachusetts, Interlink Publishing, 2006

Barrès, Auguste Maurice, *Enquête. Une enquête au pays du Levant*, Paris, Plon, 1923. Voyage described in 1914

Beauvau, Baron Henry de, *Relation. Relation Journalière du Voyage du Levant*, Nancy, Jacob Garnich, 1619

Biffi, Nicola, *Il Medio Oriente di Strabone: Libbro XVI della Geografia*, Bari, Edipuglia, 2002

Breasted, James Henry, *Ancient Records of Egypt: Historical Documents from the Earliest times to the Persian Conquest;* collected, edited and translated with commentary, Chicago, University of Chicago Press, 1906

Breydenbach, Bernhard von, *Le grant voyage de Hierusalem*, Paris, Francois Regnault, 1517. Attributed to Nicole Huen], 1522. Voyage c.1480

Bruce, Ian (Ed.), *The Nun of Lebanon: The Love Affair of Lady Hester Stanhope and Michael Bruce*, London, Collins, 1951

Buheiry, *Romantic Lebanon*, London, The British Lebanese Association, 1986. Sumptuously illustrated, intelligently written.

Carali, P. Paolo, *Fakhr ad-Din II: Principe del Libano e la Corte di Toscana 1605–1635*, Rome, Reale Accademia d'Italia, 1938

Cass, Lewis, *A Recent Visit to Lady Hester Stanhope by an American*, The United States Magazine and Democratic Review 1837–1851, May, 1838

Chiha, Michel, *Liban d'aujourd'hui*, Beirut, Editions du Trident, 1949

Churchill, Colonel Charles, *The Druzes and the Maronites under Turkish Rule from 1840 to 1860*, London, Bernard Quaritch, 1862

Cleveland, Duchess of, *The Life and Letters of Lady Hester Stanhope*, London, Wm Clowes & Sons Ltd, 1897

Croisades, *Recueil des Historiens des Croisades*, Paris, les soins de l'Académie des Inscriptions et Belles-Lettres, 1834–1884

d'Arvieux, Chevalier Laurent, *Mémoires du Chevalier d'Arvieux, Envoyé extraordinaire du Roy à la Porte, Consul d'Alep, d'Alger, de Tripoli & d'autres Echelles du Levant*, Paris, Chez Charles-Jean-Baptiste Delespine, 1735. Lebanese travels 1653–60

d'Aveiro, Frey Pantaliam, *Itinerario da Terra Sancta, e suas Particularidades*, Lisbon, Simao Lopez, 1593. Chapter 89: Beirut; 90: Tyre and Sidon; 91: Tripoli; 92: Mount Lebanon. Describes travels begun in 1552.

Daher, Paul, O.L.M., *Cedar of Lebanon*, Dublin, Browne and Nolan Limited, 1956

Dalrymple, William, *From the Holy Mountain: A Journey in the Shadow of Byzantium*, London, HarperCollins, 1997

Dandini, R. F. Jerome, *Voyage to Mount Libanus, wherein is an Account of the Customs, Manners, etc. of the Turks … with Curious Remarks upon several Passages relating to the Turks and Maronites*, London, J. Orme, printed for Abel Roper at the Black Boy in Fleet-Street, 1698

Darwish, Mahmoud, *Memory for Forgetfulness: August, Beirut, 1982*, translated from the Arabic by Ibrahim Muhawi, Berkeley, California, University of California Press, 1995. Original *dhakira li-l-naswan*, published in *Al-Karmel*, 1986

de Bruyn, M. Corneille, *A Voyage to the Levant; or, Travels in the Principal parts of Asia Minor, the Islands of Scio, Rhodes, Cyprus etc.*, London, Jacob Tonson & Thomas Bennet, 1702. Done into English by W. J.

de la Roque, Jean, *Voyage de Syrie et du Mont-Liban*, Paris, André Cailleau, 1722; Amsterdam, Herman Uytwerf, 1723 de Monconys, *Journal des Voyages de Monsieur de Monconys, Conseiller du Roy en ses Conseils d'Estat & Privé, & Lieutenant Criminel au Siège Présidial de Lyon*, Lyon, Horace Boissat & George Remeus, 1657. Travels 1645–47.

De Quincey, Thomas, *Suspiria, the Daughter of Lebanon*, London, De la More Press, *c.*1845

Deeb, Lara, *An Enchanted Modern: Gender and Public Piety in Shi'a Lebanon*, Princeton, New Jersey, Princeton University Press, 2006

El-Atrache, Jaber, *On the Druze Religion*, from 'Sur la religion des Druzes' in *Cahiers de l'Est*, edited by Camille Aboussouan, Beirut, Imprimerie catholique, Deuxième série no. 1, 1947

Fani, Michel, *Liban 1880–1914: Atelier photographique de Ghazir*, Beirut and Paris, 1995

Fedden Robin, *Syria and Lebanon*, London, John Murray, 1965

Féghali, Mgr. Michel, *Contes, légendes et coutumes populaires du Liban*, Louvain, Institut Orientaliste, 1978

Féghali, Nabil As'ad el-, *Diwan shahrour al-wadi*, Beirut, Joseph Raidy Presses, 2000

Flaubert, Gustave, *Voyage en Orient*. In *Œuvres complètes de Gustave Flaubert: Notes de voyage*, vols. I and II, Paris, Louis Conard, 1910

Frazer, Sir James George, F.R.S., F.B.A., *The Golden Bough: a Study in Magic and Religion*, London, Macmillan, 1922

Friedman, Thomas, *From Beirut to Jerusalem*, New York, Farrar Strauss Giroux, 1989

Gardiner, Alan H., *Sinuhe. Notes on the Story of Sinuhe*, Paris, Librairie Honore Champion, 1916

Gibran, Kahlil, *The Broken Wings*, translated from the Arabic by Anthony R. Ferris, London, Heinemann, 1957

Gibran, Kahlil, *The Prophet*, New York, 1923

Herodotus, *Histories*, translated by A .D. Godley, Harvard, Loeb Classics, 1963

Hitti, P. K., *Lebanon in History*, London, Macmillan, 1967. The best single book on the history of Lebanon up to the middle of the twentieth century.

Homer, *The Odyssey*, translated by George Chapman, London, Richard Field, n.d., *c.*1616

Hourani, Albert Habib, *Syria and Lebanon*, Oxford, Oxford University Press, 1946

Ibn al-Qalanisi, Hamza, *The Damascus Chronicle of the Crusades*, extracted and translated by H. A. R. Gibb, Mineola, New York, Dover Publications, 2002

Ibn Battuta, *The Travels of Ibn Batuta*, translated by the Rev. Samuel Lee, B.D., London, Oriental Translation Committee and J. Murray, 1829

Ibn Jubair, *The Travels of Ibn Jubayr*, edited by William Wright, Leyden, Brill, 1852; second edition, Leyden, Brill, 1907

Ibn Munqidh, Usama, *An Arab-Syrian Gentleman and Warrior in the Period of the Crusades: Memoirs of Usamah Ibn Munqidh* (*Kitab Al-Itibar*), translated by Philip K. Hitti, with a Foreword by Richard W. Bulliet, New York, Columbia University Press, 2000

Izzard, Ralph and Molly, *Smelling the Breezes*, London, The Travel Book Club, 1959

Joinville, Jean, Sire de, *Histoire de Saint Louis*, texte original, accompagné d'une traduction, edited M. Natalis de Wailly, Paris, Firmin Didot, 1874

Josephus, Flavius, *Antiquities of the Jews*, translated by William Whiston, London, Thomas Nelson, 1757

Keenan, Brian, *An Evil Cradling: the Five-Year Ordeal of a Hostage*, London, Hutchinson, 1992

Khairallah, K. T., *Le Problème du Levant. Les Régions Arabes Libérées: Syrie-Irak-Liban. Lettre ouverte à la Société des Nations*, Paris, Editions Ernest Leroux, 1919

Kinglake, William Alexander, *Eothen*, London, J. M. Dent, 1908

La Mazière, Pierre, *Partant pour la Syrie (Off to Syria)*, Paris: Librairie Baudinière, 1928

Lamartine, Alphonse de, *Travels in the East*, Paris, 1839

Lawrence, T. E., *Seven Pillars of Wisdom*, London, Jonathan Cape, 1937

Liban: l'Autre rive, Paris, Flammarion and Institut du Monde Arabe, 1999. The chapter on writing and printing in Lebanon by Hareth Boustany and Camille Aboussouan is particularly worth reading.

Loti, Pierre, *Galilee*, Paris, 1895

Lucian of Samosata, *De Dea Syria*, in *Lucian*, Volume IV, edited with an English translation by A. M. Harmon, Cambridge, Massachusetts, Harvard University Press, 1925

Maalouf, Amin, *The Rock of Tanios*, translated by Dorothy S. Blair, London, Abacus, 2000

Makarem, Sami, *The Druze Faith*, New York, Caravan Books, 1974

Makdisi, Jean Said, *Beirut Fragments: a War Memoir*, New York, Persea Books, 1990. See pp. 49-65.

'Mandeville', *The Buke of John Maundevill, being the Travels of Sir John Mandeville, Knight*, edited by George F. Warner, London, Nichols and Sons, 1889; *The Travels of Sir John Mandeville*, edited by A. W. Pollard, London, Macmillan and Co., 1900; The Bodley Version of Mandeville's Travels, edited by M. C. Seymour, Oxford, Oxford University Press, 1963. Originally written in Anglo-Norman French *c.*1357

Maundrell, Henry, *A Journey from Aleppo to Jerusalem at Easter A.D. 1697*, Oxford: printed at the [Sheldonian] Theater, 1703

McCarthy, John, and Morrell, Jill, *Some Other Rainbow*, London, Corgi Books, 1993

Mikdadi, Lina, *Surviving the Siege of Beirut*, London, Onyx Press, 1983

Mourani, Mishka Moujabber, 'The Fragrant Garden', in *Hikayat: Short Stories by Lebanese Women*, edited by Roseanne Saad Khalaf, London, Telegram Books, 2006

Nantet, Jacques, *Histoire du Liban*, Préface de François Mauriac, Paris, Les Editions de Minuit, 1963

Nasir-I-Khusrau, *Diary of a Journey through Syria and Palestine*, translated and with a preface by Guy Le Strange, London, Palestine Pilgrims' Text Society, 1893

Nasrallah, Emily, 'The Green Bird' from *A House not her Own: Stories from Beirut*, Charlottetown, P.E.I., Canada, Gynergy Books, 1992

Nerval, Gérard de, *Voyage en Orient*, Paris, Imprimerie nationale de France, 1851

Nicolay, Nicholas, *The Navigations, peregrinations, and voyages, made into Turkie by Nicholas Nicholay Dauphinois, Lord of Arfueile, Chamberlaine and Geographer to the King of France* ... , London, Thomas Dawson, 1585. Voyage described 1550–51

O'Rourke, P. J., *Holidays in Hell*, London, Picador, 1989

Pritchard, *Ancient Near Eastern Texts. Ancient Near Eastern Texts Relating to the Old Testament*, edited by James B. Pritchard, Princeton, New Jersey: Princeton University Press, 1955. A scholarly rendition of the texts used from Breasted's more readable version.

Regnault, Antoine, *Discours du Voyage d'Outre Mer au Saint-Sépulcre de Jérusalem, et autres lieux de la terre Saincte*, Lyon, privately printed, 1573. Voyage in 1548–49

Renan, Ernest, *Mission de Phénicie*, Paris, 1864

Rihany, Amin al-, *Qalb Lubnan* (*The Heart of Lebanon*), Beirut, Sader-Rihany, 1947

Rizk, Salom, *Syrian Yankee*, Garden City, New York, Doubleday, Doran & Co., Inc., 1943

Roger, Eugène, *La Terre Sainte, ou Description topographique très-particulière des Saints Lieux & de la Terre de Promission … : Histoire de la vie et mort de l'Emir Fechreddin, Prince des Drus.*, Paris, Antoine Bertier, 1674

Runciman, Stephen, *The Kingdom of Jerusalem; The Kingdom of Acre*, London, The Folio Society, 1994

Sandys, George, *Journey. A Relation of a Journey begun Anno Dom. 1610. Foure Bookes Containing a description of the Turkish Empire of Aegypt, of the Holy Land, of the Remote parts of Italy, and Ilands adjoyning*, first edition, London, W. Barrett, 1615; second edition, London, W. Barrett, 1621; third edition, London, Ro. Allot, 1632; fourth edition, London: Andrew Crooke, 1637

Stewart, Desmond, *Turmoil in Beirut*, London, Wingate, 1958

Strabo, *The Geography of Strabo, Literally translated with notes, the first six books by H. G. Hamilton Esq., the remainder by W. Falconer, MA*, London, Henry G. Bohn, 1857

Thevenot, Monsieur de, *Relation d'un Voyage fait au Levant*, Paris, Chez Thomas Jolly, 1665. See chapter LX, 'Beirut, Tripoli, and Mount Lebanon'. Voyage described in 1655

Thubron, *The Hills of Adonis: a Quest in Lebanon*, London, Heinemann, 1968

Timerman, Jacobo, *The Longest War: Israel in Lebanon*, New York, Vintage Books, 1982

Tueni, *Lebanon, Poems of Love and War: A bilingual anthology*, translated from the French by Samuel Hazo and Paul B. Kelley, Syracuse, Syracuse University Press, 2006

Twain, Mark [Samuel Clemens], *Innocents Abroad, or, the New Pilgrim's Progress*, Hartford, Connecticut, American Publishing Company, 1871

van Egmont, J. Aegidius and Heyman, John, *Travels through part of Europe, Asia Minor, the Islands of the Archipelago, Syria, Palestine, Egypt, Mount Sinai &cc.*, translated from the Low Dutch, London, L. Davis and C. Reymers, 1759

Vogüé, Viscount Marie Eugène Melchior de, *Syrie, Palestine, Mont Athos: Voyage aux pays du passé* ['Lands of the Past'], Paris, 1876

Volney, C-F, *Travels through Syria and Egypt in the years 1783, 1784, and 1785. Containing the present natural and political state of those countries, their production, arts, manufactures and commerce; with observations on the manners, customs and government of the Turks and Arabs*, translated from the French, in two volumes, London, G. G. G. and J. Robinson, 1787; Dublin, White, Byrne et al, 1788 and 1793

Waite, Terry, *Taken on Trust*, London, Hodder and Stoughton, 1993

William of Tyre, Archbishop, 'History of Deeds done beyond the Sea', in Croisades, *Historiens (Historiens occidentaux I)*; also translated by Emily Atwater Babcock and A. C. Cross, New York, Columbia University Press, 1943

Wilson, Anna (Ed.), *Lebanon, Lebanon*, London, Saqi Books, 2006

Yermiya, Dov, *My War Diary*, Jerusalem, Mifras Publishing House, 1983. Another Israeli account of the 1982 conflict, by a soldier rather then a journalist.

Ziyade, Khalid, *yawm al-jum'a, yawm al-ahad* (Friday, Sunday), Beirut, Dar an-Nahar, 1994

Zuallardo, Giovanni [Jean Zwallart], *Viaggio. Il devotissimo viaggio di Gerusalemme*, Rome, Zanetti & Ruffinelli, 1587. See Book V: 'Return Voyage through Lebanon'.

About the Authors

Andrée Féghali Gorton was born in Lebanon and educated at the American University of Beirut and St Hugh's College, Oxford. She has worked for the Ministry of National Heritage in the Sultanate of Oman, lectured at George Mason University and the Smithsonian Institution, and published a book on Egyptian antiquities.

Ted Gorton was born in Texas and educated at the American University of Beirut, the University of Oklahoma, and St John's and Linacre Colleges, Oxford. He has taught Arabic at the University of St Andrews, lectured at Georgetown University, and spent 25 years in the international oil business. He has published widely on Arabic and Hispano-Arabic poetry (including two volumes in Eland's *Poetry of Place* series).

They are married (to each other), have four children and live in London and south-west France.